Jonathan Edwards's Bible

Jonathan Edwards's Bible

The Relationship of the Old and New Testaments

STEPHEN R. C. NICHOLS

Foreword by Oliver D. Crisp

☙PICKWICK *Publications* · Eugene, Oregon

JONATHAN EDWARDS'S BIBLE
The Relationship of the Old and New Testaments

Copyright © 2013 Stephen R. C. Nichols. All rights reserved. Except for brief quotations in critical publications or reviews, no part of this book may be reproduced in any manner without prior written permission from the publisher. Write: Permissions, Wipf and Stock Publishers, 199 W. 8th Ave., Suite 3, Eugene, OR 97401.

Pickwick Publications
An Imprint of Wipf and Stock Publishers
199 W. 8th Ave., Suite 3
Eugene, OR 97401

www.wipfandstock.com

ISBN 13: 978-1-61097-767-8

Cataloguing-in-Publication data:

Nichols, Stephen R. C.

    Jonathan Edwards's bible : the relationship of the old and new testaments / Stephen R. C. Nichols ; foreword by Oliver D. Crisp.

    xviii + 230 pp. ; 23 cm. Includes bibliographical references and index.

    ISBN 13: 978-1-61097-767-8

    1. Edwards, Jonathan, 1703–1758. 2. Bible. New Testament—Relation to the Old Testament. 3. I. Crisp, Oliver D. II. Title.

BX7260.E3 N54 2013

Manufactured in the U.S.A.

To Katy, John and Simeon
and in memory of my father

"He Himself is before all things,
and in Him all things hold together."
—Colossians 1:17 (NRSV)

Contents

Foreword by Oliver D. Crisp ix
Preface xiii
Acknowledgments xv
Abbreviations xvii

Introduction 1

1 Prophecy 17

2 Typology 58

3 "Doctrine and Precept" 108

4 Case Study: A Harmony in Soteriology 142

General Conclusion 188

Bibliography 197
Index 219

Foreword

"He was a man of many parts." That adage certainly describes Jonathan Edwards. He was a man of many interests too, like a number of other early modern thinkers. Perhaps this was because he lived at the intersection of several different worlds. There was the academic world of letters, which had its epicenter across the Atlantic, far from the parochial shores of colonial New England. Edwards was an avid reader of the new learning that issued from European presses, of works by Locke, and Newton, the Cambridge Platonists, Malebranche and other continental writers, as well as of scholastic theology and the heartfelt religion of the Puritans. He sought to assimilate and synthesize the imported learning he managed to seize, and rejected that which he thought antithetical to his Reformed Christianity, such as Thomas Hobbes' materialism (the *bête noir* of English-speaking Protestantism) and the skepticism of David Hume.

Then there is another intersection of worlds that he inhabited, namely, the crossroads between study and pulpit, or between the retired life of the scholar and the active life of the pastor. This he negotiated with less skill: parishioners were invited to visit him, but he spent much of his time locked in his study tracing out his ideas across myriad scraps of paper, blackening his fingers with ink in the process. That said, he made a fine preacher, itinerant, and missionary, and pursued his calling with determination and a high sense of duty.

Another confluence of worlds: the medieval, where knowledge was the preserve of a Christian elite that could potentially master a body of material, and the broadly theistic Enlightenment, where knowledge was distributed through the presses and increased at a rate that outstripped the ability of any one created intellect. He was interested in many branches of learning. But he had not assimilated all of them, although his erudition was astonishing for someone removed from the centers of polite society for much of his working life.

We could go on. There are many other ways in which Edwards, as a man of parts, straddled different worlds, e.g. the evangelical and the intellectual, the church and the academy, the aristocratic classes of the settled ecclesiastical order and *hoi poloi* of the emerging evangelicalism. Although Edwards was a man of many parts, Edwardsian scholarship has tended to focus on only some of them. The evangelical Edwards of religious affections and pious devotion, the mission-focused Edwards and hagiographer of David Brainerd, the philosophical and/or theological Edwards, and, lest we forget, the Hellfire preacher immortalized in "Sinners in the Hands of an Angry God." Curious, then, that a man who made his living as a minister of religion should have much less scholarly time spent on his more biblical works. With the completion of the Yale Edition of the Works of Jonathan Edwards much of the unpublished material he wrote on this topic has begun to see the light of day.

The world-intersection pertinent to this study pertains to this biblical material and its theological implications. Specifically, Stephen Nichols considers the normativity and authority of Scripture and theological reflection upon them—matters that were beginning to be pulled apart in Edwards's lifetime, leading to the sort of rupture in the biblical and theological literature of the nineteenth century. Edwards was adamant that the Bible was the Word of God. It was to be trusted in all matters touching faith and doctrine. And, so he thought, this was entirely consistent with a responsible approach to the life of the mind. The head and the heart were not to be separated on this matter.

At the time in which Edwards wrote historical biblical criticism was in its infancy. Rather than addressing himself to those concerns, he turned instead to the development of a sophisticated, even convoluted or Byzantine account of the way in which Scriptural types and antitypes are tracked in Scripture, and how the whole creation is in fact a massive system of signs, signifying theological things that only one steeped in the biblical tradition could hope to understand. Not only that, the relationship between the two testaments was itself a source of important theological data for him, not the least of which was the way in which Christ was the at the heart of both dispensations of the covenant of redemption. The saints of the Old Testament knew and trusted in Christ just as did the apostles of the New. Some have seen in this aspect of Edwards's work an unhelpful, backwards-looking pre-critical mind at work. There is nothing to retrieve from the biblical Edwards, these critics aver, and much we might want to forget (such as his monomania over tracking the 'end times' alongside major world events of the period). But this judgment is, to say the least, overhasty—as Nichols's argument shows.

Of considerable interest among these discrete papers and notebooks is Edwards's unpublished work on "The Harmony of the Old and New Testament." Using this alongside other aspects of the Edwards *corpus*, Stephen Nichols presents us with a facet of his work that has hitherto been neglected at least in part because it has been hidden in library stacks awaiting publication. We find here that Edwards is not merely engaged with Scripture, but obsesses over it in every detail of his life. It connects the dots, making sense of his piety and experimental Christianity as well as his deep theological and philosophical concerns. But, as with other portions of his theology, Nichols shows how Edwards's work on the Bible moves beyond the paradigms he inherited, making an original and distinctive contribution to the tradition. If we do not pay attention to this material, we cannot hope to understand Jonathan Edwards. Nichols has done Edwardsian scholars and the wider intellectual community a real service. Not only does he offer careful critical reflection on under-examined aspects of Edwards's work. He has shown how these things matter for some of the deep structures of the Sage of Northampton's thought. In this respect, his study helps to flesh out one more of the parts that comprise Jonathan Edwards.

Oliver D. Crisp
Fuller Theological Seminary

Preface

THE PRESENT WORK—A WORK of historical theology—offers an account of the relationship of the Old and New Testaments in the theology of the New England divine, Jonathan Edwards (1703–58). It examines Edwards's *corpus* of writing, paying particular attention to his notes for one of his major unwritten works, hitherto largely neglected, "The Harmony of the Old and New Testament." Following Edwards's proposed structure, the present study explores his conception of the relationship of the Old and New Testaments in terms of: (a) prophecy and fulfillment; (b) types and their antitypes; (c) doctrine and precept.

Against the challenge to the unity of the Bible posed by the Deist, Anthony Collins (1676–1729), Edwards holds that the Old Testament is coherent only when its discrete witness is taken to be Messianic. The inter-connectedness of Messianic Old Testament prophecy, coupled with Edwards's novel typology, which unites the Testaments typologically in Messianic witness at every point, yields for him closeness in doctrine and precept throughout the Bible that takes Edwards beyond his tradition. In contrast to interpretations of the Bible reliant solely on human reason, Edwards's harmonious account of Scripture is seen to be dependent on the reader's possession of the Spirit-given "new sense." The three aspects of Edwards's Testamental relationship are brought together in a case study of salvation in the Old and New Testaments, which challenges the current "dispositional" account of Edwards's soteriology and argues instead that Edwards holds there to be one object of saving faith in Old and New Testaments, namely Christ. While there are difficulties in Edwards's account, it is nevertheless of value in contemporary discussions of the unity of the Bible.

Acknowledgments

I HAPPILY ACKNOWLEDGE MY debt to many institutions and individuals over the last four years of research and writing this book, which was originally my doctoral dissertation. My study was funded by an award from the Arts and Humanities Research Council and a postgraduate bursary from Bristol University's Faculty of Arts. In addition, grants were generously given by the Whitgift Foundation and the Ministry Division Research Degrees Panel of the Church of England. I am indebted to the staff of both Bristol University's Arts and Humanities Library and the Bodleian Library, Oxford. Mrs. Jennifer Eveson, administrator and librarian of the London Theological Seminary, graciously provided me with journal articles that the bigger libraries do not hold.

The beginning of my research coincided with a summer school on Jonathan Edwards taught at the London Theological Seminary by Dr. Stephen J. Nichols. I profited greatly from his enthusiastic introduction to the world of Edwards as well as from informal conversation with him. Also of enormous benefit was the "Jonathan Edwards in Europe" conference in 2007, sponsored by Yale University's Jonathan Edwards Center and hosted by Karoli Gaspar University, Budapest. The gathering of so many great Edwardsean scholars was of inestimable benefit to someone just "starting out." Prof. Stephen Stein, who has contributed more than any scholar to understanding Edwards's biblical study, offered encouragement as I ventured into this neglected vast tract of Edwards's thought. Others gave helpful comments on various parts of my work or generously shared their own expertise, among them: Dr. Brandon Withrow, Dr. Michael McClenahan, Dr. Bill Schweitzer, Dr. Michael Reeves, Dr. Paul Blackham and fellow Edwards student, Kyle Strobel. Prof. Kenneth Minkema of the Jonathan Edwards Center at Yale University shared his enthusiasm for this project and generously sent me copies of Edwards's recently transcribed notes for

Acknowledgments

the "The Harmony of the Old and New Testament," without which my research would have been impossible. He also fielded questions and offered encouragement. I gladly join the generation of Edwardsean scholars in expressing my debt to him.

Finally, my supervisor, Prof. Oliver Crisp, throughout the project, offered patient guidance, incisive comment, and generous encouragement. His own care and precision as a scholar was a model to me. He read the following work more times than should reasonably be expected of anyone. My sincere thanks go to him.

Abbreviations

PRRD   Richard A. Muller, *Post-Reformation Reformed Dogmatics: The Rise and Development of Reformed Orthodoxy, ca. 1520 to ca. 1725*, 4 vols. (Grand Rapids, MI.: Baker, 2003-06)

WJE   *The Works of Jonathan Edwards*, 26 vols. (New Haven: Yale University Press, 1957–2008)

Hereafter I cite the Yale edition of Edwards's *Works* as *WJE* followed by volume and page number. I will italicize the works Edwards published and indicate with inverted commas ("...") his notebooks and unpublished works.

WJE BoT   *The Works of Jonathan Edwards*, ed. Edward Hickman. 2 vols. (London: Westley and Davis, 1834; repr. Edinburgh: Banner of Truth, 1974)

Introduction

Situation of the Present Study

There remains at present a lack of scholarship of the Bible in the thought of the colonial pastor-theologian, Jonathan Edwards (1703–58).[1] In response to this, the present work is a study of Edwards's conception of the relationship of the Old and New Testaments. Familiar for decades in the secondary literature has been Edwards the philosopher, scientist, rhetorician and religious psychologist.[2] The influence upon him of such figures as John Locke (1632–1704), Bishop George Berkeley (1685–1753), Sir Isaac Newton (1642–1727) and the Cambridge Platonists has dominated studies of Edwards ever since Perry Miller inaugurated the present study of Edwards some six decades ago.[3] Less familiar, however, is Edwards the interpreter of Scripture. Yet oversight of the importance of the Bible to Edwards has kept us from the true Jonathan Edwards.

Edwards was first and foremost a pastor-theologian, an interpreter of the Bible and a creative defender of Reformed orthodoxy. Stephen Stein, who is responsible perhaps more than any other for attempting to rehabilitate Edwards the biblical scholar, commented in 1988 that "early estimations overstated Edwards's scientific and philosophical precociousness and contributed to the masking of [the central role of the Bible in] his

---

1. Since I begin each chapter below with a survey of the state of the relevant secondary literature, only a brief general introduction to it will be offered here.

2. See for example, Miller, *Jonathan Edwards*; Daniel, *Philosophy of Jonathan Edwards*; Lee, *Philosophical Theology of Jonathan Edwards*; Helm and Crisp, *Jonathan Edwards*; Anderson, "Editor's Introduction," *WJE* 6:1–143; Goen, "Editor's Introduction," *WJE* 4:1–95; Kimnach, "Editor's Introduction," *WJE* 10:3–258; Kimnach, "Edwards as Preacher," 103–24; Eversley, "Pastor as Revivalist," 113–30. See also the works listed in Lesser, *Reading Jonathan Edwards*.

3. Miller, *Jonathan Edwards*.

thought."[4] Gradually these estimations are being corrected. Through the recent completion of a critical edition of *The Works of Jonathan Edwards* in print and the continued publication of remaining manuscript fragments online scholars now have unprecedented access to Edwards's biblical observations.[5] In 2003 Douglas Sweeney pleaded that greater scholarly attention be paid to the importance of the Bible in Edwards's thought, noting that Matthew Poole (1624–79), Arthur Bedford (1688–1745) and Humphrey Prideaux (1648–1724) were Edwards's interlocutors even more than Locke, Berkeley and Newton. It is to be hoped that greater access to Edwards's biblical notes will bear fruit in future studies of Edwards's wider *corpus*.[6] Robert E. Brown's work on the influence of critical ideas on Edwards's exegesis constitutes welcome progress in the study of this area of Edwards's thought. Brandon Withrow's historical examination of Edwards's approach to Scripture pays attention to the commentarial tradition that Edwards draws upon and helpfully demonstrates the centrality of the doctrine of justification in Edwards's exegesis, as well as its significance to the question of who may interpret Scripture.[7]

Perhaps the reason why the importance of the Bible to Edwards's thought has been neglected hitherto is the perception that Edwards's

---

4. Stein, "Editor's Introduction," *WJE* 15:21–22. See also the following works by Stein: "Notebook on the Apocalypse," 623–34; "Number of the Beast," 293–315; "Providence and Apocalypse," 250–67; "Quest for the Spiritual Sense," 99–113; "Jonathan Edwards and the Rainbow," 440–56; "'Like Apples of Gold in Pictures of Silver,'" 324–37; "Spirit and the Word," 118–30; "Editor's Introduction," *WJE* 5:1–93; "Editor's Introduction," *WJE* 15:1–46; "Editor's Introduction," *WJE* 24:1–117; "Edwards as Biblical Exegete," 181–95. More recently McDermott, *Understanding Jonathan Edwards*, 10, comments, "Far too little scholarly work has been done on [Edwards's] use of the Bible, which rivals in quality and insight that of any in the history of Christianity." Other notable contributions include: Turnbull, "Jonathan Edwards—Bible Interpreter," 422–35; Pfisterer, *Prism of Scripture*; Gerstner, *Rational Biblical Theology*.

5. In addition to the twenty-six print volumes of *The Works of Jonathan Edwards*, The Jonathan Edwards Center at Yale University continues to publish Edwards's remaining manuscripts online at http://www.edwards.yale.edu. Of particular interest to the present study is the recent publication of Edwards's "Miscellaneous Observations on the Holy Scriptures," also known as the "Blank Bible," *WJE* 24. A Bible in which pages of biblical text are interleaved with blank pages for personal notes, the "Blank Bible" contains more than 5,500 entries by Edwards spanning the years 1730–58. See Stein's "Editor's Introduction," *WJE* 24:1–117.

6. Sweeney, "'Longing for More of it'? [*sic*]," 25–37. For a brief introduction to Edwards's influences as apparent in his catalogues of reading, see Thuesen, "Editor's Introduction," *WJE* 26:1–113.

7. Withrow, "'Full of Wondrous and Glorious Things.'"

exegesis is irretrievably anachronistic. In 1940 Ola Winslow described Edwards's theology as "an outworn dogmatic system" that "needed to be demolished."[8] Perry Miller noted that "part of the tragedy of Edwards is that he expended so much energy upon an [exegetical] effort that has subsequently fallen into contempt."[9] The assessment was shared by Peter Gay nearly twenty years later when he judged Edwards's biblicism to have been "medieval" and its results "pathetic"; Edwards "philosophized in a cage that his father had built and that he unwittingly reinforced."[10] In 2001 Bruce Kuklick's conclusion upon reading Edwards's recently-published "Notes on Scripture" was that "this powerful mind . . . chained itself to a vision that is not likely to compel the attention of intellectuals ever again."[11] Recent scholar of Edwards and the Bible, Robert E. Brown notes that while many have found ways to make Edwards's philosophy, ethics and analysis of religious experience interesting or relevant to contemporary thought they have struggled to do this with his exegesis: "There is simply no way to make Edwards a twentieth-century, and thus presumably relevant, thinker in this regard."[12] And yet before considering the contemporary value of aspects of Edwards's thought, his thought must first be adequately understood. This can only be done if proper attention is paid to the importance of the Bible to him. Edwards must first be understood before assessments of retrieval can be made.

On one level the criticisms just mentioned that are leveled at Edwards seem justified. A direct transfer of his theological convictions from his world to ours is indeed impossible for the simple reason that contemporary theological scholarship no longer operates according to the "pre-critical" presuppositions of the Northampton divine.[13] An "eclipse of biblical narrative" has occurred, to use the phrase of Hans Frei.[14] Or to change the metaphor, a conceptual chasm has opened that separates Edwards's world from our own. To suppose that Edwards's goods may be

---

8. Winslow, *Jonathan Edwards*, 325–30.
9. Miller, *Images or Shadows of Divine Things*, 25.
10. Gay, *Loss of Mastery*, 105, 113, 116.
11. Kuklick, "Edwards for the Millennium," 115.
12. Brown, *Edwards and the Bible*, xix.
13. Edwards was aware of the critical challenges of his day. See, for example, his discussion of the interpretation of prophecy in "Miscellanies," no. 1172, *WJE* 23:88 and his lengthy defense of the Mosaic authorship of the Pentateuch in "Notes on Scripture," no. 416, *WJE* 15:423–69. See also Brown, *Edwards and the Bible*, passim; Stein, "Editor's Introduction," *WJE* 15:12–21.
14. Frei, *Eclipse*.

transferred wholesale across that chasm is at best mistaken. But this does not mean that Edwards's theological system is utterly irretrievable and of no contemporary use. Rowan Williams notes that figures from the past are helpful to us, "not because they are just like us but in fancy dress, but because they are who they are in their own context."[15] When understood on their own terms such figures are capable of "de-centering" contemporary theological assumptions and challenging cherished shibboleths. Crucial therefore to an estimation of the contemporary theological value of Edwards is a better understanding of Edwards in his own context.

One aspect of Edwards's approach to the Bible that has hitherto remained neglected is his understanding of the relationship of the Old and New Testaments. Several studies acknowledge the issue, but given Edwards's expressed desire to write a major study on this very topic ("The Harmony of the Old and New Testament"), the oversight is surprising.[16] The present study seeks to address this omission. Though my enquiry will take in Edwards's entire *corpus*, my particular concern is with Edwards's notes for the "Harmony," a work he did not live to complete. Lest my argument be thought to be an exercise in building "castles in the air" (to quote Edwards), it is important to recognize the considerable volume of notes Edwards left for this work (over 500 pages of manuscript) which represents his "accumulated knowledge on the subject," built up over a lifetime of biblical study, dutifully recorded in his various biblical notebooks and expressed in his sermons and treatises.[17] Kenneth P. Minkema, Executive Editor of the *Works of Jonathan Edwards* and Director of "The Jonathan Edwards Center" at Yale University comments that at Edwards's death the first two-thirds of the "Harmony" (the parts concerned with prophecy and types) had been drawn up into "nearly final form," while the final third (that concerned with doctrine and precept) was "well under way."[18] The importance to Edwards of both the "Harmony" and the other unwritten

15. Williams, *Why Study the Past?* 26.

16. Minkema, "Great Work," 52–65; Brown, *Edwards and the Bible*; Schweitzer, "Interpreting the Harmony of Reality."

17. *Freedom of the Will*, WJE 1:387. Minkema, "Great Work," 54. For a description of the manuscript, see Minkema, "Great Work," 52–65.

18. Minkema, "Great Work," 63, n. 4. The manuscripts of the first and third sections of the "Harmony" have only recently been made available online as vol. 30 of the *Works of Jonathan Edwards* at http://www.edwards.yale.edu. I am very grateful to Prof. Kenneth Minkema of the Jonathan Edwards Center at Yale University for generously sending me copies of his recently-completed transcriptions before they were published. Edwards's notes for the second section of the "Harmony" ("Miscellanies," no. 1069, "Types of the Messiah") may be found in *WJE* 11:191–328.

Introduction

great work, "A History of the Work of Redemption," is shown in his letter to the trustees of the College of New Jersey of 19 October 1757, replying to their invitation to become the college's new President.[19] Edwards writes: "My heart is so much in these studies that I cannot find it in my heart to be willing to put myself into an incapacity to pursue them anymore, in the future part of my life . . ."[20] Nevertheless, Edwards did reluctantly accept the offer of the college presidency. Yet in the end his completion of both the "Work of Redemption" and the "Harmony" was cut short, not by the pressures of academic and administrative responsibilities, but by an inoculation against smallpox delivered on 23 February 1758; Edwards died a month later on 22 March. That Edwards's "Harmony" was not posthumously completed and published by his disciples as others of his works were, owes more to the interests of his disciples than the relative incompleteness of the "Harmony" manuscript itself.[21]

"The Harmony of the Old and New Testament"

When in October 1757 Edwards replied to the invitation of the trustees of the College of New Jersey to become its new President, he outlined to them the two major works that he had already begun work on and intended to complete: "A History of the Work of Redemption" and "The Harmony of the Old and New Testament." Since I will refer to Edwards's description of the latter work a number of times in the chapters that follow I quote it at length below:

---

19. On Edwards's unfinished "A History of the Work of Redemption," see the transcription of his notebooks for this work in vol. 31, *Works of Jonathan Edwards*, http://www.edwards.yale.edu. For discussion of the notes, see Wilson, "Editor's Introduction," *WJE* 9:61–72 and "Appendix B: Jonathan Edwards' Notebooks for A History of the Work of Redemption," *WJE* 9:543–56; McClymond, "Different Legacy?" 16–39.

20. Letter, no. 230, "To the Trustees of the College of New Jersey, Stockbridge," October 19, 1757, *WJE* 16:728–29.

21. In 1765 Samuel Hopkins and Joseph Bellamy collaborated in issuing Edwards's "Two Dissertations" in Boston: *Concerning the End for Which God Created the World* and *The Nature of True Virtue*. Edwards's son, Jonathan Edwards Jnr. transcribed and edited his father's 1739 sermon series which was published in Edinburgh in 1774 by Edwards's Scottish correspondent, the Rev. John Erskine. A selection of Edwards's "Miscellanies" were also transcribed by Jonathan Edwards Jnr. and published by Erskine as *Miscellaneous Observations* and under Edwards's name as *Remarks on Controversies*. On the fate of Edwards's manuscripts after his death see Wilson's discussion in his "Editor's Introduction," *WJE* 9:17–28.

5

> I have also for my own profit and entertainment, done much towards another great work, which I call *The Harmony of the Old and New Testament,* in three parts. The first considering the prophecies of the Messiah, his redemption and kingdom; the evidences of their references to the Messiah, etc. comparing them all one with another, demonstrating their agreement and true scope and sense; also considering all the various particulars wherein these prophecies have their exact fulfillment [sic]; showing the universal, precise, and admirable correspondence between predictions and events. The second part: considering the types of the Old Testament, showing the evidence of their being intended as representations of the great things of the gospel of Christ: and the agreement of the type with the antitype. The third and great part, considering the harmony of the Old and New Testament, as to doctrine and precept. In the course of this work, I find there will be occasion for an explanation of a very great part of the holy Scripture; which may, in such a view be explained in a method, which to me seems the most entertaining and profitable, best tending to lead the mind to a view of the true spirit, design, life and soul of the Scriptures, as well as to their proper use and improvement.[22]

The harmonizing of parts of Scripture has an ancient pedigree, stretching back to the second century. Harmonies of Scripture were popular in Edwards's own day. One such "Harmony" that Edwards had read, that by the Westminster divine, John Lightfoot (1602–75), offered a list of more than one hundred similar works.[23] So, in his "Blank Bible" Edwards adopts a familiar method when he seeks to overcome textual difficulties by recourse to harmonizing any "seeming inconsistence" in the gospel accounts.[24] His own "Notes on Scripture" contain a modest attempt to harmonize the four gospel accounts of the Resurrection, and in his "Blank Bible" there is an attempt to harmonize the events surrounding Jesus' departure from Jericho according to Matthew and Luke's accounts.[25] Yet for

---

22. Letter, no. 230, *WJE* 16:728–29.

23. Edwards names two "harmonists" in his "Catalogue": [61.] Lightfoot, *The harmony, chronicle, and order* and [578.] Pilkington, *Evangelical history and harmony*, *WJE* 26:131, 266–67. There is no indication that Edwards read the former work which lists 103 other harmonists, though the Dummer collection of books available to Edwards at Yale College included a copy of the work. Edwards's "Catalogue" reveals that he had used the second work, which lists 74 other "harmonists."

24. *WJE* 24:861.

25. "Notes on Scripture," no. 220, *WJE* 15:154–56. "Blank Bible," *WJE* 24:861.

Edwards the concept of "harmony" is more than merely a critical tool to reconcile apparent textual conflicts. It is a concept pregnant with theological significance.

I will discuss Edwards's metaphysics in more detail in chapter 2 when I consider his typology. However, it is impossible to appreciate the significance of "harmony" to Edwards without at least a brief foray into his philosophical commitments. Edwards begins his philosophical notebook, "The Mind" in ca. 1723 with an aesthetic study of the nature of excellency: "Some have said that all excellency is harmony, symmetry or proportion; but they have not yet explained it," he complains.[26] He sets himself this very task by asking a further question: why is proportion more excellent, that is more pleasing to the mind, than disproportion? The answer, he claims, is to be found in the notion of equality, or likeness of ratios. "Excellency therefore seems to consist in equality."[27] Edwards discusses excellency in the physical world, contrasting simple and complex beauty (denominated according to the pervasiveness of equalities) and the potential of disproportion to be beautiful if seen in a sufficiently wide context. He then turns from the physical to the spiritual world: "Spiritual harmonies are of a vastly larger extent; i.e., the proportions are vastly oftener redoubled, and respect more beings, and require a vastly larger view to comprehend them, as some simple notes do more affect one who has not a comprehensive understanding of music."[28]

Before addressing these spiritual harmonies as revealed in Scripture it is important to return to Edwards's initial enquiry and notice one further point concerning beauty and being. The reason why beauty consists in harmonious relations, why equality pleases the mind and inequality is displeasing in both the physical and spiritual realms, is that disproportion or inconsistency is contrary to being. "For being, if we examine narrowly, is nothing else but proportion. . . . One alone, without reference to any more, cannot be excellent. . . . [I]n a being that is absolutely without any plurality there cannot be excellency, for there can be no such thing as consent or agreement."[29]

---

26. Anderson, *WJE* 6:332 n. 2, suggests that Edwards might have had in mind here the Earl of Shaftesbury, "whose moral theory bases virtue upon a 'natural affection' that arises from the love of truth, proportion, order, and symmetry in external things, a passion very distinct from self-interest."

27. "The Mind," no. 1, *WJE* 6:332.

28. Ibid., 335–36.

29. Ibid., 336–37.

In 1724 after he had begun writing on excellency in "The Mind" Edwards composed "Miscellanies," no. 117 with the heading, "Trinity." The entry concludes: "Again, we have shown that one alone cannot be excellent, inasmuch as in such case, there can be no consent. Therefore, if God is excellent, there must be plurality in God."[30] Harmony then is a term that may be applied to God as well as to creation. (Edwards describes the relations between the divine Persons as "the supreme harmony of all").[31] More correctly, it ought to be said that harmony is a description applicable to creation only because it first describes God. The harmonies observable throughout sensible reality are shadows of the harmonies of God's own being. The "mutual sweet consents of being to being are resemblances of the consent of God who is himself the being of being, the '*ens entium*.'"[32]

Not only does the Book of Nature image the harmonious character of its creator, however, but in common with his theological tradition, Edwards believes that the Book of Scripture displays the attributes of its divine author. For Edwards, chief among these is its harmony. A young Edwards notes that there is in Scripture a "wondrous universal harmony and consent and concurrence in the aim and drift, such an universal appearance of a wonderful glorious design, such stamps everywhere of exalted and divine wisdom, majesty and holiness in matter, manner, contexture and aim; that the evidence is the same that the Scriptures are the word and work of a divine mind, to one that is thoroughly acquainted with them, as 'tis that the words and actions of an understanding man are from a rational mind, to one that has of a long time been his familiar acquaintance."[33]

Only one "thoroughly acquainted" with the Scriptures may perceive their harmony and therefore recognize their divine origin. And as Edwards notes, this "acquaintance" is of a kind that may be likened to a relational experiential knowledge, rather than a mere knowledge *of* or *about* something. There is a difference between mere "notional" or "speculative" understanding in which only the mind beholds something, and "spiritual"

---

30. "Miscellanies," no. 117, *WJE* 13:284.

31. "Miscellanies," no. 182, *WJE* 13:329.

32. "Beauty of the World," *WJE* 6:305. Edwards describes God thus in "Of Atoms," Prop. 2, corol. 11, *WJE* 6:215. The context is his discussion of "the certain unknown substance" that materialist philosophers thought supported a body's properties, which Edwards argues is actually the exercise of God's power causing there to be resistance and perseverance at a given place and time. "So that speaking most strictly, there is no proper substance but God himself . . ." (I discuss this aspect of Edwards's thought in more detail in chapter 2 in connection with his typology).

33. "Miscellanies," no. 333, *WJE* 13:410.

understanding or the "sense of the heart" in which the mind does not only speculate but the heart relishes and feels. In Edwards's classic illustration, "He that has perceived the sweet taste of honey, knows much more about it, than he who has only looked upon and felt it."[34] Edwards expresses the regenerate's experiential knowledge when he notes that as a young minister in New York reading the Bible, "Oftentimes . . . every word seemed to touch my heart. I felt an harmony between something in my heart, and those sweet and powerful words."[35] But how is this "sense of the heart" engendered? What is its origin?

I will discuss the "new sense" in more detail in chapter 4, when I consider how it is, according to Edwards, that the Old Testament saints were saved. However, at present it is sufficient merely to note that the spiritual sense arises from the Holy Spirit who indwells the saint as a new vital principle in the soul.[36] The Spirit's light does not merely shine upon the saint, but is communicated to him or her. (I will reserve discussion of the nature of the Holy Spirit's union with the soul until chapter 4). Thus through the saving influences of the Holy Spirit there is laid down in the regenerate "a new inward perception or sensation" which is "entirely different in its nature and kind from anything that ever their minds were the subjects of before they were sanctified." Consequently, "something entirely new is felt or perceived, or thought."[37] And yet Edwards is explicit that the divine and supernatural light immediately imparted to the soul by God "reveals no new doctrine, it suggests no new proposition to the mind, it teaches no new thing of God, or Christ, or another world, not taught in the Bible; but only gives a due apprehension of those things that are taught in the Word of God."[38] The person indwelt by the Holy Spirit is thus enabled to see things in a "new appearance" that he never saw before.[39] His new sight of things is not *quantitatively* different, in the sense that he does not have access to new information. It is, however, *qualitatively* different; that is, he now relishes the excellencies of spiritual things. The regenerate is enabled to see "an excellency in God; he sees a sweet loveliness in Christ. . . ." And of particular concern at present, "he sees the wonderfulness of God's

---

34. *Religious Affections*, WJE 2:272.
35. "Personal Narrative," WJE 16:797.
36. "A Divine and Supernatural Light," WJE 17:411.
37. *Religious Affections*, WJE 2:205.
38. "A Divine and Supernatural Light," WJE 17:412.
39. "A Spiritual Understanding of Things Denied to the Unregenerate," WJE 14:70–96.

designs and a harmony in all his ways, a harmony, excellency and wondrousness in his Word: he sees these things by an eye of faith, and by a new light that was never before let into his mind."[40] The perception of spiritual harmonies is the preserve of the regenerate. Only one who consents to God may begin to perceive the consents that comprise spiritual reality.

Returning to Edwards's proposal to write "The Harmony of the Old and New Testament," it is now perhaps possible to discern the purpose of the project. The work was to be apologetic—a presentation of the most reasonable reading of Scripture, in which its coherence would be shown to lie in thing concerning the Messiah. Yet Edwards knew that such a project would ultimately only be persuasive to the regenerate.[41] Though his "Harmony" would inevitably be shaped by the debates of his day as I argue below, Edwards's expressed intention, to "lead the mind to a view of the true spirit, design, life and soul of the Scriptures, as well as to their proper use and improvement," was one that he knew would only persuade the saints.

There is no doubt that the "Harmony" would have been one of Edwards's major published works. The size of Edwards's notes for the project confirms his admission that it would have provided an "occasion for an explanation of a very great part of the holy scripture." The work would have been the culmination of many years of close biblical study and would have brought together Edwards's observations expressed in sermons, the "Miscellanies," "Notes on Scripture" and the "Blank Bible." Even in its unfinished state there are sufficient structural similarities among the "Harmony" "Miscellanies" to indicate not only the general direction of what Edwards's argument would have been had he completed the work, but that in keeping with his notion of harmony the work would have embodied great intricacy and beauty. Just as to Edwards the Scriptures bear witness to their divine authority by their "wondrous universal harmony and consent and concurrence in . . . aim and drift," so his own work would

40. "Spiritual Understanding," *WJE* 14:79.

41. Edwards follows Calvin, *Institutes*, 1.7.5, in believing that while Scripture is self-authenticating there are evidences that support its credibility, to those who "have embraced it devoutly as its dignity deserves." Calvin claims that "the highest proof of Scripture derives . . . from the fact that God in person speaks in it," a point Edwards echoes when he preaches that "the Scriptures themselves are an evidence of their own divine authority." Calvin, *Institutes*, 1.7.4. "The Duty of Hearkening to God's Voice," *WJE* 10:462. Further discussion of Edwards's apologetics is beyond the scope of the present enquiry, but see Nichols, *Absolute Sort of Certainty, passim*. Schweitzer, "Harmony of Reality," chs. 4–6, similarly demonstrates the aim of the "Harmony" to be apologetic, in common with Edwards's "Rational Account" and his other unwritten "great work," "A History of the Work of Redemption."

likely have been constructed in such a way as to display something of the harmony that he saw in the Bible.[42]

SUMMARY OF CHAPTER CONTENTS

For this culmination of a lifetime of biblical study Edwards treats the relationship between Old and New Testaments under three headings: (a) prophecies of the Messiah and their fulfillment; (b) types of Christ and their antitype; (c) doctrine and precept, or faith and practice. I follow Edwards's lead in structuring my own study. In chapters 1–3 of this work I will explore Edwards's three areas of Testamental harmony in turn. In each I will begin with an examination of Edwards's wider *corpus* before looking at his notes for the unwritten "Harmony." Chapter 4 draws on the conclusions of the previous three chapters and functions as a systematic case study of the soteriological harmony Edwards sees between the Old and New Testaments. The reason for highlighting this is the challenge it poses to the current dominant account of Edwards's soteriology, an account known as "dispositional soteriology."[43] A fuller explanation will be given in what follows, but in brief this account holds that dispositions are ontologically real and that possession of a saving disposition is sufficient for an individual's salvation, irrespective of whether that disposition is expressed in an act of faith. Proponents of "dispositional soteriology" argue that it explains how the elect of the Old Testament were saved when they had no opportunity to exercise faith in Christ. However, it is my contention, as I have already noted, that lack of attention to Edwards's biblical observations has resulted in misunderstanding Edwards and misrepresenting his position. When sufficient attention is paid to Edwards's biblical notebooks it is apparent that, in line with the Reformed tradition he inherited, Edwards assumes that the Old Testament saints were saved not by possession of some unexercised disposition, but by exercising faith in the object common to both Old and New Testaments, namely Christ.

---

42. "Miscellanies," no. 333, *WJE* 13:410–11.

43. The position is associated with Anri Morimoto and Gerald R. McDermott, though it builds on the account of Edwards's ontology offered by Sang Hyun Lee in, among others, Lee, *Philosophical Theology*, *passim*. For the classic accounts of dispositional soteriology see Morimoto, *Catholic Vision*; McDermott, *Edwards Confronts the Gods*.

Chapter 1

Chapter 1 explores Edwards's understanding of the relationship of the Old and New Testaments in terms of Messianic prophecy and fulfillment. It first seeks to situate Edwards in the context of the trans-Atlantic debate concerning Jesus' Messiahship and the fulfillment of Old Testament prophecies. Central to the debate was the Deist, Anthony Collins (1676–1729), who argued that the truth of Christianity stood or fell on the ability to prove from prophecy that Jesus was the Messiah.[44]

While Edwards does not respond to Collins' challenge directly, both his reading and his own output reveal an awareness of it. Edwards shares Collins' convictions that interpretation must operate according to a ruled use of language and take notice of the intention of the human author, but his own commitment to the divine authorship of Scripture means that he cannot finally endorse the univocity Collins demands of the biblical text. Figurative language (metaphor) and figurative history (types) are part of the divinely intended literal sense and combine to speak ultimately of the Messiah, according to Edwards. This spiritual sense is communicated to the regenerate by the indwelling divine author of Scripture, the Holy Spirit, through close attention to the analogies of Scripture and of faith. Previous accounts have depicted Edwards as unrestrained in his exploration of the Bible's spiritual sense. In this chapter I argue that he is in fact guided by Scripture in his exploration to a degree hitherto unrecognized. While a conceptual impasse thus exists between Collins and Edwards, Edwards's intention in the "Harmony" is not to offer the proof from prophecy that Collins demanded, but to show the reasonableness and coherence of a Messianic reading of the ancient Hebrew prophecies. In the second part of the chapter I turn to Edwards's "Harmony" notes. Analysis of the structure of these notes reveals an intention to engage with the criticisms voiced by Anthony Collins. Confining himself to the Old Testament, the ground from which Collins had launched his attack on the Bible's unity, Edwards seeks to "outflank" those who would divide Old and New Testaments by

---

44. Discussion of the origins of modern biblical criticism and the intellectual roots of Deism is beyond the scope of the present enquiry and has been rehearsed many times. See, for example: Frei, *Eclipse, passim*; Greenslade, *West from the Reformation to the Present Day, passim*; Mulsow and Rohls, *Socinianism and Arminianism*; Reventlow, *Authority of the Bible*; Scholder, *Birth of Modern Critical Theology*; Sæbo, *Hebrew Bible/Old Testament*; Sheehan, *Enlightenment Bible*; Stephen, *English Thought*; Weinsheimer, *Eighteenth-Century Hermeneutics*. For recent discussions of Edwards's engagement with Deist thought, see *inter alia* Chai, *Limits of Enlightenment Philosophy*; McDermott, *Edwards Confronts the Gods*; Moody, *Edwards and the Enlightenment*.

establishing as constituent of the Old Testament's literal sense such phenomena as figurative language and predictive prophecy. The increasing complexity and cumulative nature of Edwards's argument, taking in temporally disparate and marginal texts, yields a comprehensive interpretation of the Old Testament, the true scope and sense of which is, according to Edwards, an anticipation of the Messiah.

Chapter 2

Chapter 2 examines the typological harmony Edwards observes between the Old and New Testaments. The typology Edwards inherited was an interpretative tool that linked the Old and New Testaments together in a limited and explicit relationship of temporal Christological prefiguring and fulfillment. In his hands this tool underwent a transformation, consonant with his philosophical commitments to a form of idealism and a notion of being as relational and communicative within a teleological scheme of divine self-glorification. Typology became for Edwards a language found not only in the Bible but writ large in nature and history. The grammar of this language was to be found in Scripture which, under the Holy Spirit, consequently closely guided Edwards's typological observations. As with his exegesis of prophecy, so too with his typology: the degree to which Scripture constrained Edwards's typological exegesis has thus far been unrecognized. The result of this is that previous accounts have depicted Edwards's typology as simultaneously conservative (in respect to Scripture) and liberal (in respect to nature and history). In response I will argue that Edwards's typology comprised a single coherent system.

When Edwards turned his universal typology to the question of the relationship of the Old and New Testaments it delivered a Christological relationship manifest not only at finite specific points, but at every moment. To Edwards the Old Testament in every detail shadowed forth the "more excellent" end and spiritual substance. Thus the typological relationship between the Old and New Testaments was for Edwards infinitely closer than it had been for his predecessors. In his "Harmony" notes on types ("Miscellanies," no. 1069) Edwards confines himself to discussion of the Old Testament, just as he did when addressing the matter of prophecy for his "Harmony" ("Miscellanies," nos. 891, 922, 1067–68 and 1347). His aim, once again, is to ground the unity of the Bible on a demonstration that the Old Testament itself is coherent only as a witness to Christ.

Chapter 3

Chapter 3 examines Edwards's Testamental harmony of "doctrine and precept," or belief and practice. (This chapter will concern itself largely with precept, leaving the harmony in doctrine to the following chapter, a case study in soteriology). Redemption history and a covenantal system, apparent in Edwards's wider *corpus*, provide the unseen framework to this part of his "Harmony." Edwards follows Calvin and a continental Reformed tradition in holding to the substantial similarity but administrative difference of what the Reformed called the "covenant of grace" in Old and New Testaments. The response of the saints to the gospel is similarly temporally-conditioned. Yet as Edwards develops the complexity of the Old Testament "veil," expanding the category of types and the Messianic nature and interconnectedness of prophecy whose meaning is made available to those in possession of the "new sense," so he inevitably emphasizes the substantial similarity between Old and New Testament expressions of the covenant of grace. As with prophecies and types, Edwards is willing to find parallels in doctrine and precept that go beyond the familiar categories employed by his tradition.

Chapter 4

Chapter 4 is less concerned with Edwards's "Harmony" project, offering instead a more systematic approach to his biblical theology. It functions as a case study of the harmony Edwards sees between the Old and New Testaments in terms of soteriology; in doing so it seeks to draw together the threads of the previous three chapters. The scope of chapter 4 is deliberately narrow, being concerned principally to answer the question of how, on Edwards's approach, the Old Testament saints were saved. A framework for the chapter is provided by interaction with the thesis of dispositional soteriology advanced by Anri Morimoto. Morimoto's thesis is dependent on an account of God's being and creation as dispositional. The chapter will therefore engage with Edwards's doctrine of God and argue that far from rejecting the metaphysics of substance and accidents for a dispositional account of God's being, Edwards is committed to an *actus purus* doctrine of God. The soteriological harmony Edwards observes between Old and New Testaments is ultimately expressed in a common object of saving faith, namely Christ, as was common to Edwards's tradition. Edwards maintains that the Old Testament saints "closed with Christ" in a manner fitting to their dispensation, though they may have grown in their subjective awareness of their salvation, just as the saints of his own day sometimes did. Though he affirms the greater revelatory clarity of the new dispensation, his multiplication of (Messianic) types and the interconnectedness of (Messianic) prophecy whose content is revealed to the regenerate, mean that in practice Edwards often seems to grant the Old Testament saints a content of faith normally associated in his tradition with the New Testament.

Finally, I have already noted the need that greater attention be paid to the centrality of the Bible to Edwards's thought. In order to understand Edwards's entire project better his theology of the Bible must be better understood since he was first and foremost a pastor and theologian. In this spirit the present work seeks to offer an account of the relationship between the Old and New Testaments in the thought of Jonathan Edwards and by studying this neglected tract of his thought, contribute to a more accurate understanding of his entire project.

I have noted Williams' encouragement that there is value in hearing the strange voices of earlier theologians since they challenge and "de-center" accepted contemporary theological norms. However, the present work seeks not only to offer a presentation of Edwards's theology in all its "de-centering" strangeness, though it attempts to do that, but it also asks whether aspects of Edwards's understanding of the relation of the Old and New Testaments may be retrieved for contemporary theological use. Discussion of this latter question will be drawn together in my general conclusion in which I will argue that among the difficulties of Edwards's account is its dependence on the Spirit-given "new sense" to guide the saint into the true scope and meaning of a text. Though Edwards's method and his reliance on the "new sense" may be explained, it seems less likely that his exegesis could be perfectly replicated by another saint. Nevertheless, his approach does indeed remain of value for a number of reasons. First, despite the shortcoming just mentioned, Edwards takes seriously the nature of the Bible as the Scriptures of the Christian church, whose scope is available to those who profess faith in Jesus the Messiah and who are indwelt by the Holy Spirit. Second, the scale of "The Harmony of the Old and New Testament" is such that it cannot be ignored by contemporary pursuits of the unity of the Bible. Third, Edwards's typology rooted in the Bible in principle offers a way of relating the world the Christian experiences to the world he or she professes to inhabit. Finally, by grounding the unity of the Bible in a unity of the Old Testament whose discrete witness is Messianic, Edwards again in principle offers to resource a conversation between the church and the synagogue.

ONE

Prophecy

INTRODUCTION

IN 1988 STEPHEN STEIN noted that in recent scholarship of Jonathan Edwards the major theme of prophecy had been almost completely overlooked; little has changed since then.[1] Though John Gerstner has examined Edwards's understanding of prophetic inspiration, Stein himself is responsible for nearly all the recent study of Edwards's biblical exegesis.[2] However, Stein's own interest in Edwards's treatment of prophecy has been largely confined to prophetic eschatology and millennialism, by his own admission, "a far more limited notion."[3] Both Prof. Stein and Prof. Kenneth Minkema have published articles on Edwards's "Harmony of the Old and New Testament," the first third of which was to be devoted to the issue of prophecies of the Messiah and their fulfillment.[4] But given the importance of prophecy in the seventeenth and eighteenth-century debates surrounding Jesus' claims to Messiahship and the truth of Christianity, it is remarkable that Jonathan Edwards's understanding of prophecy has remained so neglected.

In *The Reasonableness of Christianity* John Locke reduced Christian confession to that of Jesus as the Messiah, whose coming was foretold in

---

1. Stein, "Spirit and Word," 118–30.
2. Gerstner, *Rational Biblical Theology*, 1.140–54. Gerstner's discussion first appeared as, Gerstner, "Jonathan Edwards and the Bible," 1–71. An abbreviated version of the article appears under the same title in Hannah, *Inerrancy and the Church*, 257–78. On Stein's study of Edwards's exegesis see above, Introduction, n. 4.
3. Stein, "Spirit and Word," 124.
4. Stein, "Spirit and Word"; Minkema, "Great Work," 52–65.

Hebrew prophecies and whose mission was authenticated by miracles.⁵ His friend and disciple, the Deist Anthony Collins (1676–1729) made the fulfillment of prophecies the sole criterion for judging the truth of the Christian religion, and entitled chapter 6 of his *A Discourse of the Grounds and Reasons of the Christian Religion*, "VI. That if those proofs [to Jesus' Messiahship] are valid, Christianity is invincibly establish'd on its true foundation."⁶ But, Collins warned, "... if the proofs for christianity [*sic*] from the Old Testament be not valid; if the arguments founded on those books be not conclusive; and the prophecies cited from thence be not fulfill'd; then has Christianity no just foundation: for the foundation on which Jesus and his apostles built it is then invalid and false." With attention to five examples Collins argued that the Apostles had taken literal prophecies from the Jewish Scriptures and interpreted them not in the sense in which they were intended in the Old Testament, but in a "secondary, or typical, or mystical, or allegorical, or enigmatical sense" to demonstrate their fulfillment and thereby establish the Messianic identity of Jesus of Nazareth.⁷ Collins' conclusion was devastating: "In fine, the

---

5. Locke's goal in *Reasonableness* was to demonstrate that the confession of Jesus as the Messiah was sufficient for salvation. On Locke's project, see John Higgins-Biddle's introduction to, Locke, *Reasonableness*, xv–cxv.

6. Collins, *Grounds and Reasons*, pt. 1, ch. 6. Not all of Collins' detractors shared his confidence in the proof from prophecy. O'Higgins, *Anthony Collins*, 161, notes that it is not clear what prompted Collins to write *Grounds and Reasons*, but it is possible it was the publication in 1722 of a review of the Dutch theologian, William Surenhusius' book, Βίβλος Καταλλαγῆς in which Surenhusius claimed to have discovered twenty-five lost rules by which the Jews of the New Testament times cited and interpreted the Hebrew Scriptures. Collins critiqued Surenhusius' "rules" which included vowel re-pointing and the substitution of consonants, portraying them as unprincipled "wire-drawing" in order to force a particular meaning on the Hebrew prophecies, though O'Higgins, *Anthony Collins*, 167–68, argues that Collins' report of Surenhusius is questionable. Another publication that may have animated Collins' pen was William Whiston's *True Text of the Old Testament*. Collins accused Whiston of "clipping and docking" the prophecies in the attempt to recover a pristine Old Testament text. Noting that the citations of the Old Testament in the New are not always verbally identical, Whiston had argued that the text of the Old Testament had been deliberately corrupted by the Jews in an attempt to cast doubt on Jesus' fulfillment of Messianic prophecies. According to Whiston, the corruption of the prophecies forced exegetes to "go roundly and frequently into that strange notion of the double sense of prophecies, to the great reproach of the Gospel." Whiston, *True Text of the Old Testament*, 92. On the "double sense" and Edwards's relation to it, see my discussion below. Whiston's work, *Scripture Prophecies* followed his 1707 Boyle Lectures in which he rejected any interpretation of Scripture's prophecies as types and argued that they had only one referent, the Messiah.

7. Collins' discussion centers on Matt 1:22–23; 2:15; 2:23; 11:14; 13:14.

prophecies cited from the Old Testament by the authors of the New, do so plainly relate, in their obvious and primary sense, to other matters than those which they are produc'd to prove; that to pretend they prove, is, to give up the cause of Christianity to the Jews and other enemies thereof; who can so easily show, in so many undoubted instances, the Old and New Testaments to have no manner of connection in that respect, but to be in an irreconcilable state."[8]

Grounds and Reasons provoked some thirty-five angry responses, to which Collins in turn replied.[9] In the summary of Hans Frei, Collins presented his readers with a choice: either admit the rules for literal interpretation of the Old Testament prophecies, in which case the New Testament writers' application of those prophecies is false; or admit that the New Testament writers employed non-literal rules for interpreting the Old Testament, in which case their interpretation had little to do with the prophets' words and is therefore meaningless. At the heart of the choice was Collins's insistence on a ruled use of language appropriate to the human author.[10]

The recent publication of Edwards's "Catalogue" and "Account Book" have opened Edwards's world of reading to close examination.[11] The former notebook comprises an annotated list of books Edwards had either read or wished to read. The latter includes a list of books Edwards lent to friends and fellow ministers and the dates on which he lent them.[12] From these notebooks a picture may be drawn of Edwards's reading interests and (of particular concern here), his awareness of the debates in the Old World

---

8. Collins, *Grounds and Reasons*, 31, 40, 48. Collins does not explicitly conclude that Christianity is groundless, though as this extract demonstrates, his argument certainly tends to that direction. The degree to which Collins' writings cautiously implied atheistical convictions is beyond the scope of the present enquiry, but is debated in the secondary literature. While O'Higgins, *Anthony Collins*, 234 portrays Collins' religious position as "ambiguous," being "just on, or just over the fringe of Protestant Christianity," Berman, *History of Atheism*, 71 argues that it is "highly probable" that Collins was "a strong-minded atheist." My concern is simply to highlight the hermeneutical challenge Collins posed to the unity of Old and New Testaments. O'Higgins, *Anthony Collins*, 155–99 offers a detailed exposition of *Grounds and Reasons*.

9. Collins, *Scheme of Literal Prophecy*. For an account of the reception of *Grounds and Reasons* and the ensuing debates see: Stephen, *English Thought*, vol. 1, 212–28; Frei, *Eclipse*, 66–85; O'Higgins, *Anthony Collins*, 174–222.

10. Frei, *Eclipse*, 69.

11. *Catalogues of Books*, WJE 26.

12. For a critical introduction to these notebooks and to Edwards's reading in general see, Thuesen, "Editor's Introduction," WJE 26:1–113.

surrounding Messianic prophecy and the relationship of the Old and New Testaments. Of the leading Deists Edwards only attacked Matthew Tindal directly in his own writing, though he was acquainted with others through the compilations of Philip Skelton and John Leland.[13] Conspicuous by his absence from Edwards's "Catalogue" is Anthony Collins. Indeed nowhere in Edwards's *corpus* is Collins named. Yet it is inconceivable that Edwards was unaware of this leading Deist thinker or the significance of his claims outlined above. The presence of the compilations of Skelton and Leland, coupled with the number of volumes in Edwards's "Catalogue" that confront Collins' arguments, strongly suggests Edwards was indeed aware of Collins though his access to him was a mediated one, the result perhaps of his geographical remove from the Old World.[14] Edwards's awareness of Collins' claims and the storm they provoked are the context of his own observations concerning the proper interpretation of Scripture prophecy. In this chapter I will argue that the first part of Edwards's "Harmony" shows evidence of awareness of the criticisms Collins raised. In turn it offers a defense of the unity of the Bible by arguing that a Messianic interpretation of the Hebrew Scriptures is a thoroughly reasonable and coherent interpretation of those Scriptures.

After *Grounds and Reasons* the apologetic debate in Britain moved on from the proof of prophecy to that of miracles.[15] The first part of Edwards's

---

13. "Miscellanies," nos. 1337, 1340, *WJE* 23:342–45, 359–76. Edwards used another Deist, Thomas Chubb as an Arminian foil in *Freedom of the Will*. Chubb's *Collection of Tracts* also appears in the "Account Book." In the "Catalogue" are: [515.] Skelton, *Deism revealed*; [677.] Leland, *Principal Deistical Writers*.

14. Among the responses to Collins listed in Edwards's "Catalogue" are *inter alia*: [305.] Chandler, *Defence*; [325.] Harris, *Practical Discourses*; [553.] Chandler, *Vindication of the Christian Religion*; [556.] Gill, *Prophecies of the Old Testament*; [569.] Bentley, *Remarks upon a Late Discourse*. In addition to Skelton's compilation, Edward Chandler's and William Harris' works are crossed out with a vertical line, likely indicating that Edwards had read them. After leaving Yale College Edwards's access to the scholarship of the Old World was primarily through the library of the Hampshire Association of ministers. When this collection of books was divided in 1742 Edwards's Scottish correspondents, notably the Rev. John Erskine, replaced the Association as his principal source. See Thuesen, "Editor's Introduction," *WJE* 26:36–50.

15. For an account of this shift see O'Higgins, *Anthony Collins*, 175–99. By way of example, Clarke, *Obligations of Natural Religion*, The Boyle Lectures, II, 317, had argued in 1705 that "the divine authority of the Christian religion is positively proved, by the exact completion both of all those prophecies concerning our Lord, and of those that he himself delivered." Following *Grounds and Reasons*, in a new edition of the same Boyle lecture Clarke, *Connexion of the Prophecies*, 28, argued that prophecies were not a proof that Jesus was the Messiah, but a *sine qua non* to his being such: "yet neither any nor all of these characters, could prove any man to be the promised

"Harmony" however, appears to assume that a proof from prophecy is possible. Edwards expresses to the trustees of the College of New Jersey his intention to consider "all the various particulars wherein these prophecies have their exact fulfillment [sic]" and show the "universal, precise, and admirable correspondence between predictions and events."[16] It would be curious were Edwards employing an argument abandoned in Britain some two decades earlier, but he is not. Such an argument is simply not consonant with his commitments displayed elsewhere in his *corpus*. As I noted in my introduction Edwards follows Calvin in the subordination of external proofs to Scripture's self-authentication.[17] Although Calvin offers proofs to support Scripture's credibility, preceding them all, the "same Spirit . . . who has spoken through the mouths of the prophets must penetrate into our hearts to persuade us that they faithfully proclaimed what has been divinely commanded."[18] In the same way to Edwards the noetic effects of sin are such that the unregenerate are denied a spiritual understanding of things. When reading Scripture there is in them a "want of observing the nature and design of the Old Testament."[19] Only the saint illuminated by the Holy Spirit may see "a harmony, excellency and wondrousness in [God's] Word," and of interest here, the "true scope and sense" of the prophecies.[20] Therefore, Edwards's intention in the first part of his "Harmony" is not to offer convincing proofs to those like Collins who questioned Jesus' Messianic identity based on the fulfillment of prophecy. Rather his aim is both to highlight "the unreasonableness of [the] deists" and to offer a more reasonable way of reading the prophecies.[21]

In what follows I will first establish the general features of Edwards's understanding of prophecy, comparing it with that of Anthony Collins. I will then turn to his "Harmony" notes in which he constructs a reasonable

---

Messiah; but the want of any one of them, would prove that man was not he. The proof of Jesus being the Christ were the works which his Father gave him to finish."

16. Letter, no. 230, *WJE* 16:728.

17. See above, Introduction, n. 41.

18. Calvin, *Institutes*, 1.7.4. Calvin offers thirteen proofs to "fortify the authority of Scripture" in *Institutes*, 1.8.1–13. Discussion of Edwards's apologetics is beyond the scope of this enquiry, but see for example Nichols, *Absolute Sort of Certainty*, 21–45; Schweitzer, "Harmony of Reality," esp. ch. 4, "The Harmony of Scripture."

19. "Work of Redemption," *WJE* 9:290.

20. "Spiritual Understanding," *WJE* 14:79; Letter no. 230, *WJE* 16:728.

21. "Work of Redemption," *WJE* 9:282. Edwards makes this comment in the context of arguing that all the works and words of God since the creation of the world were preparatory to Christ's incarnation.

defense of the harmony of the Christian Scriptures and the identity of Jesus the Messiah, in order to show how he "rebuts" the criticisms voiced by Collins.

Authorial Intention, the Literal Sense and a Ruled Use of Language

An account of Reformation and post-Reformation exegesis is beyond the scope of the present work.[22] The quest for the literal sense of the text was inherited by the orthodox from the Reformers. Broadly speaking this involved rejecting the notion of diverse senses of a text as the basis of doctrinal argument (the principle, *theologia symbolica non est argumentativa*). Common to such exegesis was the distinction between types and figures intrinsic to the text (and therefore comprising its literal sense), and those extrinsically and imaginatively applied by the exegete.[23] An influential preaching manual on both sides of the Atlantic, *The Arte of Prophesying* by William Perkins (1558–1602) affirmed that, "There is one onelie sense and the same is the literall."[24] And nearly a century later one of Jonathan Edwards's favorite Reformed divines, Francis Turretin (1623–87) analyzed this "only one true and genuine sense" with characteristic precision, noting that the literal sense can be either "simple" where the historical sense declares a historical event, doctrine or precept, or "composite" as in prophecy, where part of the sense lies in the type and part in the antitype. Furthermore, the "simple" sense may be either "proper and grammatical" where the literal sense is indicated by the words themselves, or "figurative and tropical" where the sense lies in what the words signify.[25] These

---

22. See, for example, Muller and Thompson, *Biblical Interpretation*; Muller, *PRRD*, 2, *passim*. For a recent study of Edwards's seventeenth-century interlocutors, see Withrow, "Wondrous and Glorious Things," 19–90.

23. See Muller's helpful discussion of "The 'Divers Senses' and the Unity of Scripture," in *PRRD*, 2.469-82; Frei, *Eclipse*, 75-85. See for example, Keach, *Tropologia*, I. ii, "Of Parables, VI," 240.

24. Perkins, *Arte of Prophecying*, 30-31. Edwards owned the three volume *Works* of Perkins (London, 1608-31), twice lending a volume to Samuel Hopkins. Hall, *World of Wonder, Days of Judgment*, 48, notes that probate inventories from seventeenth-century New England frequently show common laypeople to have owned at least one volume of the *Works*. On the influence of Perkins on New England preaching see Toulouse, *Art of Prophesying*, esp. 15–23; Hall, *Faithful Shepherd*, *passim*.

25. Turretin, *Institutes* 2.19.2. Edwards recommends both Turretin and Mastricht as "excellent" to the Rev. Joseph Bellamy: "Turretin is on polemical divinity; on the Five Points and all other controversial points; and is much larger in these than Mastricht;

distinctions do not represent multiple senses of the text. There is only one sense, the literal one, defined as "that which is intended by the Holy Spirit and is expressed in words either proper or figurative."[26] The "mystical" or "spiritual" sense of the text, being "that in which the thing expressed in the literal sense signifieth another thing in a mystery, for the shadowing out of which it was used by God," is not properly separate from the literal sense but is grounded in it.[27] To anticipate the argument that follows, Edwards follows this tradition, namely that the spiritual sense is not a distinct sense from the literal one but arises from it by divine design. His expansion of types coupled with his confidence in the saint's "new sense" gives him particular freedom in interpreting Scripture's spiritual sense. Yet Edwards is guided in this by Scripture, and this to a degree hitherto unrecognized.

Stephen Stein helpfully highlights the fact that Edwards uses the term, "spiritual sense" in two ways, both to describe "the process and product of God's grace."[28] The term refers to both an epistemological category (that of affective knowledge), and a hermeneutical category ("the fuller understanding of the Bible which is one of the results of the sense of the heart implanted by God").[29] First, as I outlined in the "Introduction," to have a "spiritual sense" or a "spiritual understanding" of the gospel, according to Edwards, is not to possess new information about it, but rather to appreciate its excellency, beauty and fitness. This is the preserve of the regenerate. This spiritual knowledge stands in contrast to the "notional" or "speculative" knowledge available to all men. Spiritual knowledge, arising from the "new sense of the heart" is a spiritual sense engendered by the Holy Spirit at conversion. Second, according to Stein, Edwards uses the term "spiritual sense" to denote the product of God's grace: a fuller understanding of the Bible which is one of the results of the sense of the heart implanted by God.

---

and is better for one that desires only to be thoroughly versed in controversies. But take Mastricht for divinity in general, doctrine, practice and controversy; or as an universal system of divinity; and it is much better than Turretin or any other book in the world, excepting the Bible, in my opinion. . ." Letter, no. 73, "To the Reverend Joseph Bellamy," Northampton, January 15, 1746/7, *WJE* 16:216–18. Like Turretin, Leigh, *Treatise of Divinity*, 1.9, 171–72, distinguishes the literal sense into "plain and simple" and "figurative," citing as an example of the latter Christ's words in John 10:16 that describe the Gentiles as "other sheep which are not of this fold."

26. Turretin, *Institutes*, 2.19.3.
27. Leigh, *Treatise*, 1.11, 172.
28. Stein, "Spiritual Sense," 109.
29. Ibid.

Jonathan Edwards's Bible

In a passage in *Religious Affections* Edwards brings together the two ways in which Edwards uses the term "spiritual sense." He argues that spiritually to understand the Scriptures is to have one's eyes opened to what was always in the Scripture. According to Edwards, it is not the grasping of a *new* meaning, but the recognition of the "true meaning," the true scope and sense of Scripture, to which the reader was before spiritually blind:

> Spiritually to understand the Scripture, is rightly to understand what is in the Scripture, and what was in it before it was understood: 'tis to understand rightly, what used to be contained in the meaning of it; and not the making of a new meaning. When the mind is enlightened spiritually and rightly to understand the Scripture, it is enabled to see that in the Scripture, which before was not seen, by reason of blindness. . . . Spiritually to understand the Scripture, is to have the eyes of the mind opened, to behold the wonderful spiritual excellency of the glorious things contained in the true meaning of it, and that always were contained in it, ever since it was written. . . .[30]

More controversially, Stein argues that although "Edwards spoke of the Bible as the source and the norm of his theology. . . often it appears that the Scripture was more the occasion than the origin or measure of his reflections."[31] He argues that in contrast to the Reformation accent on the sufficiency of the singular literal sense of the Bible, Edwards "underscored the multiplicity of levels of meaning in the text and the primacy of the spiritual."[32] He accuses of Edwards of poetic "flights of exegetical fancy" and of exercising his "exegetical imagination without limit."[33] "[T]he Bible did not function for [Edwards] as a theological norm or source in any usual Protestant fashion because the literal sense of the text did not restrict him. On the contrary, the freedom and creative possibilities of the spiritual sense beckoned, and he pursued them with abandon."[34]

Although Stein's identification of Edwards's two uses of the term "spiritual sense" is helpful, in the present chapter (on prophecy) and the following chapter (Edwards's typology) I will argue that surprising though some of his conclusions may be to modern sensibilities, Edwards's exegesis is not the flight of fancy that Stein contends, but is tightly constrained by

---

30. *Religious Affections*, WJE 2:280–81.
31. Stein, "Spiritual Sense," 101.
32. Ibid.
33. Stein, "Edwards and the Rainbow," 440.
34. Stein, "Spiritual Sense," 113.

his reading of Scripture. Of particular use to Edwards in his pursuit of the "true meaning" of Scripture is the principle that Scripture is its own interpreter. The degree to which he relies on this has been underestimated in previous accounts of his exegesis, as I will seek to demonstrate.

Central to Edwards's immediate exegetical heritage is the principle that Scripture is its own interpreter. Perkins notes, "The principall interpreter of the Scripture is the holy Ghost . . .." and, "The supreme and absolute meane of interpretation is the Scripture it self." He then describes three "subordinate means" to aid in the interpretation of a passage of Scripture. The first is the analogy of faith, to Perkins, a summation of the doctrines of the faith expressed in the Apostles Creed, coupled with love explicated in the Decalogue. Second, the *sui interpres* principle must take account of the "circumstances," or context of the text propounded. Third, Scripture interprets itself by comparison or "conference" of similar and dissimilar places.[35] He then offers an example of his method, interpreting 1 Cor 11:24 ['This is my body which is broke for you'] thus: Taken "naturally" the words disagree both with the analogy of faith since the Creed states that Christ "ascended into heaven" and with the nature of a sacrament which is "a memoriall of the bodie of Christ absent." Therefore the words are taken figuratively: "the bread is a sign of my body; by a Metonymie of the subject for the adjunct." This agrees with the analogy of faith, it "consenteth with the circumstances of the place propounded" and it agrees with "like places."[36] The figure is part of the literal sense intended by the divine author.

John Edwards (1637–1716) Anglican author of the ministerial advice manual, *The Preacher*, similarly notes that "as Scripture offers some difficulties to us, so it solves them best of all. The Bible itself is the best interpreter and reconciler."[37] He shares Perkins' subordinate principles also. First, like Perkins John Edwards asserts, "The only rule of faith is the best rule of interpretation."[38] Second, regarding the importance of a text's context: "We must not diminish nor curtail any text, or any part of the Bible: we must take it all together, one part with another, and never determine anything from a single sentence or passage separated from the rest,

---

35. Perkins, *Arte of Prophecying*, 31–32.

36. Ibid., 46–51.

37. Edwards, *Preacher*, 94. Jonathan Edwards lists the work in his own "Catalogue": [200.], *WJE* 26:155 and was interested in obtaining other works of his namesake, four of which he mentions in the "Catalogue" [nos. 129., 132., 281., 452.]

38. Edwards, *Preacher*, 94.

where we know there is a connection." Third, the conference of texts is crucial to correct interpretation: "If a man heedfully peruses the Scripture and diligently compares one place with another, and lets plain texts expound those that are dark, and the larger ones those that are but brief and concise, he will never fail of the true meaning of these Holy Writings."[39] The *sui interpres* principle expounded in these three ways by both Perkins and John Edwards underlie Jonathan Edwards's exegesis of prophecy to a degree that Stein has unfortunately not recognized, as I will seek to demonstrate below. However, since in what follows I will examine Edwards in the context of the challenges posed by Anthony Collins, I will first briefly outline the latter's own rules of exegesis.

Collins' debt to John Locke's epistemology of sensation is apparent. Locke had argued that we cannot know an object itself, only our sensation of it. Simple ideas, sensibly related to external objects have relation only to those objects. Our words are signs of our experienced ideas, so that in the communication of those ideas words are significant and meaningful only to the extent that they can be understood as referring to those intended ideas.[40] Prophets, the recipients of the "original revelation," as Locke termed it, signified their new simple ideas by their words. To everyone else access to this revelation was through the reading of Scripture and was therefore one stage removed from "original revelation"; Locke termed this indirect communication, "traditional revelation."[41] In the activity of reading Scripture, as with any indirect communication, meaning could not be understood except by ideas derived from the stock of ideas the reader already possessed. Whatever the "original revelation" may have been, the reader of Scripture only had access to it through the propositions of "traditional revelation" and these propositions must comply with the normal rules for the meaningful use of language.[42] If language were to be used in

---

39. Ibid.

40. Locke, *Essay*, 3.9.1–4.

41. The inadequacy of words to communicate simple ideas leads Locke to the conclusion that there is unavoidable obscurity surrounding the ancient authors, which should lead to caution in reading them and charity in consideration of the interpretations offered by others. Locke, *Essay*, 3.9.10, 22–23. Locke notes a further limitation of traditional revelation: "Whatsoever Truth we come to the clear discovery of, from the Knowledge and Contemplation of our own Ideas, will always be certainer to us, than those which are conveyed to us by Traditional Revelation" because we can never be as sure that this revelation originated from God as we can be of the agreement or disagreement of our own ideas. Locke, *Essay*, 4.18.4.

42. Ibid., 4.18.3. The notion that the same exegetical rules applied to the Bible as to every other text has a history beyond the scope of the present work. It is explicit in the

a ruled and rational way, propositions could not refer to more than one thing at the same time.[43]

Collins appears to have shared Locke's assumptions, though he drew radical conclusions from them when he began his attack on what he perceived to be the New Testament's interpretation of literal Old Testament prophecies. He argued: "To suppose that an author has but one meaning at a time to a proposition (which is to be found out by a critical examination of his words) and to cite that proposition from him, and argue from it in that one meaning, is to proceed by the common rules of grammar and logick; which, being human rules, are not very difficult to be set forth and explain'd. But to suppose passages cited, explain'd, and argu'd from in any other method, seems very extraordinary and difficult to understand, and to reduce to rules."[44]

Edwards concedes that the New Testament writers sometimes applied Old Testament texts in ways not envisaged by their human authors. In contrast to Locke and Collins, the Reformed theologian appears to believe that a single text might have more than one referent. For example, he notes that "many prophecies of the Old Testament are applied in the New, to other things than what they most directly signified. Many of the prophecies of Scripture are applicable to many things."[45] Edwards agrees that Scripture's language, like all language, must obey certain rules if it is to be meaningful. And like Locke and Collins, Edwards roots the ruled use of language in the intention of a rational author. But for Edwards discussion of authorial intention is inadequate if attention is not also paid to the intention of the rational divine author.

Ava Chamberlain notes that Edwards's "Miscellanies" of the 1730s express his attempt to construct a defense of the rationality of the Christian religion against Deist criticisms. She argues that Edwards's response to the Deist challenges he encountered shifted in the 1730s from a systematic

---

Tractatus Theologico-Politicus of Benedict [Baruch] Spinoza (1632–77), who suggested that prophecies were phenomena of culturally-expressed meaning, not universal truth; their significance was the historical function they played in the culture of their time. Spinoza's method pivoted on the assumption that the same epistemological rules should be applied to the Bible as to any other text since its authors were men like any other men. On Spinoza's contribution to the development of rationalist biblical criticism see Harrisville and Sundberg, *Bible in Modern Culture*, 30–45.

43. Locke asserts this in numerous places in his *Essay*, but considers it in depth in his discussions, "Of the Abuse of Words" and "Of the Remedies of the foregoing Imperfections and Abuses," Locke, *Essay*, 3.9 and 11 respectively.

44. Collins, *Grounds and Reasons*, 51. On these supposed "rules" see above, n. 6.

45. "Notes on Scripture," no. 188, *WJE* 15:104–5.

defense of orthodoxy to a historical defense based upon prophecy and that this is reflected in Edwards's abandonment of the "Rational Account," his adoption of the historical mode in his 1739 redemption discourse and his two great writing projects, "A History of the Work of Redemption" and "The Harmony of the Old and New Testament."[46] Crucially, Edwards's attempt employs a standard of rationality not shared by his opponents. Thus while Edwards concurs with Locke's claim that religious belief must conform to the principles of reason, for Edwards it is the "new sense," engendered in the saint by the Holy Spirit and not unaided human reason that is necessary for reading Scripture properly.[47] The analogy of Scripture is closed to the mere "principles of nature." What is needed is a new "spiritual principle" animating the exegete: "When the ideas themselves appear more lively, and with greater strength and impression, as the ideas of spiritual things do [to] one that is spiritually enlightened, their circumstances and various relations and connections between themselves and with other ideas appear more... and therefore hereby a man sees the harmony between spiritual things, and so [comes] to be convinced of their truth. *Ratiocination, without this spiritual light, never will give one such an advantage to see things in their true relations and respects to other things and to things in general.*"[48]

Edwards further argues that common language cannot adequately describe spiritual things and therefore the common use of words must not be allowed to determine the way Scripture uses those same words. Instead, "the rule is the use of words in Scripture language: what is said in fact to be the use of words in the Bible, by comparing one place with another.... that must determine the sense in which we must understand them."[49] "Most of the jangles about religion in the world," Edwards notes, stem from the inability to distinguish between the meaning of words in divinity from what is intended in their normal use.[50] Similarly, in a sermon of May 1748 the Northampton pastor challenges his congregation to

---

46. Chamberlain, "Editor's Introduction," *WJE* 18:26–34.

47. In the following chapter I will note that Edwards speaks of his expanded conception of typology as "a certain sort of language," whose idiom may be acquired under the tutelage of the Holy Spirit by "good acquaintance with the language... by having our senses as it were exercised to discern it." "Types," *WJE* 11:150. But of present significance is that Edwards views Scripture's language in the same way.

48. "Miscellanies," no. 408, *WJE* 13:469–70. Emphasis added.

49. "Saving Faith and Christian Obedience Arise from Godly Love," *WJE* 25:497–535 (512).

50. "Miscellanies," no. 83, *WJE* 13:249.

apply itself to the interpretation of Scripture, warning it against supposing that the meaning of Scripture's types will be immediately suggested by the Spirit of God. Instead the Holy Spirit's usual method of instructing his people in the meaning of types is by "enlightening . . . minds to see the glory and excellency of holy and divine things, and giving . . . a right taste and relish, and sanctifying and assisting . . . reason to search out the meaning of the Scripture by study or by searching the Scripture, or by comparing one scripture with another, or 'comparing spiritual things with spiritual' as the Apostle speaks [1 Cor 2:13]."[51] Consequently, a failure to grasp the true sense and scope of Scripture is a moral or spiritual issue, not an intellectual one. "[M]ost persons are to blame for their inattentive, unobservant way of reading the Scriptures."[52] They read the histories as if they were "only the histories of the private concerns of such and such particular persons, such as the histories of Abraham, Isaac and Jacob . . . " whereas in fact they are "accounts of vastly greater things, things of greater importance and more extensive concernment than they that read them are commonly aware of." "Infinitely greater things" contained or pointed at in the histories are "passed over and never taken account of."[53] Divine illumination is necessary for reading Scripture, but Scripture reading is no mystical experience detached from exegetical rules. Readers must, "be assiduous in reading the holy Scriptures" and must "content not [themselves] with only a cursory reading."[54] They must observe what they read and follow Christ's injunction to "search the Scriptures."[55] The pursuit of the true scope or sense of any word or passage may be established under the illumination of the Holy Spirit but it is by the "conference" of similar texts and comparison of dissimilar ones. Scripture is a self-contained, self-interpreting world whose meaning is made available to the saint only by its divine author, the Holy Spirit. It is a world that the reader must inhabit by faith, but one in which he or she is an energetic and studious participant.

Underlying Edwards's convictions regarding access to the true scope and sense of the Bible is the assumption of a divinely-intended harmony of meaning and message, the analogy of Scripture. And as its title suggests,

---

51. "Extraordinary Gifts of the Spirit are Inferior to Graces of the Spirit," *WJE* 25:309.

52. "Work of Redemption," *WJE* 9:291.

53. Ibid.

54. "The Importance and Advantage of a Thorough Knowledge of Divine Truth," *WJE* 22:101.

55. Ibid.

Edwards's "Harmony of the Old and New Testament" rests firmly on this assumption. Edwards depends on the analogy of Scripture and the analogy of faith to answer many of the objections to the Christian religion that he notes in his "Miscellanies." For example, in "Miscellanies," no. 842 Edwards answers those who object to Christianity on the basis that the apostles seemed to speak of Christ's coming to judgment "as if they thought it near at hand" when it has still not appeared many centuries later. Turning to Ephesians 2:7 ["That in the age to come He might shew the exceeding riches of His grace in His kindness toward us through Christ Jesus"] Edwards engages in a study of the phrase "ages to come," noting that the Apostle uses it to indicate a time that was "not to be till many generations were passed, yet it was at hand, in a sense that is agreeable to the common language of the Holy Spirit." By a comparison of texts he observes that the incarnation was also spoken of as being "at hand" by the prophets Haggai, Malachi and Isaiah though it lay centuries ahead. And when the Apostle Peter says in connection with Christ's second coming, that "a thousand years in God's sight is but as one day [2 Pet 3:8], 'tis no new conceit of his own, to save their own reputations; but God's language, that he had used of old, that justifies him in so saying."[56] Thus to Edwards apparent exegetical difficulties can be resolved by careful attention to Scripture's rule of language elsewhere, the literal sense intended by the rational divine author being conveyed by the Holy Spirit to the saint.

For Edwards the Holy Spirit's superintendence of Scripture's writing has an important implication: while Edwards is able to endorse what Locke and Collins say concerning the intention of the human author or "penman" as Edwards frequently calls him, he denies with respect to the divine author the univocity Collins demands of the text. The rational human author might have had only one meaning in mind as he wrote, but the rational divine author who directed the writing frequently intended harmonious relation to more than one historical referent. This is becoming of "him who is infinite in understanding and has everything in full and perfect view at once." Scripture, he continues, "often includes various distinct things in its sense. [God] knows how to adapt his words to many things, and so to speak infinitely more comprehensively than others, and to speak so as naturally to point forth many things: I say, it becomes such a One, when he speaks, to speak so as [to] include a manifold instruction in his speech."[57] Thus while Abraham had only Isaac in mind when

---

56. "Miscellanies," no. 842, *WJE* 20:57–64.
57. "Miscellanies," no. 851, *WJE* 20:80.

he spoke of the sacrificial lamb in Gen 22:8, the Holy Spirit's intention encompassed his. Consequently, Abraham's words referred also to Jesus Christ, the Lamb of God.[58] While the linking of type and antitype as dual historical referents to a single prophecy places Edwards firmly within a "pre-critical" hermeneutical tradition, Edwards also expands the notion of a text's multiple referents, bringing to the fore the importance of the analogy of faith in his exegesis. In doing this he makes explicit a move, analogous to his transformation of typology which will be considered in the following chapter.[59] In terms of Scripture Edwards argues that two or more meanings of a word or text can validly co-exist even where they are *not* linked through a typological referent, providing it is agreeable to the analogy of faith and appears to be the intention of the divine author. For example, commenting on Dan 5:25ff. Edwards compares the words in the ancient languages and relates their meaning: "The signification of these words is, 'he hath numbered, he hath weighed, and they divide.' *Mene, mene*; that's repeated for the thing is certain. It signifies, both in Hebrew and Chaldee, 'he hath numbered and finished.' *Tekel*; that signifies in Chaldee, 'thou art weighed,' and in Hebrew, 'thou art too light.' *Upharsin*, which should have been rendered *Pharsin* or *Peres*; *Pharsin* in Hebrew signifies the Persians; *Paresin* in Chaldee signifies 'dividing.' Daniel puts both together."[60] The analogy of faith guides Edwards's exegesis so that polyvalence is not confined to typological relationship. A word "may allow of two senses or translations entirely different and not dependent or related one to another as type and antitype . . . And when both senses are what the language properly allows, both are instructive and agreeable to the analogy of faith, we may well interpret 'em of both."[61] Again, to Edwards the pursuit of the literal sense as that intended by the Holy Spirit entails attention to the occasion, context and scope of a text as well as to the "conference" of Scriptures, guided by reference to the theological commitments of the analogy of faith. Only under the guidance of the Holy Spirit and by exercise of the Spirit-given "new sense" may the interpreter perceive Scripture's ruled use of language and interpret faithfully.

---

58. Gen 22:8, "Blank Bible," *WJE* 24:164–65.

59. In chapter 2 I discuss Edwards's conception of types as images found not only in Scripture, but also throughout history and the natural world, vehicles of God's self-communication, the interpretation of which similarly depend on the analogies of Scripture and faith.

60. Dan 5:25ff, "Blank Bible," *WJE* 24:764.

61. Ibid.

In short, Edwards's approach is not the unprincipled exercise of imagination that Stein suggests. It does operate according to certain principles, overarching all of which is that Scripture is its own and best interpreter. The Northampton divine does read Scripture according to certain rules or principles, but for Edwards (unlike for Collins) these are rules of a dynamic language of divine communication, the sense of which is only available to those in possession of the Holy Spirit.

Given their importance to Edwards's interpretation of prophecy, particularly in his "Harmony," discussion of the authorial intention and the literal sense must take account of two figurative features: types and metaphorical language. I will treat each in turn.

Prophecy and Types

Edwards concedes that the prophets might have had "other concerns" besides their chief Messianic concern. Though God may have intended more through the prophets' words than they themselves knew, the prophets predicted Christ's redemption by the Spirit of Christ that was in them. Edwards explains the relationship between "other concerns" and the chief concern as that between type and antitype.

Opponents of Collins differed over the matter of the double-referent of prophecies.[62] As I have noted above, William Whiston (1667–1752) rejected the notion of types altogether.[63] The dissenting minister, Samuel Chandler (1693–1766) believed that while some prophecies might have a double fulfillment, in the majority of cases the prophecy could be divided such that part might be said to concern an immediate fulfillment, while part referred to a more distant event.[64] By contrast Anglican theologian and philosopher, Samuel Clarke (1675-1729) defended the notion of prophesied types when he noted that the same words might have reference "to some nearer event" but also "to the great event which providence had in view."[65] Anglican clergyman, Arthur Ashley Sykes (ca. 1684–1756) found the notion of types absurd and would only allow the use of typology when

---

62. In this brief summary I follow O'Higgins, *Anthony Collins*, 175.

63. See above, n. 6.

64. Chandler, *Vindication*, 253.

65. Clarke, *Connexion of the Prophecies*, 23. The work appears as [419.] in Edwards's "Catalogue," *WJE* 26:214, crossed out with a vertical line, indicating that Edwards had read it.

the prophet made it clear he was employing it.⁶⁶ In contrast to Whiston and Sykes, Edwards was enthusiastically committed to types as a unifying feature of redemption history witnessed in Old and New Testaments. As I will demonstrate below, at times Edwards notes, like Samuel Chandler, that a prophecy may be dissected in such a way that it is seen to respect two events: one immediate, the other more distant. And at times, like Clarke, he endorses the notion of prophesied types. Yet however Edwards explains the phenomenon, he is certain of the fact of prophecy's double-referents, though he is less certain of degree to which the prophets understood the full range of referents of their own messages.⁶⁷

Sometimes Edwards suggests that the prophets were well aware of the typical nature of the referent they intended. They knew that their messages had both an immediate material referent and an ultimate spiritual referent.⁶⁸ Sometimes they spoke of the ultimate referent (the antitype) in terms of the more immediate referent (the type), or moved seamlessly from one to the other in the same message. Edwards observes this practice in Jesus' own discourses with the Jews. In John 2:19f Christ, speaking of his body, challenged the Jews to "destroy this temple and in three days I

---

66. Sykes, *Truth of the Christian Religion*, 178, 204, 205. This response to Collins also appears in Edwards's "Catalogue," as [573.], *WJE* 26:264–65, though there is no indication Edwards read it.

67. Brown notes that this very question became a subject for discussion at the Hampshire Association of ministers in 1744–45. He conjectures that perhaps Edwards was responsible for pushing the agenda at the Association since he has an extensive entry ("Miscellanies," no. 842, *WJE* 20:57–64, ca. 1740) on this theme. Edwards raises the subject again ca. 1753 in "Miscellanies," nos. 1198–99, *WJE* 23:119–23. Brown, *Edwards and the Bible*, 22, 211 n. 82, 239 n.55. Edwards's notebooks for his unwritten "A History of the Work of Redemption" suggest that he intended settling the question there. He notes: "When Come to MOSES observe how Revelation was given & upheld in the Ch[ur]h of God till that Time. & then observe the Nature of Prophecy. how the Prophet & Persons that had Revelations knew 'em to be Revelations from God how They knew before Moses & how afterword. & how true Prophets were known to others, about the Continuance of Prophecy." "A History of the Work of Redemption," Bk. 1, vol. 31, *Works of Jonathan Edwards*, http://www.edwards.yale.edu. Whether or not Edwards was responsible for raising the question at the Association, it was one that he seems to have wrestled with inconclusively.

68. Likewise, Turretin, *Institutes*, 12.5.15 notes, "The same spiritual promises were given to them with us, although often under the shell and veil of promises." In *Institutes*, 11.5.18–20 he repeats that the promises were taken by the Old Testament saints as respecting spiritual, not temporal deliverance. In this Edwards follows the notion of a distinction between substantial similarity and administrative difference of the covenant of grace in Old and New Testament. Since I discuss this in chapter 3 I will pass over it here.

will raise it up." Edwards reasons that since it was the Spirit of Christ who spoke through the prophets, could not the prophets also have spoken consciously of the antitype in terms of the type? Could they not have spoken knowingly in the same message of two stages of fulfillment?[69] Again, commenting on the LORD God's promise in Gen 3:14–15 that his Seed would crush the serpent's head, Edwards notes: "In this first prophecy that ever was uttered, we have a very plain instance of what is common in divine prophecies through the Scripture, viz. that one thing is more immediately respected in the words, and another that is the antitype principally intended, and so of some of the words being applicable only to the former, and others only to the latter, and of God's beginning to speak in language accommodated to the former, but then as it were presently forgetting the type, and being taken up wholly about the antitype."[70]

Edwards's position does not appear entirely consistent, however. On occasions he notes that sometimes the prophets did not speak intentionally of the Messiah at all; their chief concern may have been only a more immediate referent which redemption history would later reveal to have been a divinely-intended type.[71] Therefore, in contrast to Collins Edwards asserts that in reading the prophets "we need not seek an interpretation which it would be natural for the prophets themselves to understand by it, for the Holy Ghost spoke in what words he pleased to, and meant what he pleased, without revealing his meaning to the prophets."[72]

Edwards, the revival pastor teaches that new "immediate revelation" (which he defines as, "God's making known some truth by immediate suggestion of it to the mind, without its being made known by sense or reason, or by any former revelation") is unavailable now that the canon of Scripture has closed. Immediate revelation was designed as a temporary aid to the church in her minority until, with the closing of the canon, she would be furnished with a "perfect and complete standing rule, sufficient to guide her in all things." Edwards, the optimistic post-millenialist believes

---

69. "Miscellanies," no. 1287, *WJE* 23:231–32.

70. "Notes on Scripture," no. 456, *WJE* 15:537.

71. "Miscellanies," no. 1308, *WJE* 23:267–68 comprises an extract from Stapfer, *Institutiones*, 2.1088 (trans. by Douglas Sweeney). Stapfer notes that it is not proper that a prophecy's meaning should be perfectly plain: "For it is not necessary that they are understood before the event; nor is it needed that human industry and wisdom contribute anything to their fulfillment. The latter would certainly occur if human beings knew clearly beforehand everything by which something ought to happen. Nor, finally, ought divine counsels be returned void from the foreknowledge of human beings."

72. "Notes on Scripture," no. 118, *WJE* 15:83.

Prophecy

that the church will continue to grow in her understanding of the Bible and in God's time will come to "a very glorious state here in this world and to a very great degree of perfection in knowledge and resemblance of an heavenly state of perfect light and knowledge."[73] He even uses the growth in understanding of the gospel in the Old Testament in an argument that the end of the world and the millennium must still be some way off from his own day. Just as "there are a multitude of things in the Old Testament which the church then did not understand, but were reserved to be unfolded to the Christian church, such as *most of their types and shadows and prophecies*, which make up the greatest part of the Old Testament . . ." so, according to Edwards, the present-day church still has much progress to make in understanding the Scriptures before she reaches the degree of perfection described in such Scriptures as Isa 30:26 ["Moreover the light of the moon shall be as the light of the sun, and the light of the sun shall be sevenfold, as the light of seven days, in the day that the LORD bindeth up the breach of his people, and healeth the stroke of their wound . . ."].[74] This is because the Scriptures were "designed chiefly for the latter age of the world, in which they shall have their chief and, comparatively, almost all their effect; and they were written for God's people in these ages, of whom at least 99 in an hundred must be supposed incapable of such knowledge [of antiquity and ancient figures of speech] by their circumstances and education, and 999 in a thousand of God's people that hitherto have been saved by the Scriptures."[75]

While it appears that Edwards struggles to determine what the prophet understood or intended by his own message, his commitment to the polyvalence of the Holy Spirit's words meets his typology of history and by the meeting of the two he is able to claim that *all* prophecy speaks ultimately of the Messiah.[76] Edwards denies that typical and antitypical fulfillment comprise two distinct "senses" of the prophecy, in the way that

73. "Extraordinary Gifts," *WJE* 25:279–311.

74. "Miscellanies," no. 351, *WJE* 13:426–27. Emphasis added. "Extraordinary Gifts," *WJE* 25:281.

75. "Efficacious Grace," *WJE* 21:232.

76. The attraction to Edwards of Stapfer's account of the double referents of prophecies is thus apparent. "Miscellanies," no. 1307, *WJE* 23:266–67 comprises a lengthy extract from the Stapfer, *Institutiones*, 2.1086–88, in which Stapfer seeks to reconcile the differing interpretations of a single prophecy by highlighting the typical nature of "the City of God." Such is the harmony between the physical and mystical worlds that whatever happens in the typical world also occurs in the antitypical world. Consequently, interpreters who look for the prophecy's fulfillment in this typical world "dissent, but properly agree" with those interpreters who seek the fulfillment in the antitypical world.

Collins employed the term to describe literal and figural readings of the same text. Rather, for Edwards there is one literal sense that embraces more than one historical referent. By way of illustration, in a note on Ezek 38:17 Edwards argues that the fact that Ezekiel, who prophesied during the captivity in Babylon, spoke of the destruction of Israel's enemies as "that which is to be accomplished long after that time, and after the people had been resettled in their own land after a long captivity," shows that the similar message of the former prophets did not have respect *only* to the destruction of Babylon and return from exile, but *also* to an event in the distant future.[77] Edwards returns many times to consider the apparent multiple stages of a prophecy's fulfillment. In a note on Matt 16:28 he discusses Jesus' promise that some of his disciples would not die before seeing his kingdom come in power. Commenting that some of Jesus' disciples saw his transfiguration, some saw the descent of the Holy Spirit and some saw the coming of his kingdom in the destruction of Jerusalem he concludes: "And 'tis plain and evident that 'tis a common thing in Scripture, that things are said to be fulfilled that have been spoken of in the same context when they are fulfilled in their type, and not in that which is ultimately intended." Rather than distinguish between these events, Edwards argues that they should be understood as "several parts or ... degrees" of the one event. Jesus' promise could therefore be considered met even when only one stage of its fulfillment had been achieved.[78] The "conference" of Scriptures and the analogy of faith in pursuit of the one literal sense similarly guide Edwards's interpretation of Enoch's prophecy of the Lord's coming in judgment [Jude 14–15] and indeed of Old Testament prophecies of Christ in general: "It don't seem to be confined to any particular coming of Christ, but it has respect in general to Christ's coming in his kingdom and is fulfilled in a degree in both the first and second coming of Christ. ... It is very parallel in this respect with many other prophecies of the coming of Christ that were given of Christ under the Old Testament."[79]

Edwards owned *The Divine Legation of Moses* by the Anglican Bishop of Gloucester, William Warburton (1698–1779), a work he occasionally appears to have consulted regarding prophecy's multiple referents.[80] In a short note entitled, "Double Sense of Scripture," written in the early 1750s

---

77. Ezek 38:17, "Blank Bible," *WJE* 24:757.

78. "Notes on Scripture," no. 197, *WJE* 15:115–19. See also the related, "Notes on Scripture," nos. 414, 464, *WJE* 15:421–22, 554 respectively.

79. "Work of Redemption," *WJE* 9:144.

80. Warburton, *Divine Legation*.

Prophecy

Edwards refers to Warburton's work and comments, "The prophecies of the seventy years captivity had a twofold accomplishment."[81] Similarly an entry in the "Blank Bible" on Joel 1–2 Edwards again cites Warburton's work regarding the desolation of the land by locusts and by the Assyrian army.[82] However, Edwards rarely uses the term "double sense." The nomenclature he prefers is that of "type," underlining once again his commitment to Christ being the true scope and sense of all Scripture.

Collins had applied Locke's theory of language to prophecies, turning them into deliberate predictions by the human author. He had subordinated the meaning of a text to its historical referent on the ground of the interpreter's assessment of the human authorial intention. A prophecy could only have one meaning, that which the interpreter deemed to have been intended by the human author. Edwards operates on the assumption that the divine authorship of Scripture permits multiple referents in the literal sense. Though Edwards employs the terms "figural sense" and "literal sense" he uses them in a different way from the way Collins does, to refer to the two stages of historical fulfillment.

Metaphorical Language

Locke had conceded that "figurative Speeches, and allusion in Language, will hardly be admitted, as an imperfection or abuse" of language. Figurative language in general was more entertaining than "dry truth," but as a method of instruction, it was misleading, aimed at moving the passions and thereby misleading judgment.[83] This stands in contrast to Edwards's thought, according to which God employs a figurative language (types) in Scripture and the natural world in order to communicate spiritual reality to his creatures through a nexus of images, a feature I will explore in more

---

81. "Miscellanies," no. 1172, *WJE* 23:88. Warburton discusses Joel 1–2 in *Divine Legation*, 2.635ff.

82. Joel 1–2, "Blank Bible," *WJE* 24:792. In the relevant passage Warburton comments: "This Art in the Disposition of the Prophecy is admirable; and renders all Chicane to evade a *double sense* ineffectual. For in some Places of this Prophecy, *Dearth by Insects* must needs be understood; in others, *Desolation by War*. So that both Senses are of Necessity to be taken in.... [I]t joins the two Senses so closely as to obviate all Pretence for a Division to the Injury of the Holy Spirit. Here then we have a Double Sense, not arising from the Interpretation of a single Verse, and so obnoxious to mistake, but of a whole and very large descriptive Prophecy." Warburton, *Divine Legation*, 2. 638–39. Emphasis original.

83. Locke, *Essay*, 3.10.34.

detail in the next chapter.[84] His communication in this way is directed towards both the understanding and inclination of the saint. Indeed to Edwards the "principles of human nature render types a fit method of instruction: it tends to enlighten and illustrate, and to convey instruction with impression, conviction and pleasure, and to help the memory..."[85] Therefore, to bearers of the divine image, a "rhetoric of sensation" that represents spiritual reality under an image is not the inadequate mode of instruction that it was to Locke, but is perfectly fitting as a mode of communication.[86] To Edwards, under the guidance of the Holy Spirit and the analogies of Scripture and faith, the saint's freedom in the identification and interpretation of types is mirrored by his freedom to explore Scripture's metaphors.

In contrast to Collins Edwards argues that often God directed the prophets' words to point beyond what they had intended "both where their

---

84. As will become clear in my discussion of metaphorical language, Edwards also subscribes to a form of *accommodatio* or *condescensio*, the notion that an infinite God must in some way condescend or accommodate himself to human ways of knowing in order to reveal himself. In 1723 Edwards preached on Rev 21:18: "Although things on earth are insufficient to represent to us these glories [of heaven], nor are we capable of conceiving of it, yet God condescends, when he speaks of these things, to our way of apprehension, and because we are most apt to [be] affected by those things which we have seen with our eyes, and heard with our ears and had experience of." "Nothing Upon Earth Can Represent the Glories of Heaven," *WJE* 14:139–40. Metaphorical language is one example of such accommodation; types are another since in Edwards's thought they constitute a language of divine communication. Edwards's confidence that the Spirit-given "new sense" can grasp the meaning of divine communication through Scripture and types does not negate his commitment to *accommodatio* since the doctrine refers to the manner or mode of revelation, not to the quality of revelation or to the matter revealed. Turretin, *Institutes*, 2.17.3, frames his discussion of the perspicuity of the Scriptures around the question of "the obscurity of the mode in which these most abstruse things are delivered and which we maintain are so wonderfully accommodated (*synkatabasei*) by the Lord that the believer (who has the eyes of his mind opened) by attentively reading may understand these mysteries sufficiently for salvation." For a recent study of *accommodatio* in Calvin, see Balserak, "God of Love and Weakness," 177–95; *Divinity Compromised*. On the doctrine in the Reformed tradition see Muller, *PRRD*, 2, *passim*.

85. "Miscellanies," no. 1069, *WJE* 11:191. See Edwards's comment on Gen 1:26 in his "Blank Bible," *WJE* 24:126, that at creation the Son endued humanity with understanding, while the Spirit endued human beings with a holy will and inclination. I will return to Edwards's conception of the *imago dei* in chapter 4.

86. The phrase, "rhetoric of sensation" was coined by Perry Miller. Miller, "Edwards, Locke and the Rhetoric of Sensation." On the development of Edwards's imagistic sermon rhetoric, see Minkema, "Preface to the Period," *WJE* 14:24–34; Kimnach, "Editor's Introduction," *WJE* 10:227–33.

meaning was not agreeable to strict philosophical verity" and "likewise where the more immediate and remote meanings were properly true."[87] According to Edwards, many Old Testament prophecies make no sense at all if read "literalistically."[88] Edwards addressed the issue of biblical metaphors directly in a sermon on Luke 16:24. With attention to those "Freethinkers . . . of the present age" who deny the greatness of hell's sufferings, some of whom "have written to this purpose," Edwards assembles eight arguments to defend his doctrine: "*The torments of hell are exceeding great.*"[89] In the third of these arguments he begins to address the significance of Scripture's metaphors of the wicked as "stubble," "briars," and "thorns" which are easily consumed by the flames. Edwards does not hesitate to draw a doctrinal conclusion from these metaphors: "These similitudes hold forth no less than the perfect destruction of the creature." However, conscious of those who claimed that the interpretation of metaphors must

---

87. "Miscellanies," no. 229, *WJE* 13:347–48. In his "Notes on the Apocalypse" Edwards comments: "the Scripture does not represent things, especially in prophecy and vision, according to philosophical verity, but as they appear to our eyes." *WJE* 5:140–41. Brown highlights also "Miscellanies," no. 133, *WJE* 13:294. Edwards argues against the notion that the literal location of hell is under the earth. This is but a "metaphor expression" of the state of the dead, the symbolic language of a vision: "when taken for reality, it is childish." "Miscellanies," no. 60, *WJE* 13:229–33. See also "Notes on Scripture," no. 274 [composed ca. 1737], in *WJE* 15:230–31, on Jonah's description of hell as being in the bowels of the earth, and at the bottom of the sea. Brown argues that Edwards attempted to reconcile the vulgar language of "biblical descriptions and their traditional 'literal' interpretation to a modern understanding of the cosmos and to the laws that governed it." He notes that Edwards's refusal to identify Scriptural language with "philosophical verity" was intended to defend traditional doctrine, whereas Whiston's extreme literalism in his *Hell's Torments*, a work known to Edwards, was intended to buttress a doctrinal departure. Brown, "Sacred and the Profane Connected," 45.

88. "Miscellanies," no. 1068, § 23. I intend "literalistic" to convey the idea Muller expresses as "a reductionistically grammatical reading that takes no cognizance of figures of speech in the text itself or that atomizes the text in such a way that the broader context or 'circumstances' of the place, the larger analogy of faith, and the divine authorship are not taken into consideration." Muller, *PRRD*, 2.477–82 (477).

89. "The Torments of Hell are Exceeding Great," *WJE* 14:301–28 (303). It is possible that among the "freethinkers" that Edwards has in mind is the Anglican Archbishop John Tillotson (1630–94), whose published sermons were widely circulated both in England and New England. On 7 March 1690 Tillotson preached a sermon, "Of the Eternity of Hell Torments" (pub. London, 1708) which Isabel Rivers notes "caused great offence through the suggestion that hell's torments might not be eternal." *Dictionary of National Biography*, s.v. John Tillotson, cited in McClenahan, "Jonathan Edwards' Doctrine of Justification," 207. On Edwards's defense of hell's torments in his later "Miscellanies," see Pauw, "Editor's Introduction," *WJE* 20:17–24.

not be pushed too far, he asserts, "This is not a straining at all beyond the proper meaning of those places that speak of the utter destruction and absolute ruin of the sinner."[90] Edwards reports the objection that "sometimes the Scripture uses metaphors that, if they should be taken in an equality to the literal sense, 'twould carry the matter beyond the strict truth; as sometimes when the Scripture only speaks of a temporal destruction, it uses such metaphors." Crucial to Edwards's argument is a distinction between Scripture's metaphors of "temporal things" and those of "another world." He admits that the former "often are hyperbole" and that taken ["literalistically"] they express more than is intended.[91] But rather than curtail his argumentative use of metaphors, hyperbolic metaphors of the temporal world are evidence to Edwards of the typological nature of sensible reality. They "allude to some spiritual thing [of which] the temporal thing was the image." So, the bondage of the Israelites in Egypt is called the "iron furnace" [Deut 4:20; Jer 11:4], not because the Israelites ("literalistically") experienced the punishment of being burned alive, but because their experience was a type of hell. Furthermore, since spiritual realities are the "*ultimum*, the very highest things that are aimed at by all metaphors and similitudes," it is impossible, according to Edwards, to exhaust the meaning of figurative language. Biblical metaphors "fall short rather than go beyond" in their portrayal of spiritual reality. Yet even though they are inadequate in this way, the Bible *must* employ metaphors because there is a "want of words to express... [spiritual reality] any other way."[92] "God's aim when he tells us about hell is not to set it out with uncertain metaphors and similitudes, but really to let us know what hell is."[93]

To Edwards figurative language and figurative history are divinely cut from the same cloth. As with types, Edwards expects the saints to explicate Scripture metaphors by the analogies of Scripture and faith. The argumentative use of metaphors is fundamental to Edwards's establishing the Messianic coherence of prophecy. For example, in his "Harmony"

90. "Torments of Hell," *WJE* 14:308, 309.

91. I have substituted the term "literalistically" for Edwards's own "literally" for the sake of clarity, in line with my discussion above of the changing meaning of the literal sense of a text in eighteenth-century hermeneutics.

92. "Torments of Hell," *WJE* 14:312. Anderson, "Editor's Introduction," *WJE* 11:38-39, notes that Edwards's argument at this point in the sermon encapsulates the central thesis of his "Images" notebook on natural types which he may have begun at around this time. However, his sermon of 1723, "Nothing Upon Earth . . ." suggests that Edwards had been considering this five years earlier. See above, n. 84.

93. "Torments of Hell," *WJE* 14:313.

Prophecy

notes his exposition of the metaphor of the "Branch" becomes a significant organizing theme of the work.⁹⁴ Edwards takes the prophecy of the Branch from the roots of Jesse in Isa 11 and traces it through the prophets, noting from Jer 23:5-6 that this Branch is a king who would execute judgment on earth, whose name is "the LORD our righteousness," in whom Israel would dwell in safety. On 2 Sam 23:1-8 he comments: "Here you may see the thing that David speaks of, that his heart was so much upon, is one that was to be the ruler over men, that was to grow of his house. The word in the original signifies 'to BRANCH forth' being of the same root with that so often translated the *Branch* in the prophecies..."⁹⁵

Edwards's approach in his exposition of metaphors is identical to the "allusive allegory" of Benjamin Keach, whose work, *Tropologia* was being read in New England.⁹⁶ Keach (1640-1704) distinguished two kinds of allegory *within* Scripture: the "simple" and "allusive." "Simple allegory" moves directly from the signifier to the meaning, while "allusive allegory" is indirect, its interpretation relying on the reference to other texts or Scriptural figures. Though his transformation of typology, which will be explored in the following chapter, entails an expansion of the argumentative use of types, yet the argumentative use of types itself, apparent throughout Edwards's *corpus*, is characteristic of the Reformed tradition he inherited.⁹⁷

---

94. It appears in "Miscellanies," no. 891, §§ 4-12, 14, 16-17.

95. "Miscellanies," no. 891, § 7.

96. Keach, *Tropologia*. Keach's work, however, does not appear in Edwards's catalogues of reading, his preferred handbook on typology being Mather's *Figures or Types*.

97. This characteristic was not generally shared by Arminian exegetes, however, as witnessed in the dispute between William Sherlock and John Owen over the nature of the mystical union. Central to Sherlock's criticism of Owen was the use of Scripture metaphors by the Reformed tradition that Owen seemed to represent: "these men instead of explaining these metaphors, turn all Religion into an Allegory." Sherlock, *Knowledge of Jesus Christ*, 279. For recent discussion of this debate see, Kapic, *Communion with God*, 153-56. Edwards was familiar with the work of William Sherlock's son, Thomas Sherlock (1677-1761), Bishop of successively Bangor, Salisbury and London. Edwards owned Thomas Sherlock, *Use and Intent*, a work apparently written in response to Collins, *Grounds and Reasons*. Like Edwards, Sherlock argues that "no-one ever understood Isaiah 11:6 literally ['The wolf also shall dwell with the lamb...']. Nor could it now be literally applied to the 'state of the gospel.'" But while acknowledging the metaphor, the Arminian bishop followed his father in his unwillingness to explicate it: "[W]hatever the true Meaning is, this Prophecy expounded by the Rules of Language only, does no more obtrude one determinate Sense upon the Mind since the coming Christ, than it did before. But then we say, the State of the Gospel was very properly prefigured in this Description, and is as properly prefigured by an hundred

So intertwined are type and metaphor as figurative aspects of the literal sense that in his "Harmony" notes Edwards defends the typical nature of history as recorded in Scripture by defending the literal nature of figural language. His strategy is one that he employs throughout his "Harmony," as in his defense of the phenomena of prophecy and types that I will consider below: Edwards confines himself to the Old Testament and the rule of language he finds there. Basing his argument on the coherence of the Old Testament itself, he claims that the Old Testament's use of language is sufficient to demonstrate the ludicrousness of a purely literalistic interpretation: "It would be absurd to take that text literally, 'the mountains and hills shall break forth before you into singing, and all the trees of the field shall clap their hand [Isa 55:12],'" and likewise asserts that it would be ridiculous to assume the "weeks" of Dan 9:25–27 were ever intended to be understood as simple periods of seven days.[98] The problem such a reading presents is inconsistency: "Upon a supposition that the representation of outward, glorious things in the days of the Messiah are to be understood literally [i.e., 'literalistically'], the prophecies are exceeding inconsistent one with another."[99] According to Edwards, the approach represented by Collins not only ignores the rational divine rules of language, but represents a violation of the rational human rules. Only if metaphorical speech is admitted as a feature of the Old Testament are the Old Testament Scriptures themselves coherent. And once this feature is conceded, argues Edwards, then not only is the Old Testament coherent, but a significant objection to the coherence of the relationship between the two Testaments is removed also.

Yet given his commitment to the literal sense as that intended by the divine author, Edwards's "response" does not have much purchase on Collins' criticism. While Collins objected to what Edwards would have called the figurative (typical) aspect of the divine author's language, it is not clear that he denied the figurative (metaphorical) aspect of the human author's language. Despite Collins' rejection of any "secondary, or typical, or mystical, or allegorical, or enigmatical" interpretation of literal prophecies, as he perceived them, the metaphorical nature of some prophecies does not seem to have bothered him. In this he may have followed Hugo Grotius (1583–1645) whom he described as "the most judicious of interpreters" and "the great Grotius whose commentaries on the Bible will ever be

---

more of the like Kind." Sherlock, *Use and Intent*, 29–86 (38).

98. "Miscellanies," no. 1068, § 23 and § 3 respectively.

99. Ibid., § 23.

Prophecy

esteemed by all those who desire truly to understand it."[100] Grotius comments on Isa 11:6, "[M]any Things in the Sacred Writings are not to be understood according to the strict Propriety of the Words, but in a Figurative Sense. . . . [M]any Things spoke of the Times of the Messiah may be explained in this manner."[101] In summary, there is something of a conceptual impasse between Collins and Edwards. Collins' commitment to the literal sense of the text as that intended by the human author and subject to the rational rules of language, is matched by Edwards's commitment to the literal sense as that intended by the divine author, made available only to those indwelt by the Holy Spirit, and capable of polyvalence—in short, subject to its own principles of interpretation. In this way Edwards's method may be explicated, but whether it could be replicated to any practical effect seems less certain. Access to his self-contained world of the Bible is solely through the exegete's own regeneration by the Holy Spirit. His or her continued ability to read the Scripture aright is wholly dependent on the "new sense," a reality denied to the unregenerate. Edwards may be able to offer a principled defense of his reading of Scripture, but meaningful critical engagement with it seems very difficult, if not impossible.

In turning now to the "Harmony" notes it is important to remember the purpose for which Edwards applies the principles I have outlined above, lest his hermeneutics are written-off as inadequate to answer Collins. Edwards's intention in the first part of the "Harmony" is not to offer a proof from prophecy capable of convincing the unregenerate, but to undermine the criticisms voiced by Collins by demonstrating the coherence and reasonableness of a Messianic interpretation of prophecy.

---

100. Collins, *Grounds and Reasons*, 42, 244.

101. Grotius, *Truth of the Christian Religion*, 248–49. Collins, in *Grounds and Reasons*, 49, claimed that Grotius had shown that "most if not all" of the Hebrew Scriptures quoted by the Apostles "are not grounded on the literal sense." Ernestine van der Wall argues that in *Bibliothèque choisie* Arminian editor of Grotius, Jean Le Clerc claimed that Collins had misrepresented Grotius; van der Wall, "Between Grotius and Cocceius," 205 n. 27. Le Clerc also argued that Grotius' conception of the two senses of prophecy was not novel, and that Grotius believed the spiritual application properly applied to Jesus. Grotius *Opera omnia theologica*, 1.569–72, did in fact take some prophecies as applying to Jesus without any hint of a spiritual or typological interpretation, among them: Mal 4:1, 5; Hag 2:8, cited in O'Higgins, *Anthony Collins*, 158 n. 2.

The "Harmony": Prophecy and Fulfillment

Kenneth Minkema comments that although Edwards's opponents are not named in his "Harmony" notes, the tone of the work is clearly polemical and marks Edwards's contribution to the transatlantic debate over Messianic prophecy and the trustworthiness of the Christian Scriptures.[102] However, as I have argued, though the work does indeed mark Edwards's attempt to "respond" to the criticisms Collins had voiced, it is not intended to offer a proof from prophecy capable of convincing the unregenerate. Rather, it is a defense of the internal logic of a Messianic reading of the Old and New Testaments—a supporting proof from prophecy but one that is convincing only to the regenerate. Furthermore, as I will argue below, the very structure of the work that demonstrates Edwards's intention to engage with the criticisms voiced by Collins.

In his letter to the college trustees in New Jersey Edwards notes that in the first part of his "Harmony" he would consider "the prophecies of the Messiah, his Redemption and Kingdom" by "comparing them all one with another, demonstrating their agreement and true scope and sense . . ."[103] By comparing prophecy with prophecy, Edwards's aim is to demonstrate his belief that the Old Testament's prophecies as a whole are united by a single subject and concern. Though he is committed to the principle of the analogy of Scripture, as I have argued above, the shape of Edwards's contribution to the transatlantic debate may also owe something to the methodology of Thomas Sherlock, whose *Use and Intent* he regularly cites in his Old Testament notes in the "Blank Bible." Responding to Collins, Sherlock had noted that "they who consider the Prophecies under the old Testament [sic], as so many Predictions only, independent of each other, can never form a right Judgment of the Argument, for the Truth of Christianity. . . . 'Tis absurd therefore to expect clear and evident Conviction from every single Prophecy applied to Christ, the Evidence must arise from a View and Comparison of all together."[104]

---

102. Minkema, "Great Work," 52–53.

103. Letter, no. 230, "To the Trustees of the College of New Jersey, Stockbridge," October 19, 1757, *WJE* 16:724–30.

104. Sherlock, *Use and Intent*, Preface, 39. However, as I noted above, Edwards's letter to the college trustees shows that he does not follow Samuel Clarke, *Use and Intent*, 78 in considering Jesus' fulfillment of Messianic prophecy merely to be the *sine qua non* of his Messianic identity. Though Edwards carefully argues that the prophecies of the Messiah are indeed answered in Jesus Christ, he is in no doubt that they are first united in their *prediction* of the Messiah, his redemption and kingdom.

Prophecy

The structure of Edwards's treatment of prophecies in his "Harmony" notes seems designed to show that a Messianic reading of the prophets is the most coherent one and as such is the most reasonable and intended meaning of those Scriptures.

The section of the "Harmony" treating the prophecies and their fulfillment has usually been thought to comprise four "Miscellanies" entries: nos. 891, 922, 1067 and 1068.[105] The first three of these, together entitled "Prophecies of the Messiah," are united by 101 consecutively-numbered sections, each quoting and commenting on one or more Old Testament text.[106] The final part, "Miscellanies," no. 1068 entitled, "The Fulfillment of the Prophecies of the Messiah," comprises 181 numbered sections. That there are more sections dealing with fulfillment than prophecy is simply explained by Edwards's structuring of the sections. I will argue below that a further "Miscellanies" entry, no. 1347, should also be considered a part of Edwards's notes for the unwritten "Harmony."

"Miscellanies," nos. 891, 922, 1067: "Prophecies of the Messiah"

Minkema notes that Edwards arranges his material according to "a preconceived method," though he does not suggest what this method might be.[107] Edwards does not arrange the material canonically, but in a way that best presents its coherence in one concern: the Messiah, his redemption and kingdom, just as he outlined to the trustees of the college at New Jersey.[108] This threefold structure does not underline the work as a whole in its unfinished state but provides the framework of each of "Miscellanies," nos. 891 and 922. In each of these "Miscellanies" Edwards traces the threefold theme, though from a different perspective. "Miscellanies," no. 891 begins with prophecies of the virgin birth, the defeat of Satan and the rule of the Messiah (§§ 1–3). This is followed by the theme of the Messiah as the Branch of Jesse (§§ 4–12, 14, 16–17) whose rule will be permanently established and who will both shelter the righteous and judge the

---

105. Minkema, "Great Work," 58.
106. "Miscellanies," nos. 891 (§§ 1–18); 922 (§§ 19–37); 1067 (§§ 38–101).
107. Minkema, "Great Work," 54.
108. § 1. Gen 3:15; § 2. Gen 49:8–12; § 3. Isa 9:6–7.... § 95. Zech 12–14; § 96. Gen 3:20 etc. Nevertheless, there are occasions where consecutive sections deal with material from the same biblical book: § 24–34 comment almost exclusively on the book of Isaiah, particularly its "Servant Songs"; §§ 45–60 and §§ 75–87 are concerned with various Psalms; § 60 is entitled "The Book of Psalms" and § 87 is entitled "The Book of Psalms in General."

unrighteous (§§ 16–18). In "Miscellanies," no. 922 the same structure is apparent. Beginning again with the virgin birth (§ 19) Edwards underscores his freedom in the argumentative use of Scripture metaphor as he now replaces the theme of the Messiah as the "Branch" with that of the Messiah as the "Stone" or "Ruler" (§§ 20–23). He traces this theme through several disparate prophecies, arguing for their agreement. This then gives way to a discussion of the Messiah's work of redemption as the Servant in the book of Isaiah (§§ 24–34). Edwards concludes "Miscellanies," no. 922 with discussion of the Messiah's glorious universal appearance as Israel's true King and Judge (§§ 34–37). By "Miscellanies," no. 1067 the threefold structure is harder to discern. Perhaps this is because by then the work has become extremely complex and cross-referential. "Miscellanies," no. 1067 appears to be concerned largely with the establishment and character of the Messiah's kingdom.[109]

Although Edwards begins the "conference" of prophecies with the *protevangelion* of Gen 3:15 the text that exercises governing position in all three "Miscellanies" is Gen 49:10 ['The sceptre shall not depart from Judah, nor a lawgiver from between his feet, until Shiloh come; and unto him shall the gathering of the people be'].[110] Shiloh, Edwards interprets as,

> some great person . . . that was to be of the tribe of Judah, and was to sway the sceptre over God's people, and to be their lawgiver, and to have the government devolved on his shoulders, and he was a person that was to come in the latter days . . .
>
> The word Shiloh signifies secondine[111] and so denotes the same person mentioned in the other prophecy, called the seed of the woman [Gen 3:15], as being wholly from the womb and secondine of the woman without the seed of man; and it also signifies a peacemaker or safe-maker, or, in other words, a savior . . .[112]

In these notes Edwards cites Jacques Basnage, *The History of the Jews* (London, 1708).[113] The interest of Basnage (1653–1723) to Edwards was

---

109. It begins with § 38 (Amos 9:11ff.) and over the following 64 sections discusses a wide range of Old Testament texts, though the Psalms predominate. A recurring theme of Edwards's exegesis here is the ingathering of scattered Israel, including the calling of the Gentiles.

110. For example, in "Miscellanies," no. 891 alone "Shiloh" is directly referred to in §§ 2, 3, 4, 5, 8, 9, 10, 11, 15 and 18.

111. Archaic form of "secundine," or afterbirth.

112. "Miscellanies," no. 891, § 2.

113. Basnage, *History*.

the author's argument that the Old Testament prophecies that the Apostles interpreted of the Messiah were also interpreted of the Messiah by the "ancient Jews," both before and during the first century AD. In the part of the work that Edwards cites with reference to Gen 49:10 Basnage argues that the "Chaldee Paraphrasts" and "Talmudists" who would have no interest in identifying Shiloh with Jesus Christ, nevertheless explain the term of the Messiah. He concludes: "Whereas the rest either invent, or follow some very remote Explications; because they find themselves gravell'd with the proof drawn from this Oracle against them in the behalf of J. CHRIST; the Jews have no reason to complain, since we condemn them out of the Writings of their great Masters, and of our most virulent Enemies. Shiloh is therefore the Messiah."[114]

Edwards does not explain why he structures the "Harmony" according to the threefold theme, nor why his exegetical centre of gravity is Gen 49:10, although in his "History of the Work of Redemption" sermons preached some four or five years earlier he notes that Gen 49:8–12 is "a prophecy given forth of Christ *on some account more particular than ever had been before*."[115] The particularity of this prophecy is apparent in four respects. First, the prophecy speaks of the person of Christ. It shows for the first time of whose posterity he was to be: of the tribe of Judah. Second, the prophecy outlines in greater clarity Christ's redemptive work and its consequences: he defeats his enemies, goes up from the prey and receives the praise of his brothers. Third, the prophecy is more particular concerning the time of Christ's coming than any prophecy before had been.

---

114. Basnage, *History*, 346. See also "Miscellanies," no. 922, § 31 where Edwards cites Basnage, *History*, 358: "The antient Rabbies did apply the 53d Chapter of Isaiah to the Messiah." In "Miscellanies," no. 1069 ("Types of the Messiah"), *WJE* 11:203, 208, 241, 305 he again cites Basnage as an authority that the ancient Jewish rabbis "judged that all things happened to their fathers as types and figures of the Messiah" (208). Edwards similarly employs an unlikely source, the Remonstrant, Grotius' *Christian Religion*, bk. 5, §§ 14, 15, 19 in which Grotius cites first-century rabbis in support of his claims that certain Old Testament prophecies refer to the Messiah. For example, in "Miscellanies," no. 1068, § 2, "It was foretold that the Messiah should come during the continuance of the second temple," Edwards quotes Grotius: "Rabbi Josue, who saw the razing of the temple, said that the time of the Messiah was then past, as Rabbi Jacob in Caphtor testifies." Grotius, *Christian Religion*, bk. 5, § 14. (In "Miscellanies," no. 1068, § 164, on the conversion of the Gentiles in the time of the Messiah's kingdom, Edwards quotes from *Christian Religion*, bk 2. § 18). Edwards's interest in the rabbis' interpretation of prophecies was by no means unusual in the Reformed tradition. On the rise and fall of the Reformed interest in rabbinical interpretation in the seventeenth century see Steiger, "Development of the Reformation Legacy," 725–32.

115. "Work of Redemption," *WJE* 9:171. Emphasis added.

Fourth, the prophecy is plainer than ever before regarding the calling of the Gentiles.[116] In short, although the prophecy stands in a line with others, representing the gradual increase of "gospel light which dawned immediately after the fall of man" and would increase through redemption history until the coming of the Messiah, it speaks to Edwards with unprecedented clarity of the person of the Messiah, his work of redemption and the nature of his kingdom. The three elements seem, to Edwards, to be fundamental to Messianic prophecy and make Gen 49 both the natural reference point for a consideration of all other Messianic prophecies, and the template for the structure of his approach in the "Harmony" as a whole.

Second, Edwards's argument that a Messianic reading offers the only coherent reading of the Hebrew Scriptures is demonstrated in the increasing complexity of Edwards's analogy of Scripture as the work progresses. "Miscellanies," no. 891 appears relatively simple in its scope; of its eighteen sections, all but two comment on only one biblical passage, while §§ 16–17 comment on only two passages each. In "Miscellanies," no. 922 the texts treated in each section increase both in number and length and by "Miscellanies," no. 1067 Edwards is regularly dealing with whole chapters or groups of chapters, comparing them with texts from other parts of the Bible. In this way Edwards demonstrates his conviction that a Messianic hermeneutic is not simply the best way of reading certain well-known individual texts that opponents frequently touted, such as Isa 7:14 and Hos 11:1.[117] Rather, it offers coherence to disparate and "marginal" texts. For example, Edwards expounds texts such as Gen 3:20 (in which Adam names his wife, "Eve"), and Moses' song in Deut 32:18–43.[118] Furthermore, Edwards presents his reading as reasonable because it is capable of offering a coherent reading of the Hebrew Scriptures on the widest possible scale. So, in § 60 ("The Book of Psalms"), Edwards argues that the entire book of Psalms ought to be interpreted "Messianically," since the Psalmists always speak either in the name of Christ or in the name of a member of Christ mystical.[119] Similarly in § 97 ("Isaiah 40 to the end") Edwards notes

---

116. "Work of Redemption," *WJE* 9:171–72.

117. See, for example, Collins, *Grounds and Reasons*, 40–47.

118. "Miscellanies," no. 1067, § 96 and § 72 respectively.

119. It is in confirmation of a Messianic interpretation of the Psalms that Edwards makes most use of Poole, *Synopsis Criticorum*. An enormous synopsis of 120 temporally and theologically disparate commentators and linguists (such as the Remonstrant, Hugo Grotius and his Calvinist critic, André Rivet; Westminster divine, John Lighfoot; Benedictine monk, Arias Montanus), Poole (1624–79) lists his sources in his preface, ii-vi, and notes that the scope of the work is a critical examination of the

that "it is manifest that the great subject of the whole of this second part of the book of the prophet Isaiah . . . is the great salvation of the Messiah, and the glorious blessings of his kingdom and the prosperity of God's Israel in his days; excepting some occasional mention made in some few places of other things . . . and some things that relate more especially to some events that are types, forerunners and earnests of this great salvation."[120]

Third, Edwards demonstrates his belief that a Messianic reading of the prophets is coherent and reasonable by the cumulative nature of his argument. The work becomes more cross-referential as it progresses. In each section Edwards cites a new text or group of texts and then proceeds to establish the agreement of the new material with that which has already

---

words and phrases of Scripture. The eclectic nature of Poole's sources is matched only by the variety of those he mentions in the preface, vii, as having given their names in support of his work, among them: John Owen, Richard Baxter and from the Continent, Johannes Cocceius and Gisbertius Voetius; the Arminian Anglican John Tillotson; Cambridge Platonists, Ralph Cudworth and Benjamin Whichcote. Of Edwards's 792 citations of Poole in his "Blank Bible," 263 concern Wisdom literature, while only five concern the Prophets. Edwards's use of Poole for the Psalms but not the Prophets is reflected in his "Harmony" notes on prophecy: nine of his eleven references to Poole concern the Psalms, the other two being to Deut 18 ("Miscellanies," no. 1067, § 34) and Deut 10:16 ("Miscellanies," no. 1068, § 152). The pattern continues in Edwards's notes on the harmony in doctrine and precept, which I consider in chapter 3: thirteen of Edwards's sixteen references to Poole's *Synopsis* relate to the Psalms, the three exceptions relating to Lev 20:2; 2 Sam 24:1; Hos 14:6. It is not clear why Edwards relied on Poole's *Synopsis* so heavily for the Psalms, but ignored him on the Prophets (both in his "Blank Bible" and "Harmony" notes). However, other anomalies may be more easily explained. With ninety-six references, Nonconformist, Matthew Henry (1662–1714) is Edwards's favorite reference work on the Prophets in his "Blank Bible." However Edwards cites Henry, *An Exposition of the Old and New Testaments* only once in the "Harmony" notes on prophecy ("Miscellanies," no. 922, § 31 on Isa 11:1). Similarly, Edwards cites the popular work of the Nonconformist, Philip Doddridge (1702–51), *The Family Expositor* 303 times in his "Blank Bible." Doddridge is Henry's New Testament counterpart as favorite source in Edwards's "Blank Bible." All but one of Edwards's 205 references to Matthew Henry concern the Old Testament; all but six of his 303 references to Doddridge concern the New Testament. Yet despite Edwards's extensive citation of Doddridge in his "Blank Bible," he is nowhere mentioned in the "Harmony" notes. The reason for the disparity of Edwards's use of Henry and Doddridge between his "Blank Bible" and "Harmony" may be found in the respective purpose of each text. While the "Blank Bible" functions as Edwards's personal synoptic commentary and long-term central reference point for biblical observations, the "Harmony" notebooks are directed toward a particular apologetic aim in which seventeenth and eighteenth-century theological commentary is of less interest to Edwards than the philological observations of Poole, the historical comments of Josephus and the Messianic interpretations of the first-century rabbis supplied by Basnage or even Grotius.

120. "Miscellanies," no. 1067, § 97.

been discussed. For example, in § 64 (Isa 24:13–23; 25–35), one of the longest entries in the entire work, Edwards returns to the study of the book of Isaiah begun in §§ 24–34, but now brings to bear his conclusions about several of the Psalms he has just studied in §§ 36, 39, 45–60. As Edwards's case is developed, so the instances of agreement between the prophecies increase. Phrases Edwards uses to link the prophecies such as, "... is doubtless the same person..." and "... agreeable to..." pepper the entire work. Such is the weight of Edwards's cumulative case that at times it even appears to weary him and comments begin to appear, such as, "The things are so exactly the same with the things spoken of in this chapter, and in many other prophecies, that a particular observation of them is needless."[121]

Fourth, a noticeable feature of the three "Miscellanies" is the almost total absence of references to the New Testament. Edwards's analogy of Scripture is confined to the Hebrew prophecies. Edwards attempts to outflank the objections raised by Collins to the way the New Testament writers made use of the ancient prophecies. In doing so he pre-empts the criticisms of Edwards's scholar, Stephen Stein among others, that a Christian reading of the Hebrew Scriptures does violence to their Jewish integrity.[122] Edwards attempts to demonstrate that a Christian reading can operate entirely on the basis of the Old Testament, without disturbing its historic integrity. Indeed, Edwards argues that a Messianic reading is the only reasonable way of reading the Old Testament prophecies. With pre-critical assumptions regarding the authorship and provenance of the biblical texts, Edwards argues that only by reading the prophecies as a persistent anticipation of the Messiah, his redemption and kingdom, can the disparate and temporally distinct texts cohere.

"Miscellanies," no. 1347 and "Scripture Prophecies of the Messiah"

Sometime between 1754 and 1756 Edwards compiled another notebook, "Scripture Prophecies of the Old Testament."[123] In the notebook Edwards

---

121. Ibid., § 67.

122. Stein criticizes Edwards's habit of reading the Hebrew Bible in such a way as to diminish its "historical intention and the original integrity" by "transforming it into the Old Testament whose ultimate purpose and meaning depended essentially on the Christian New Testament." Stein, "Editor's Introduction," *WJE* 24:1–117 (30).

123. See Minkema's description of the manuscript in his introductory note to the Yale transcription.

Prophecy

comments that these prophecies are "besides the prophecies of the Old Testament prophecies of the Messiah, which are considered elsewhere."[124] The majority of the notes are struck through with "use lines," but Minkema comments in his introductory remarks that "where Edwards used them is not known, since these materials were not apparently added to 'Prophecies of the Messiah.'"[125] In what follows I will first argue that Edwards almost certainly expanded his "Scripture Prophecies" notebook into what is now "Miscellanies," no. 1347 and that this was intended to supplement "Miscellanies," nos. 891, 922 and 1067–68 and form part of the "Harmony."[126] I will then demonstrate how these notes contribute to Edwards's argument that a Messianic reading of the prophets is both coherent and reasonable.

The numerous entries in "Scripture Prophecies" are in little discernable order. A prophecy of the destruction of the Canaanites is followed by a reference to Noah's prophecies of his sons; a few lines later there is a note on the extent of the Promised Land. The entries comprise a list of prophecies, with very few noting a fulfillment. The vast majority are drawn from the Pentateuch, although a central section deals with prophecies found in the historical books. Virtually all of the Pentateuchal material is struck through with "use lines," but almost none of historical material is. Turning to "Miscellanies," no. 1347, under the heading, "First, the prophecies of the Pentateuch," all but one of the used entries in the Pentateuchal sections of "Scripture Prophecies" may be identified.[127] They appear in "Miscellanies," no. 1347 sometimes *verbatim*, usually in expanded form, but their source is unmistakable.[128] The heading itself ("First, the prophecies of the

124. Transcription of "Scripture Prophecies of the Messiah," 21.

125. Introductory note, 1.

126. Douglas Sweeney, notes in passing that various of Edwards's later "Miscellanies" "functioned as drafts or parts" of his unwritten "Harmony" and "A History of the Work of Redemption." As regards the former, he cites "Miscellanies," nos. 1172, 1192, 1193, 1194, 1283, 1290, 1327, 1347 and 1353a. Sweeney, "Editor's Introduction," *WJE* 23:1–36 (7, esp. n. 2). However, while it is true that Edwards addressed many issues in these entries pertinent to his intended project, with the exception of "Miscellanies," no. 1347 (c. f. "Scripture Prophecies") they do not claim to be additions to the "Prophecies of the Messiah" "Miscellanies." All, except nos. 1347 and 1353a are single-issue entries, unlike the other acknowledged parts of the prophetic section of the "Harmony" and nos. 1172, 1192–94 were all written no earlier than late August 1752.

127. This exception is: "That God would raise 'em up a prophet, Deut. 18:15, etc" (26). However, given Edwards's intention that both "Scripture Prophecies" and "Miscellanies," no. 1347 should deal with "prophecies of the Old Testament which have been fulfilled besides the prophecies of the Messiah," this exception is not surprising.

128. For example, in "Miscellanies," 1347, *WJE* 23:384 Edwards includes a large

Pentateuch") suggests a further section would have followed, one that perhaps would have dealt with prophecies from the historical books.[129] "Miscellanies," no. 1347 is unfinished and in a footnote in the published Yale edition editor, Douglas Sweeney notes that at the end of the entry Edwards left the remainder of the page and four following leaves blank.[130] It is very likely that having gathered together the Pentateuchal material from "Scripture Prophecies" Edwards intended to do the same with the historical material under a second heading, but in the event did not do so. This would explain why the historical material in "Scripture Prophecies" is free of "use lines." In short, given the weight of evidence above it is almost certain that "Miscellanies," no.1347 deserves attention alongside nos. 891, 922, 1067–68 in any discussion of the unwritten "Harmony."

What was Edwards's purpose in this supplementary "Miscellany"? In the second half of no. 1347 the vast majority of the new material concerns the fulfillment of the prophecies: "fulfilled in Saul"; "remarkably fulfilled in David"; "fulfilled in what we have an account of in 1 Sam. ch. 14 . . ."[131] That is, the entry appears to have been intended as a general defense of the notion of predictive prophecy. Edwards appears to believe that if he could demonstrate from within the Old Testament that prophecies were fulfilled, he would be establishing an important bridgehead against the rationalist criticisms of Collins that I outlined at the beginning of this chapter. Edwards had employed this very strategy ten years earlier in "Miscellanies," no. 1069, "Types of the Messiah," also part of the "Harmony" notes. As I will demonstrate in chapter 2 he first seeks to establish the phenomenon of type and antitype solely within with Old Testament before then considering its function in linking the Old and New Testaments.[132] To Edwards the reasonableness of prophetic prediction and fulfillment (or type and antitype) as a phenomenon that unites Old and New Testaments, is grounded

---

section almost *verbatim* from "Scripture Prophecies," (Yale transcription, 22–23), adding four more Scripture references to the more than seventy he has brought over from his earlier notebook. However, a few paragraphs later he develops a brief reference in "Scripture Prophecies," 23 ("Jacob's Blessing of the Tribes, Gen 49") into a 480 word section, with discussion of whether the prophecy of Benjamin ought to be taken temporally, or spiritually; if the latter, Edwards argues it was fulfilled in the Apostle Paul (Phil. 3:5).

129. This is likely because as Edwards noted at the outset, the writing prophets themselves are treated in "Miscellanies," nos. 891, 922, 1067–68.

130. "Miscellanies," no. 1347, *WJE* 23:391 n. 6.

131. Ibid., 382–91 (388).

132. "Miscellanies," no. 1069, *WJE* 11:194–202.

Prophecy

upon its identification within the literal sense of the Old Testament. If the latter is reasonable, then the former must be also.

Edwards defends the notion of predictive prophecy and fulfillment in "Miscellanies," no. 1347 by demonstrating that the promises of the land are inseparably interwoven with the Pentateuchal narratives. First, the promises made to Abraham and Jacob are so interwoven everywhere with the rest of the Pentateuch, that "if the law itself was written before they became possessed of Canaan, we must suppose those promises were written also before."[133] Second, they are so interwoven with the narratives of Moses and the exodus that "the whole history is built on the promises and can't [be] separated." Indeed, so closely bound are they that the whole story of the exodus and wilderness wanderings is "as it were a comment on these promises, strictly connected."[134] Not only does history exhibit the fulfillment of prophecy, but prophecy explicates history. This is consonant with Edwards's thought expressed elsewhere that Spirit-inspired prophecy enables the saint truly to understand pneumatologically-driven history, whether deliverance from Egypt, revival in Northampton or war with France.[135] Third, the promises are "interwoven with, and supposed and implied in, the laws and precepts of the Pentateuch." In short, the prophecies of the Israelites' possession of the land within the Old Testament were so widespread and "blended with the history and laws in general" that "all together may be looked upon as one great and vastly complicated and variegated prediction of this event."[136] To excise the promises from the narratives is to do violence to the narratives themselves and disturb the integrity of the Hebrew Scriptures. Edwards may have in mind here not only Collins' criticisms, but also William Whiston's attempt to reconstruct

---

133. "Miscellanies," no. 1347, *WJE* 23:382–91 (383). Edwards's argument rests on his commitment to the "the books of Moses" (383) as being written by Moses himself. See his lengthy entry in "Notes on Scripture," no. 146, *WJE* 15:423–69. In addition, Robert Brown notes that after 1753 Edwards began a new set of notes (running to 131 pages) on the Mosaic authorship of the Pentateuch—"a significant expansion of his earlier effort." Brown, *Edwards and the Bible*, 177.

134. "Miscellanies," no. 1347, *WJE* 23:382–91 (384).

135. On the role of Scripture in the interpretation of Edwards's types, see my argument in the following chapter. Edwards preached his 1739 redemption sermon series to show that the 1734–35 revival in Northampton illustrated the entire course of providential history: God accomplishes his work of redemption by effusions of his Spirit. See also Stein, "Editor's Introduction," *WJE* 5:1–93; "Notebook on the Apocalypse"; Zakai, *Jonathan Edwards's Philosophy of History*, passim.

136. "Miscellanies," no. 1347, *WJE* 23:382–91 (384).

a pristine Old Testament text, noted above.[137] Just as in the other "Miscellanies" which we have already had cause to note, Edwards does not attempt a proof-text piecemeal answer to Collins' five disputed prophecies, but something far more sophisticated: an exhaustive presentation of the reasonableness of "the true scope and sense" of the Hebrew Scriptures.

"Miscellanies," no. 1068: "The Fulfillment of the Prophecies of the Messiah"

As with his treatment of the prophecies, so now with their fulfillment: Edwards's intention is not to provide an unanswerable "proof" of Christianity from prophecy of the kind Collins demanded, but to demonstrate that a Messianic reading of the Hebrew prophecies is the only coherent one and therefore also the most reasonable.

There are a number of similarities between the "Miscellanies," no. 1068 and those considered above, first among which is the familiar threefold structure of the Messiah (§§ 1–15), his redemption (§§ 16–99) and kingdom (§§ 100–181). A second similarity is perhaps more surprising: the absence of quotation from the New Testament in a "Miscellany" that charts the fulfillment of Messianic prophecy. Edwards's unspoken assumption throughout the long entry appears to be that his readers will have the person and work of Jesus Christ in mind. This further underlines that Edwards's purpose in the "Harmony" was not to offer a convincing proof from prophecy to the unregenerate, but to demonstrate the reasonableness of identifying Jesus as the Messiah through the fulfillment of ancient predictions.

It is likely that Edwards's apologetic purpose also accounts for the major difference between the two parts of his prophecy notes. Unlike the preceding "Miscellanies," the present one is not organized according to Scripture texts, but under propositional titles. For example, the first block (§§ 1–7) is entitled, "The Time of the Messiah's Coming." This is then further broken down: § 1. "Before the scepter departs from Judah"; § 2. "While the second Temple stands"; § 3. "At the end of Daniel's seventy weeks" etc. With further headings such as: "Born at Bethlehem"; "Messiah rejected by the greater part of the Jews"; and "Incarnate in order to make atonement

---

137. See above, n. 6. Although Edwards nowhere mentions Whiston's *Essay*, he is familiar with the author. Various of Whiston's other works appear in Edwards's "Catalogue" including his *Chronology of the Old Testament*, [. 67] in "Catalogue," *WJE* 26:132.

for sin."[138] New Testament quotations are rendered unnecessary because readers are led systematically through the identity and work of the Jesus. Instead of relying on quotations from the New Testament to establish the fulfillment of the prophecies, Edwards systematically arranges the exegetical conclusions he has drawn from the earlier "Miscellanies" and relies on the very structure of no. 1068 to direct his readers' thoughts to Jesus of Nazareth according to the analogy of faith. The result of this is that Edwards presents Christ as the fulfillment of far more than the relatively few individual prophecies highlighted in the New Testament narratives. Earlier literature engaging with the Deists' challenge had focused on the five disputed passages Collins had cited. The battle had been over the appropriateness of the Apostles' use of the Hebrew Scriptures. Edwards does not ignore the disputed texts; at times he engages in lengthy biblical criticism himself, as in his discussion of Isa 7:14.[139] But his approach in the "Harmony" is broader. In presenting a Messianic reading of the Hebrew Scriptures in their entirety as the most reasonable reading, Edwards is able to provide context to the disputed texts.

---

138. These are the headings for §§ 11, 39 and 81 respectively.

139. Collins, *Grounds and Reasons*, 43, asked, "How could a virgin's conception and bearing a son seven hundred years afterwards, be a sign to Ahaz?" Edwards "responds" to the question in "Miscellanies," no. 1067, § 19 by noting that sometimes a sign occurs after the thing signified: "The utmost that is aimed at in this prophecy, is not the birth of Mahershalalhashbaz . . . the birth of Mahershalalhashbaz was upon no account a great wonder, who seems to be born only to be some faint type of this person here foretold. Sometimes those things that are mentioned in Scripture as signs of things predicted, do not come to pass till after the thing signified has been accomplished . . ." Among other instances in Scripture of the sign following the thing signified, he cites Exod 3:12. On the meaning of "virgin" Edwards quotes the Basel Hebraist, Buxtorf, *Lexica Hebriacum*, who notes that "the word in the original properly signifies a young woman, unmarried, living in her father's house"; he also quotes Basnage, *History*, 356, in which Basnage claims the term means a woman unknown by a man. Edwards argues that Mahershalalhashbaz's mother, the prophetess Isaiah went to (Isa 8:3) was not a virgin (she was already mother of Shearjashub, Isa 7:3). While Edwards concedes that the Hebrew word for "virgin" doesn't always mean a woman untouched by a man, he notes that it is remarkable that only the mother is mentioned in the prophecy of Isa 7:14. "This, like that first text that was mentioned, 'I will put enmity between thee and the woman, between thy seed and her seed; it shall bruise thy head', etc. [Gen 3:15]; and agreeable to Jacob's prophecy [Gen 49:8–12], in which the Messiah is called Shiloh, which signifies secondines . . ."

Conclusion

The storm created by Collins' *Grounds and Reasons* is the context of the first part of Edwards's "Harmony." Employing features apparent throughout his *corpus*, Edwards's "strange *old* world of the Bible" first offers an analogy of Scripture on a scale seemingly designed to dwarf Collins' criticisms regarding the Apostles' use of a mere five Jewish prophecies. The "Harmony" offers a coherent reading that encompasses both these disputed texts and as a vast *corpus* of temporally distinct prophecies. Second, in identifying Jesus as the Messiah Edwards confines himself to the Old Testament, the grounds from which Collins launched his attack on the unity of the Christian Scriptures. Offering a re-imagination of the literal sense of the entire Hebrew Scriptures Edwards argues that it is only as they are understood as the anticipatory "Old Testament" that they are themselves coherent or harmonious. Edwards does not consider his "proofs" capable of persuading his opponents to faith in the Messiah. Rather his presentation of prophetic harmony seems designed to undermine their criticisms concerning the fulfillment of Messianic prophecy and present a coherent and reasonable alternative reading of the Scriptures. The scale and detail of the first part of the "Harmony" means that despite the strangeness of its presuppositions today, Edwards's account cannot be ignored. Its value lies in its very strangeness to modern sensibilities, with its capacity to challenge and "relativize" cherished contemporary norms.

I have argued that Stephen Stein, who has pioneered the serious and thorough study of Edwards's biblical notebooks, is mistaken in characterizing Edwards's exegesis as "imaginative" and "unrestrained." Instead I have sought to demonstrate that Edwards's approach to the prophecies of the Old Testament is in fact tightly constrained by Scripture. His dependence on the principle, *Scriptura Scripturae interpres* is expressed in his explication of prophetic types and the argumentative use of metaphor. Under the guiding hand of this principle Edwards is able to assert that the Messiah, his redemption and kingdom comprise the true scope and sense of the prophecies of the Old Testament, made available to the saint by the indwelling Holy Spirit. Yet Edwards's approach is not without its difficulties. I have noted that Edwards frequently struggles to establish the penman's own understanding or authorial intention. In his approach divine authorial intention ultimately overwhelms that of the human author. Although Edwards believes that this divine intention may be communicated to one in possession of the Holy Spirit, the subjectivity of the whole exercise makes it all but impossible to reproduce to any practical effect. The rules that guide the saint in his or her reading of prophecy may perhaps be explicated. That they might be replicated seems less certain. In the next chapter I will argue that this subjectivity characterizes Edwards's typology also.

TWO

Typology

INTRODUCTION

THE HISTORY OF THE typological exegesis of the Bible is well documented and, beyond the most cursory sketch, would exceed the scope of the present enquiry.[1] This introduction is not intended to be a history of typology, but rather a series of representative "soundings" in order to provide context to my discussion of Edwards's typology that follows.

The work of the German literary scholar, Erich Auerbach remains foundational to studies of figural hermeneutics some fifty years after its publication.[2] Auerbach argued that the Apostle Paul's mission to the Gentiles was central to the transformation of the interpretation of the Hebrew Scriptures. In the process of being made relevant and accessible to the Gentiles, the narratives of the Jewish Scriptures were read as a prefigurative part of a divinely-governed history that found its purpose and goal in Jesus the Messiah.[3] A typological approach to reading the Hebrew Scrip-

---

1. A standard account is provided by de Lubac, *Four Senses of Scripture, passim*. In the course of this chapter I will use a number of terms which it seems wise to define at the outset. "Figural" or "figurative exegesis" will be used to describe the general approach of all non-literal reading of texts or natural phenomena. On the relationship between literal and figurative exegesis in the eighteenth century, see my discussion of Anthony Collins in the previous chapter. As a general guide, I will use the term "type" (and its adjective, "typical") to refer to the signifier in a scheme of phenomenal prefiguring, and "antitype" to that which is signified, its fulfillment. I reserve the terms "typology" (and its adjective, "typological") to refer to the methodological approach of identifying and interpreting types and their antitypes. Distinct from the horizontal prefiguring of antitype by type is "allegory," which describes the approach of vertical imaging.

2. Auerbach, *Drama of European Literature*; *Mimesis*.

3. According to Auerbach, this divine governance weakened the horizontal, causal

tures was thus a part of the church's exegetical "tool box" from its earliest days.

The word "τύπος" ("type") occurs seventeen times in the Septuagint and New Testament, and in the majority of cases conveys the meaning of "example" or "pattern."[4] The Apostle Paul uses the word group in describing the prefiguring of the future in prior history. In 1 Cor 10:11 he describes God's dealing with Old Testament Israel as being "τυπικως" ("typical"), that is, in a manner that was intended to inform and teach the church in the last days. Similarly, in Rom 5:14 Paul describes Adam as a "τύπος" of him who was to come, Christ. Pauline typology is the prefiguring of one historical event by means of another. Type and antitype (αντίτυπος) inhabit the same temporal plane. Leonard Goppelt argues that prior to the Apostle it cannot be demonstrated that the word had this meaning, but that by the time of Barnabas and Justin this usage had become firmly established.[5] However, while the word "τύπος" may not have conveyed historical prefiguration until the Apostolic era, the concept was not the Apostolic creation that literary scholar, Auerbach contends. The French theologian and historian, Jean Danielou pushes the use of what amounts to typology further back, arguing that the Hebrew prophets recalled God's work in the past as a foundation for exhorting faith in great works yet to come. For example, Ezekiel's description of a new Jerusalem in terms of a new Paradise (Ezek 47:12) is "the highlight of [a] paradisiacal presentation" by the prophets that employs the idea of Paradise in a typological way.[6] Nevertheless, the linear and historical plane on which phenomenal prophecy and fulfillment sits is the defining characteristic of typology.

---

connections between the narrative's events, while strengthening their vertical bonds. Auerbach, *Mimesis*, 16–17, 48–49. Had he heard Edwards's 1739 "Redemption" sermons it is likely he would have charged the New England divine with the same crime. However, Edwards represents no mere fusion of two conflicting historiographies. I will argue that his idealist philosophy coupled with his theology of history as history of the self-communication of God binds historical events together as tightly on the horizontal plane as it does on the vertical.

4. Baker, *Two Testaments*, 185–87. Baker notes that the word, "τύπος" has occasional other meanings, but these are closely related to the meaning, "example" or "pattern." These include: "mark" (John 20:25, twice); "image" (Amos 5:26; Acts 7:43); and "to this effect" (Acts 23:25). Its cognates, τυπικως, αντίτυπος and ὑποτύπωσις also relate in every case to the meaning, "example" or "pattern."

5. Goppelt, *Typos*, 5.

6. Danielou cites Hos 2:22; Amos 9:13 and Ezek 34:28 as examples of prophecies that employ Paradise motifs in a typological way. Danielou, *From Shadows to Reality*, 13.

It is, in Chrysostom's classic definition, "a prophecy expressed in terms of things" (ἡ πραγμάτων . . . προφητεία).⁷

Where typology links events, persons or institutions horizontally on a linear historical plane, allegory describes a vertical relationship of symbolism or representation. In allegorical exegesis the text's literal or historical sense plays a relatively minor role, being treated more as a mere symbol of the moral or spiritual truths that are the goal of the exegete. By locating the truth of a text in a spiritual, non-historical sphere, allegory offered a fruitful way of reading apparently problematic texts or historical narratives. While typology is restricted to texts that manifest signs historically antecedent to their referents, allegory can be applied to any text.

The early church witnessed a hermeneutical parting of the ways in the distinction between typology and allegory.⁸ Alexandrian exegesis, influenced by Hellenistic and Jewish modes of allegorical interpretation witnessed in the writings of Philo and Clement, tended to favor allegorical exegesis.⁹ Reacting to what it perceived to be an arbitrary and illegitimate instrument, the Antiochene church contended that the key to the true sense of a text when this was not already fully explicit in the literal historical sense was to be found in what was called "insight" (θεορία), by which was meant the spiritual reality to which the historical facts set out in the text were designed to point.¹⁰ Crucially, this did not dispense with the literal or historical sense of a text, but demanded that there should be a real correspondence between historical reality and spiritual object and that the two should be apprehended together by reflection on the whole sweep of salvation history. In an approach that sought phenomenal correspondences on the historical plane, typology found a natural home. Chiefly associated with Antioch in this regard are Diodore of Tarsus (ca. 300–ca. 390); Theodore of Mopsuestia (ca. 350–428) and Theodoret (ca. 393–ca. 460), though John Chrysostom (ca. 347–407) made prolific use of

---

7. Chrysostom, *De poenit. Hom.* 6, 4, in Kelly, *Early Christian Doctrines*, 76.

8. The distinction between Antioch's more literalist exegesis and Alexandria's more allegorical one should not be overstated, however. There was considerable unity and agreement between the two regarding the typical correspondences between the Old and New Testaments. See Kelly's discussion in *Early Christian Doctrines*, 69–75; Young, "Alexandrian and Antiochene Exegesis," 334–54. For a critical overview of typology and allegory from the Church Fathers to Calvin, see Davis, "Puritan Typology," 11–45.

9. Froehlich, *Biblical Interpretation*, 1–29; Simonetti, *Biblical Interpretation in the Early Church*; Kugel and Greer, *Early Biblical Interpretation*.

10. Nassif, "Antiochene θεωρία in John Chrysostom's Exegesis," 49–67; Kelly, *Early Christian Doctrines*, 76.

the typological method in his sermons. In seeking to offer context to the typology of an eighteenth-century colonial theologian, it is the Western Church, however, that is of more concern.

From the three senses of Origen's exegesis, the Alexandrian school developed through Ambrose, Augustine and John of Cassian into what became known as the *quadriga*, the four-fold sense of Scripture of the Middle Ages.[11] Under this approach if the literal or historical sense of a text (*sensus literalis*, or *sensus historicus*) did not engender the Christian virtues of faith, hope and love these might be discovered in the text's spiritual senses: the *sensus allegoricus*, which taught things to be believed; the *sensus tropologicus*, which taught things to be loved or done; and the *sensus anagogicus*, which taught things to be hoped for.[12]

Though the early Reformers must not be separated entirely from the late-medieval tradition they inherited and be interpreted as the first modern biblical critics, nevertheless their concern for the grammar of the historical literal sense of the text marks their significance.[13] With the Reformation typology again came to the fore in linking Old and New Testaments into one meta-narrative focused on Christ. To Luther the Old Testament bore witness to Christ in a two-fold sense. First, as law it was designed to drive people to their Savior. Second, as the promises and figures of Christ, the Old Testament was full of him. Christ is present as a Person of the God of the Old Testament who speaks to his people and makes promises to them. The promises are ultimately promises of Christ. Similarly, the Old Testament offers figures of Christ and his church, according to Luther: "If you wish to have a proper and certain interpretation then keep Christ constantly before you, for he is the man to whom all this applies."[14] Luther called this interpretation "spiritual interpretation," but distinguished it from that practiced by Origen, Jerome and others which he claimed ignored the literal meaning of the words. Luther's spiritual interpretation does not abandon the literal historical sense, but is grounded in it. When reading historical narratives Luther is particularly concerned with the meaning of the words in the text because the history they describe is prophetic. The historical event is thus a type, a phenomenal

---

11. De Lubac, *Four Senses of Scripture*, 1–40; Ocker, "Biblical Interpretation in the Middle Ages," 14–21.

12. On the doctrine of Scripture in medieval scholastic theology, see Muller, *PRRD*, 2.35–62.

13. Muller, "Biblical Interpretation in the Sixteenth and Seventeenth Centuries," 22–44.

14. Quoted in Althaus, *Martin Luther*, 96.

prophecy on the historical plane that finds its fulfillment in Christ.[15] Like Luther, English Bible translator, William Tyndale did not reject allegory *per se* but the allegorizing that discarded the simple grammatical sense in favor of another reading. He distinguished between the allegories of men and those contained in Scripture, arguing that to understand scriptural allegories was to understand the literal or "normal" sense, that which the author intended.[16] John Calvin saw all the Scriptures as revealing Christ. The difference between the Old and New Testaments is not the content of revelation, but its manner. Before his revelation in the flesh, the Son must be veiled in types and shadows. One fundamental difference between the Old and New Testament therefore "consists in figures; that, in the absence of the reality, [the Old Testament] showed but an image and shadow in place of the substance; the New Testament reveals the very substance of the truth as present." That is, "the gospel points out with the finger what the law foreshadowed under types."[17] The "key" with which to "open up [the] way" in reading the Old Testament, according to Calvin, is recognition of the type-antitype distinction between Old and New Testaments.[18] Typology thus plays a central and important role in his relating of the Old and New Testaments.

Edwards's more immediate Reformed and Puritan theological forebears enthusiastically appropriated typology in their reading of the Old Testament. On the Continent Johannes Wollebius (1586–1629), for example, employed typology to demonstrate the Christological character of the ceremonial Law, with particular attention to how the structure and contents of the Tabernacle typified Christ and his redemption.[19] And Puritan exegetes produced manuals to aid in the proper typological exposition of Scripture, the first being that by William Guild.[20] In short, the Protestant exegesis that came down to eighteenth-century New England emphasized a literal historical interpretation of Scripture.[21] It was in the

---

15. Ibid., 92–102. Hagen, "Martin Luther," 687–94, notes that allegorical, tropological and anagogical senses are present in the Luther's exegesis where they embellish the single simplest, that is the grammatical, sense which holds out Christ, the *res* of Scripture.

16. Feldmeth, "William Tyndale," 996–1000; Davis, "Puritan Typology," 29–31.

17. Calvin, *Institutes*, 2.11.4; 2.9.3.

18. Ibid., 2.10.20; c.f. 2.9.1–4.

19. Wollebius, *Abridgment*, 97–108.

20. Guild, *Moses Unveiled*.

21. Anderson, "Editor's Introduction," *WJE* 11:4–6.

literal historical sense that types were identified. Consequently, the spiritual sense of Scripture was properly part of this literal sense.

To anticipate the following discussion somewhat, Jonathan Edwards transformed typology from a tool that identified and interpreted the Bible's phenomenal prophecy into an imaging system of divine self-communication that took in not only Scripture but also history and the natural world. And yet there was already in Edwards's immediate heritage what might be termed an "imagistic consciousness," distinct from, though informed by, Scripture's typology. *Magnalia Christi Americana* (London, 1702), the ecclesiastical history of New England produced by Cotton Mather (1663–1728) expressed the parallel between the New England experiment and the great biblical drama of Old Testament Israel. In his first chapter Mather outlined his intention to present "an history of some feeble attempts made in the American hemisphere to anticipate the state of the New Jerusalem . . ." describing the settlers who landed at Cape Cod in 1620 as "this little Israel, now going into a wilderness."[22] The colonial Puritan's self-conception and Scripture-reading reinforced each other, according to literary scholar, Thomas Davis.[23] Such imagistic consciousness extended beyond historical events, however. In the natural world another of Cotton Mather's works, *Agricola* (Boston, 1727) echoed the English Puritan, John Flavel's *Husbandry Spiritualized* (London, 1669) as a litany of nature's illustration of spiritual truths.[24] To use the memorable phrase of Massachusetts pastor, Edward Taylor (1642–1729), the world was "slickt up in types."[25]

---

22. Mather, *Magnalia Christi Americana*, 46, 50. On the Puritan use of Scripture in the self-conception of the colonies, see Smolinksi, "Israel Redivivus," 357-95; Bercovitch, *Puritan Origins, passim*. Bercovitch accuses Edwards of "astonishing arrogance" in the central place he gave America in redemption history, seeing the redemption of Israel from the Babylonian exile and the rebuilding of Jerusalem as typical of the spiritual redemption that was to arise from the New World. Bercovitch, *Puritan Origins*, 155. For a critique of Bercovitch's argument (as being too optimistic an account of Edwards's conception of America's role in the divine economy), see McDermott, *One Holy and Happy Society*, 11–92 and my discussion of Edwards's notion of the "national covenant" in chapter 3.

23. Davis, "Puritan Typology," 45.

24. Mather, *Agricola*. Edwards consulted Flavel's work, as his "Catalogue" of reading reveals: [57.] Flavel, *Husbandry Spiritualized*, "Catalogue," *WJE* 26:130.

25. "Meditation. Col. 2:17. Which are Shadows of Things to Come and the Body is Christs [sic]" in Stanford, *Poems of Edward Taylor*, 83. See also, "Upon a Spider Catching a Fly" (340–41) which Taylor sees as an image of "hell's spider," Satan, entangling Adam's race in his web of stratagems. Jonathan Edwards makes a similar point as part of his observation in "Images," no. 60, *WJE* 11:107. However, as I will argue, Edwards

The literary scholar, Mason Lowance describes the resurgence of biblical typology in seventeenth-century England and New England as being "in the best tradition of typological conservatism, that of the fourth-century Antioch school," and despite efforts in the seventeenth and early eighteenth century to transform types into Platonic symbols and allegorical configurations, Lowance argues that a mainstream of conservative typological exegesis persisted, exemplified by Samuel Mather (1626–71) in his *Figures or Types of the Old Testament* (Dublin, 1683).[26] Examination of Edwards's recently published catalogues of reading reveals that he consulted Mather's *Figures or Types* more than any other work in his own study of biblical typology.[27]

Samuel Mather (Cotton's uncle) defined a type as "some outward or sensible thing ordained of God under the Old Testament, to represent and hold forth something of Christ in the New."[28] Consequently, interpreters "must not indulge their own fancies as Popish writers use to do, with their allegorical senses as they call them; except we have some Scripture ground for it. It is not safe to make anything a type merely upon our own fancies and imagination."[29] In answer to the question, "How can we tell what is a type ordained by the Lord?" Mather declared: "The answer is we cannot safely judge of this but by the Scripture." There must either be express warrant in Scripture for the type-antitype relationship, or there must be a

---

departs from his heritage in seeing nature not simply as an occasion for illustrating spiritual truths, but as a divinely designed language of God's self-communication aimed at his own glorification. See my discussion of his interpretation of natural types below.

26. Lowance, *Language of Canaan*, 6. On typology in early New England see: Bercovitch, "Special Typology Issue;" *Typology and Early American Literature*; *Puritan Origins*; Davis, "Puritan Typology," 11–45. On studies specifically of Edwards's typology against this background, see below, n. 38.

27. Mather, *Figures or Types* [43.], "Catalogue," *WJE* 26:128, 425. This is likely the work that fulfilled Edwards's desire, recorded on the first page of his "Catalogue" (also in 1723), to acquire "the best [book] upon the types of the scripture," [233.], "Catalogue," *WJE* 26:164. If this is the case, it would illuminate a diary entry also of 1723: "When I want books to read; yea, when I have not very good books, not to spend time in reading them, but in reading the Scriptures... in writing on types of the Scripture, and other things, in studying the languages, and in spending more time in private duties." "Diary," 28 August 1723, *WJE* 16:780. As I will argue below, Edwards believed types to be God's language of communication, with whose idiom the saint could grow familiar.

28. Mather, *Figures or Types*, 52.

29. Ibid., 55.

sufficient weight of evidence from various parts of Scripture to suggest a typical relationship was intended, even if not explicitly specified.[30]

In countless places in his notes on Scripture Edwards appears to follow Mather's typology.[31] In numerous places he interprets Noah's flood as a type of the final judgment in the Messiah's time; King David as a type of Christ; and the sacrifices under the Law as types of Christ's sacrifice of atonement.[32] However, as his "Images" notebook and his "History of the Work of Redemption" sermons demonstrate, Edwards also believes it is possible to exegete typologically the natural world and history since, like Scripture, they are full of types by divine design.[33] Early in his career Edwards makes an important statement about his understanding of typology, a statement I will return to later when I consider his "Harmony." In "Miscellanies," no. 362 (ca. 1728) he notes that

> the whole outward creation, which is but shadows of His being, is so made as to represent spiritual things. It might be demonstrated by the wonderful agreement in thousands of things, much of the same kind as between the types of the Old Testament and their antitypes; and by there being spiritual things so

---

30. Ibid., 53-55.

31. Although Edwards employs typology throughout his vast *corpus* of sermons, treatises and notebooks, a number of texts stand out as particularly important for understanding it: "Types"—a methodological notebook on the practice and rules of typological interpretation, compiled ca. 1744-49; "Images of Divine Things"—a series of 212 numbered observations on natural types, compiled between the late 1720s and ca. 1757; "Miscellanies," no. 1069, 'Types of the Messiah," (ca. 1744-49)—Edwards's notes for the second part of his projected "Harmony." These works all appear in *WJE* 11.

32. Many possible examples could be given of each. The following represent a tiny selection. On the typological nature of the Flood: "Work of Redemption," *WJE* 9:144, 490; "Miscellanies," no. 1069, *WJE* 11:221-25; "Blank Bible," *WJE* 24:146; "The Manner in Which the Salvation of the Soul is to be Sought," *Sermons of Jonathan Edwards*, 357-75. On David as a type of Christ see "Notes on Scripture," *WJE* 15:77, 282; 2 Sam 8:2, "Blank Bible," *WJE* 24:363; "Miscellanies," no. 1069, *WJE* 11:304-5. On the typological nature of the ceremonial law see "Miscellanies," no. 119, *WJE* 13:284; Heb 9:24 "Blank Bible," *WJE* 24:1151; "Christ's Sacrifice," *WJE* 10:594-604; "Miscellanies," no. 1069, *WJE* 11:317.

33. More controversially, Gerald McDermott has argued that Edwards also believed the history of religions to be typological. Pagan religions shadowed the spiritual truths of Christian redemption thereby preparing the way for the reception of the gospel by the heathen. In this way McDermott argues that Edwards opened the way for a more expansive notion of the salvation of non-Christians. McDermott, *Edwards Confronts the Gods*, 110-29. Since I address Edwards's soteriology in chapter 4, I will pass over McDermott's thesis here.

often and continually compared with them in the word of God. And it is agreeable to God's wisdom that it should be so, that the inferior and shadowy parts of his works should be made to represent those things that immediately concern himself, and the highest parts of His work. Spiritual things are the crown and glory, the head and soul, the very end, the alpha and omega of all other works. So what therefore can be more agreeable than that they should be made as to shadow them forth.[34]

This is fitting to God's method in other arenas, according to Edwards. The "inferior dispensation of the gospel was all to shadow forth the highest and most excellent which was its end," so that everything recorded in it was typical of gospel things.[35] No longer are history and the natural world either analogous to, or simply illustrative of, spiritual truths, as they were for Edwards's predecessors. Rather they are part of a universal system in which all sensible reality is divinely designed to communicate ideas of spiritual things.[36] Aware of his innovation and the ridicule it might invite, Edwards nevertheless confesses his belief that "the whole universe, heaven and earth, air and seas, and the divine constitution and history of the holy Scriptures, be full of images of divine things, as full as a language is of words."[37]

In contrast to his understanding of prophecy, Edwards's typology has received considerable scholarly attention.[38] In his 1948 introduction to *Images or Shadows of Divine Things* Perry Miller, father of the Edwardsean renaissance, portrayed Edwards as a conservative exegete who wanted to use biblical typology to counteract the contemporary tendency to a

---

34. "Miscellanies," no. 362, *WJE* 13:434–35.

35. Ibid., 435.

36. In what follows I will offer an account of the metaphysical foundation of Edwards's typology and demonstrate how it separates Edwards's typology from that of his predecessors.

37. "Types," *WJE* 11:152.

38. See for example: Anderson, "Editor's Introduction," *WJE* 11:3–48; Cherry, "Symbols of Spiritual Truth," 263–71; Fabiny, "Edwards and Biblical Typology," and McDermott's response, "Alternative Viewpoint: Edwards and Biblical Typology," 109–12; Holmes, *God of Grace*, 99–119; Kimnach, "Editor's Introduction," *WJE* 10:3–258; Knight, "Learning the Language of God," 531–51; the same article appears as Knight, "Typology," 190–209. See also Lowance and Watters, "Editors' Introduction," *WJE* 11:157–86; McDermott, *Edwards Confronts the Gods,* 110–29; Miller, "Introduction," *Images,* 1–41; Stein, "Editor's Introduction," *WJE* 15:2–3, 9–12; Wainwright, "Jonathan Edwards and the Language of God," 519–30; Wilson, "Editor's Introduction," *WJE* 9:40–50.

tropological hermeneutic represented by Cotton Mather's *Agricola*.[39] Miller argued that Edwards used conservative biblical typology to oppose the allegorizing of his contemporaries, yet saw the Bible as only one among several manifestations of the typical system.[40] Miller saw in Edwards's typologizing of nature an "extension of typology" which had its foundation and basis in the continuity of Old and New Testaments, but which ultimately presented the natural world as an alternative sphere of revelation, exalting it to "a level of authority coequal with [biblical] revelation."[41] Stephen Stein has challenged Miller's assessment, arguing that the latter was wrong to place nature on an authoritative par with Scripture. It was, according to Stein, "a mistaken judgment . . . which conveniently allowed Miller to link Edwards with Emerson's naturalism and which has produced a long and distinguished but potentially misleading scholarly tradition."[42] One such in this tradition is the literary scholar, Mason I. Lowance Jr., who has established himself as the leading recent scholar of Edwardsean typology.[43] Lowance argues that Edwards's typology represents an attempt to reconcile two visions of typology that were in competition in early eighteenth-century New England: the "conservative" notion of the type as a (horizontal) temporal prefiguration, and the "liberal" notion of the type as (vertical) ahistorical Platonic symbol.[44] Edwards's "transformation of the Puritan types was a significant attempt to reconcile natural epistemology and scriptural exegesis. He wound up borrowing the nomenclature of typology while endowing the natural world with spiritual significance."[45] However, according to Lowance different elements of Edwards's typology are prominent at different places in his *corpus*. As points on a spectrum of conservative-liberal typology, the 1739 Redemption sermons portray the "conservative" approach; Edwards's "Images" notebook displays the more allegorical, "liberal" approach; and his "Miscellanies" show evidence

---

39. Miller, "Introduction," *Images*, 9–24.

40. Ibid., 27.

41. Ibid., 28.

42. Stein, "Spirit and Word," 125. Examples of works that have linked Edwards with Emerson include: Miller, "Introduction," *Images*, 1–41; "From Edwards to Emerson," 589–617; Brumm, *American Thought*, 86–108; Bercovitch, *Puritan Origins*, 157ff.; *American Jeremiad*; Lowance, *Language of Canaan*, 277–95.

43. See for example, Lowance, "'Images or Shadows of Divine Things'"; *Language of Canaan*; "Editors' Introduction", *WJE* 11:157–82.

44. Lowance, *Language of Canaan*, 51, 252–53.

45. Ibid., 5–6, 276.

of both.⁴⁶ The result, however, is an Edwards who appears at odds with himself: conservative in some places, liberal in others.⁴⁷

In the course of this chapter I will argue that Miller's and Lowance's accounts are ultimately unsatisfactory. Both fail to pay sufficient attention to the priority and constraining role of Scripture in Edwards's identification and interpretation of types.⁴⁸ In response I will argue that Edwards's typologizing of Scripture, history and nature are all of one piece, explicable by reference to his philosophical commitments, in particular his idealism and his notion of being as relational and communicative within a teleology of divine self-glorification.⁴⁹ Though Edwards departs from Samuel Mather's conservative approach to typology by transforming it into an imaging system capable of reading not only Scripture, but also nature and history, it is Scripture that helps Edwards identify and interpret the (eschatological) types he sees. To Edwards the typological relationship between the Testaments is itself evidence of a universal nexus of types and antitypes that runs throughout creation and history in which "God glorifies himself

---

46. Lowance, *Language of Canaan*, 251–56. As an example of the third approach, Lowance cites "Miscellanies," no. 1069, "Types of the Messiah." Since I will consider this entry in some detail later in the present chapter, I will not address it here.

47. Lowance, *Language of Canaan*, 249–76. Paula Cooey challenges Lowance's account, arguing that if the purpose of allegory is exclusively edification, then the process by which nature becomes a source for prophetic types is not allegorization. For nature to become prophetic presupposes the historicization of nature and the appropriate term for this approach is not "allegory," according to Cooey, but "anagogy." She concludes: "Once the anagogic character of Edwards's interpretation of nature is recognized, his theology no longer easily divides into the categories of liberal and conservative." Cooey, *Jonathan Edwards on Nature and Destiny*, 8. Cooey's analysis is to be welcomed in its portrayal of Edwards's typology as a coherent whole but, like Lowance, she fails to recognize the guiding role of Scripture in his identification and interpretation of types. This, as I will argue, is central to Edwards's approach to types.

48. Mason Lowance and David Watters note the guiding role of prophecy and biblical typology in Edwards's approach in "Miscellanies," no. 1069, but do not explore this. "Editors' Introduction," *WJE* 11:178. Lowance neglects it entirely in his treatment of Edwards's wider *corpus*.

49. Edwards's integrated typology is arguably reflected also in the terminology he employed throughout his typological writings. His interchangeable use of the terms "type," "shadow," "correlation" and "representation" reflects his more expansive view of types than his contemporaries possessed. While Wilson Kimnach notes that Edwards experimented with various titles for his "Images" notebook but staunchly refused to employ the word "Types," it would be wrong to read too much into this; the notebook's individual entries frequently use the language of "type," just as they do "representation," "shadow" and "image." Kimnach, "Editor's Introduction," *WJE* 10:45n.

and instructs the minds he has made."⁵⁰ When Edwards reads the Bible through the lens of this universal imaging system, he sees in Scripture a degree of typological harmony that far surpasses that acknowledged by Mather. Although at times Edwards appears to conform to the "conservative" typology of Mather in his scriptural exegesis as Lowance claims, I will argue that the conservative results are in fact consistently delivered on the basis of his new typology. This is confirmed by examination of Edwards's biblical notebooks, sources largely ignored by Lowance, in which apparently-conservative results are found alongside innovative and unfamiliar ones. To Edwards, Old and New Testaments are not linked at finite explicit points, but in every place, at every moment. I will argue that, far from following the approach he had inherited from Samuel Mather, there is evidence of Edwards's single typology throughout his biblical *corpus*. And this is the crucial context for understanding Edwards's notes for the unwritten "Harmony," which I will examine in the final part of this chapter.

Before turning to Edwards's biblical notes it is necessary to establish the unitary nature of his approach. I turn therefore first to Edwards's metaphysics.

THE METAPHYSICS OF EDWARDS'S TYPOLOGY

Being and Knowing

Foundational to Edwards's metaphysics was his early refutation of Hobbesian materialism.⁵¹ Thomas Hobbes (1558–1679) had argued that "body in the most general acceptation, signifieth that which filleth, or occupieth some certain room, or imagined place; and dependeth not on the imagination, but is a real part of what we call the universe."⁵² All substance was material, presenting itself to our senses in terms of its "accidents" or appearances. While Newton and Descartes responded that the *regulation* of the material reality depended constantly on the operation of God's power, Edwards rejected the assumption that bodies could exist by themselves as substances at all. To him the very *existence* of bodies depended on the continual action of God.⁵³ Edwards asserted that it was not the essence of

---

50. "Miscellanies," no. 362, *WJE* 13:435.
51. Hobbes, *Leviathan*, XXXIV.2; XLVI.15, 261, 446–47.
52. Ibid., XXXIV.2.
53. Anderson, "Editor's Introduction," *WJE* 6:53–59. In *Freedom of the Will*, Pt IV, § 6, *WJE* 1:374, Edwards admitted that he had never read Hobbes. Rather, it is likely

matter to resist division. He contended that the materialist assumption, that matter was supported by an underlying "substance," neither explained how matter acquired the power to resist division, nor why a particular body should exist at all. Rather than the answers to these problems being found in a substance that underlay all matter, Edwards questioned the very category of material substance.[54] In his 1721 essay, "Of Atoms," he argued that a body could not be broken into infinitely small pieces without ceasing to exist.[55] Solidity, therefore, was a body's perseverance, or

---

that his familiarity with Hobbes came through reading his critics, notably the Cambridge Platonist, Henry More. More, *Antidote*; *Immortality* and *Enchiridion* were part of the "Dummer Collection"—a body of some eight hundred books donated to Yale College by Jeremiah Dummer, London agent for the Massachusetts and Connecticut colonies in 1714. Edwards would have had access to the collection in his senior year (1720), while he studied for his masters degree (1720–22) and as a tutor (1724–26). On the Dummer books see Pratt, "The Books Sent from England," 7–44; Thuesen, "Editor's Introduction," *WJE* 26:8–13. For an inventory of the books see Bryant and Patterson, "The List of Books," 423–92. In addition to More's work the Dummer collection also introduced Yale to such works as Malebranche, *Search After Truth* and Locke, *Essay*. Perry Miller depicted a thirteen-year old Edwards as experiencing something of an epiphany as he read Locke's *Essay*—the defining moment in his intellectual life. This dating first appeared in Hopkins, *Life and Character*, reprinted in Levin, *Jonathan Edwards*, 5–6. Morris, *The Young Jonathan Edwards*, *passim*, qualifies Miller's account by arguing that although the thirteen-year old Edwards read Locke's *Essay* in his second year at college, sometime between June and October 1717, he was influenced by a far wider range of authors than Miller assumed. However, the recent publication of Edwards's "Catalogue" in *WJE* 26 has furthered the challenges to Miller's assumption first voiced by Norman Fiering and Wallace Anderson, namely that Edwards first read Locke's *Essay* as a graduate student or even as a tutor at Yale and that the influences upon the young Edwards were disparate. Fiering, *Jonathan Edwards's Moral Thought*, 33–40 and Anderson, "Editor's Introduction," *WJE* 6:15–18, 25–26. See Thuesen, "Editor's Introduction," *WJE* 26:90.

54. Controversially, Sang Hyun Lee has argued that Edwards rejected the concept of substance metaphysics altogether, replacing it with a dynamic dispositional ontology in which God's being is one of eternal becoming, and creation is in some sense a further actualization of his being. Lee's position is most fully expressed in his *Philosophical Theology*. Despite its dominance as an interpretation of Edwards's philosophical theology, it is not without its critics. Stephen Holmes argues Lee's account is anachronistic, Edwards being committed to the classical doctrine of God's being as *actus purus*. Holmes, "Dispositional Ontology?" 99–114. Also responding to Lee, Oliver Crisp argues that Edwards's ontology is more simply explained as being a version of essentialism, the doctrine that divides what exists into substances and their properties. He also argues that Edwards's commitment to a form of occasionalism renders Lee's notion of "unrealized dispositions" inoperable. Crisp, "Jonathan Edwards's Ontology," 1–20. See also Crisp, "Divine Simplicity," 23–41. On the similarity of Edwards's position to Berkeleyan essentialism, see my discussion below.

55. "Of Atoms," Prop. 1, corol. 4, *WJE* 6:211–12.

its resistance to being annihilated. If asked what was responsible for this resistance, Edwards answered that it was not the substance of a body itself, but the exercise of God's power.[56] If solidity resulted from the immediate exercise of God's power, "causing there to be indefinite resistance in that place where it is,"[57] and if body and solidity were the same, "it follows that all body is nothing but what immediately results from the exercise of divine power in such a particular manner."[58] In "Of Atoms" Edwards suggested that substance even be conceived as God himself. "[I]t follows that the unknown substance, which philosophers used to think subsisted by itself, and stood underneath and kept up solidity and all other properties, which they used to say it was impossible for a man to have an idea of, is nothing at all distinct from solidity itself; or, if they must needs apply that word to something else that really and properly does subsist by itself and support all properties, they must apply it to the divine Being or power itself... How truly, then, is he said to be *ens entium*."[59]

Edwards pursued his conception of substance in another of his philosophical journals, "The Mind," (composed between ca. late 1723 and ca. late 1740s).[60] He again asserted that the very substance of the body itself was "nothing but the divine power, or the constant exertion of it."[61] In this Edwards was responding to the claims of the new science. He denied that nature's laws were independently operative, being grounded in the nature of matter itself, and he denied that God merely regulated the world. Rather, the very existence of bodies depended on the constant operation of God's power, observable through what *appeared* to be fixed natural laws.[62]

---

56. For Edwards's rejection of the notion of an underlying substance in which properties inhere, see also "Miscellanies," no. 267, *WJE* 13:373 and "The Mind," no. 61, *WJE* 6:376–80.

57. "Of Atoms," Prop. 2, corol. 8, *WJE* 6:215.

58. "Of Atoms," Prop. 1, corol. 4, *WJE* 6:211; "Of Atoms," Prop. 2, corol. 9, *WJE* 6:215

59. "Of Atoms," Prop. 2, corol. 11, *WJE* 6:215. John Locke is the most likely source of Edwards's reflections on the one "substance" that supports the properties of bodies. See Locke, *Essay*, 2.23, 295–317 in which he argues that the substance of an object, that in which its properties inhere, is sensibly unknowable. See also, Anderson, "Editor's Introduction," *WJE* 6:54–68.

60. See Anderson, "Note on 'The Mind,'" *WJE* 6:313–29, for a discussion of the dating of the entries in this notebook.

61. "The Mind," no. 27, *WJE* 6:350–51.

62. "Miscellanies," no. 1263 ("God's Immediate and Arbitrary Operation,") *WJE* 23:201–12. The interpretation of this entry is disputed. Lee quotes it in support of his notion of dispositional ontology, arguing that in it Edwards appears to believe that

Edwards's speculations on ontology led him further: to consider the location of being. In "Of Being" (1721) he had argued that it was impossible to conceive of "nothing" existing; "so we see it is necessary some being should eternally be."[63] In other words, if we were able to think away all things, we would still be left with space, which is not "nothing." Rather, space is God and God "contains, envelops all other reality."[64] "Space is this necessary, eternal, infinite and omnipresent being ... But I had as good speak plain: I have already said as much as that space is God. And it is indeed clear to me, that all the space there is not proper to body, all the space there is without the bounds of the creation, all the space there was before the creation, is God himself."[65]

Wallace Anderson charts the development in Edwards's philosophical thought from his early concern with the nature of being to his assertion of idealistic phenomenalism.[66] Further entries in "Of Being" reveal Edwards's belief that "nothing has any existence anywhere else but in consciousness."[67] In this, Edwards's belief bears striking resemblance to the "immaterialism" of George Berkeley (1685–1753).[68] Central though

---

God creates arbitrarily, and then conserves his creation in an occasionalistic manner but according to established physical laws. Lee, *Philosophical Theology*, 51–67, 102–07, esp. 63. However, Crisp argues that the context of the entry is the discoveries of natural philosophy that meant many were now willing to allow "a present continuous immediate operation of God on the creation" according to fixed laws that God himself determined from the beginning of creation and according to which he must act in conservation, so that "though they allow an immediate divine operation in those days, yet they suppose it is [now] limited by what we call laws of nature, and seem averse to allow an arbitrary operation to be continued or even to be needed in these days." One possible reading of the entry is that the "natural laws" are illusory, being entirely dependent on God's arbitrary creation *ex nihilo* at every moment, and on this reading "Miscellanies," no. 1263 is consistent with the occasionalism Edwards develops in *Freedom of the Will* and *Original Sin*. Crisp, "How 'Occasional' was Edwards's Occasionalism?" 61–77.

63. "Of Being," *WJE* 6:202.

64. Jenson, *America's Theologian*, 21.

65. "Of Being," *WJE* 6:203. In his assertion that space is God Edwards was likely influenced by the Cambridge Platonist, Henry More, as Anderson notes, *WJE* 6:203 n. 3.

66. Anderson, "Editor's Introduction," *WJE* 6:52–136.

67. "Of Being," *WJE* 6:204.

68. Berkeley, *Principles*, Pt I, §§ 3, 6, 10, 28–33. The recently-published catalogues of Edwards's reading indicates that Edwards had read Berkeley's *Principles* [no. 318] "Catalogue," *WJE* 26:184. Thuesen notes that three references to Berkeley in the various catalogues, in addition to Anderson's contention that Edwards used Berkeley's *New Theory of Vision* in "The Mind," "belie Perry Miller's contention in Miller, *Jonathan Edwards*, 62, that 'nowhere [in Edwards's manuscripts] is there any sign of a first-hand

the idealist assertion was to Edwards's metaphysics, it was not his primary claim, nor was Edwards's challenge directed against the skepticism or atheism that resulted from materialist accounts of reality, as was the case with Berkeley.[69] As noted at the beginning of this section, Edwards had settled to his own satisfaction the question of material substantiality prior to developing his own idealism. Edwards's idealism was the logical consequence of his assertion that nothing could be without being known. Again the resonance with Berkeley is striking. Berkeley's *dictum*, "*esse est percipi*" ("to be is to be perceived") could be echoed by Edwards.[70] To Edwards it was impossible to believe that "there should be being from all eternity without its being conscious to itself that it was; that there should be being from all eternity and yet nothing know, all that while, that anything is."[71]

In an oft-quoted illustration Edwards asked how a room full of objects yet empty of people could have being in any other way than in the

---

acquaintance with Berkeley." Anderson, "Editor's Introduction," *WJE* 6:372 n. 1; Thuesen, "Editor's Introduction," *WJE* 26:93. However, while there are similarities between Edwards and Berkeley, it is not clear that Edwards had read Berkeley by the time he formulated his own idealism, the earliest expression of which ("Miscellanies," no. pp) can be dated to early 1723. Edwards's arguments for idealism were shaped very specifically to deal with the peculiarities of his own earlier views concerning the existence of bodies. As Anderson observes, "Edwards' [sic] arguments are not at all concerned with one question that was central to the other idealists of the time, namely whether bodies are substances, capable of existing by themselves. He had already decided that question in the negative, and did not trouble to reconsider the matter." Anderson, "Editor's Introduction," *WJE* 6:77. The question of the source of Edwards's idealism therefore remains an open one; see Anderson's survey in his "Editor's Introduction," *WJE* 6:76-77 n. 3. In general attempts to identify major influences on Edwards's idealism have failed to prove that Edwards had read the sources in question by the time of his own expression of idealism. Berkeley was not the only idealist known to Edwards. He was also familiar with the Cambridge Platonists, Henry More (1614–87) and Ralph Cudworth (1617–88). Though Edwards nowhere names More in his *corpus*, his influence on Edwards's "Of Atoms" is very likely. Anderson notes that in "Of Atoms" Edwards's argument and vocabulary are similar to those of More's *Immortality*. "Of Atoms," *WJE* 26:208 n. 2; see also 63-64. In "The Mind," no. 40, *WJE* 6:359 (ca. 1726), Edwards quotes from Cudworth's *Intellectual System* regarding Plato's cave: "All this is a Description of the State of those Men, who take Body to be the only Real and Substantial thing in the World, and to do all that is done in it . . ." Cudworth, *Intellectual System* ch. 1, § 19. I will return to the significance to Edwards of the Cambridge Platonists in my discussion of the *prisca theologia* below.

69. See Anderson's discussion of this in his "Editor's Introduction," *WJE* 6:77, 102–3.

70. Berkeley, *Principles*, Pt I, § 3.

71. "Miscellanies," no. pp, *WJE* 13:188.

consciousness of God.[72] Likewise, how could another universe devoid of intelligent beings exist?[73] Both the uninhabited room and the uninhabited universe have being only as they are known in God's consciousness. If they could cease to be known by God, they would cease to be.[74] Going a stage further, Edwards argued that even the created mind that perceives a body exists because *it* is perceived in the mind of God. Thus, both the perception of a thing in a created mind and the existence of the thing independent of human perception are the result of the thing's perception in the mind of God. Whereas Edwards had earlier argued that all things exist in God by virtue of their location in space, he now argued that they exist by virtue of God's knowledge of them. The universe is an ideal one, existing in the mind of God. Edwards concludes "The Mind," no. 27 with the assertion: "The world is therefore an ideal one; and the law of creating, and the succession of these ideas, is constant and regular."[75] Space is "God's field: space is the field of the universal consciousness that God is."[76] Consequently the power that creates places of indefinite resistance and therefore being, is God's power of thought.

Before exploring the typological implications of Edwards's idealism it is necessary to consider the relationship he saw between material creation and spiritual reality. This is the subject of our next section.

Communicative Being

If the first part of Edwards's metaphysics consonant with his typology is his idealism, a second necessary part is his conception of being as relational and communicative. In his notebook, "The Mind," Edwards attempted to explain why excellency or beauty was to be found in harmony and proportion, and in doing so he brought the category of substance under that of relations.[77] A thing's being was dependent on its relationship to other things: "For being, if we examine narrowly, is nothing else but proportion."[78]

---

72. Ibid. Edwards developed the case of the unoccupied room in "Of Being," *WJE* 6:204-06 and "The Mind," *WJE* 6:356-58.

73. "Of Being," prop.1, *WJE* 6:204.

74. Ibid.

75. "The Mind," no. 27, *WJE* 6:351. For Edwards's discussion of how these "laws" are dependent on the arbitrary power of God, see "Miscellanies," no. 1263, *WJE* 23:201-12.

76. Jenson, *America's Theologian*, 28-29.

77. "The Mind," prop. 1, *WJE* 6:332ff. Anderson, "Editor's Introduction," *WJE* 6:83.

78. "The Mind," prop. 1, *WJE* 6:336.

Thus, "One alone, without reference to any more, cannot be excellent."[79] Every created thing was related in some way to every other created thing. But every material thing also imaged spiritual reality.[80] "The beauty of the world consists wholly of sweet mutual consents, either within itself, or with the Supreme Being. As to the corporeal world, though there are many other sorts of consents, yet the sweetest and most charming beauty of it is its resemblance of spiritual beauties."[81]

Edwards conceived of spiritual reality as the "substance" of the inferior and material creation. "Type" stands in relationship to "substance," its antitype, in a way that assumes that the substance is made real and accessible through the type. The way in which the substance is communicated by God is expressed in this oft-quoted extract from "The Mind": "The secret lies here: that which truly is the substance of all bodies is the infinitely exact and precise and perfectly stable idea in God's mind, together with his stable will that the same shall gradually be communicated to us, and to other minds, according to certain fixed and exact established methods and laws: or in somewhat different language, the infinitely exact, precise and stable will with respect to correspondent communications to created minds, and effects on their minds."[82]

Material type was connected with spiritual antitype. And to Edwards the substance, in some sense more real than the material world, was communicated through its shadow or type.[83] But Edwards not only described the antitype as the "substance" of the type. It was also the "end" and "consummation" of the type. God's communication served a greater end: his own glorification. Thus in one of his earliest "Miscellanies" Edwards asserted that knowledge of God was the purpose of the universe. God did not create the world for nothing. It would be "useless" if there were no intelligent beings but God "for God could neither receive good himself nor

---

79. Ibid., 337. See also, "Miscellanies," no.117, *WJE* 13:283–84.

80. See for example Edwards's notes for his "A Rational Account of the Main Doctrines of the Christian Religion Attempted," in which he comments: "Creation: the ends of it. Things made in analogy to spiritual things." "A Rational Account," *WJE* 6:394.

81. "Beauty of the World," *WJE* 6:305.

82. "The Mind," no. 13, *WJE* 6:344.

83. In his "Editor's Introduction," *WJE* 10:227–36, Kimnach argues that Edwards's pursuit of a new rhetoric of images grew out of the pastoral concern of a preacher to connect the real world of his congregation's senses to the true spiritual world, thus awakening in the hearts of his congregation the spiritual realities to which the material world pointed.

communicate good."[84] Religion was the purpose of creation; the world was ontologically a communicative thing. In "Miscellanies," no. 247 Edwards tied this communication to God's self-glorification: "For God to glorify himself is to discover himself in his works, or to communicate himself in his works, which is all one; for we are to remember that the universe exists only mentally, so that the very being of the world implies its being perceived or discovered. . . . So that the glory of God is the shining forth of his perfections; and the world was created that they might shine forth, that is, that they might be communicated."[85]

Edwards's new typology had a new metaphysical basis. Material creation, comprising an imaging system of spiritual reality, was designed to be read typologically. Just how much this differed from Edwards's immediate heritage is clear when he is compared once again with Samuel Mather. Mather outlined rules for correctly understanding types, noting that, "Before the Gospel there were no Gospel types. . . . There were some things extant before that were made types afterward; but they had not that *schesis*, that habitude and relation to Christ and the Gospel, 'til there was a Gospel or promise of life by Christ, that blessed Seed."[86] To Mather God imbued creation with typological significance at the moment of the *protevangelion* of Gen 3:15. In the divine economy aspects of creation were endowed with the ability to shadow forth the gospel to humanity. Edwards, however, believed that "things even before the fall were types of things pertaining to the gospel redemption."[87] Material creation had always shadowed forth spiritual truths. Creation was the vehicle of God's self-communication and the means to his self-glorification. As such the biblical history expressed

---

84. "Miscellanies," no. gg, *WJE* 13:185. Edwards believes that God's communication *ad extra* comprises both idea and will, as is fitting to his being and activity *ad intra*. I will discuss Edwards's conception of the Trinitarian character of God's communication in chapter 4, a case study in the harmony in Edwards's soteriology in the Old and New Testaments.

85. "Miscellanies," no. 247, *WJE* 13:360–61. See also for example, "Miscellanies," nos. 1218, 1225, *WJE* 23:150–53, 157 which are both preparatory to the first of Edwards's twin dissertations: *Concerning the End for Which God Created the World*, *WJE* 8:405–536.

86. Mather, *Figures or Types*, 55–56.

87. "Miscellanies," no. 479, *WJE* 13:523. See also "Images," no. 8, *WJE* 11:53. For Edwards the very act of material creation was typological so the *protevangelion* was declared in Gen 1:1. The question of Edwards's position regarding the ordering of the divine decrees is beyond the scope of the present enquiry. Discussions may be found in Crisp, *Metaphysics of Sin*, 5–24; Gerstner, *Rational Biblical Theology*, 2.142–88; Holmes, *God of Grace*, 126–34.

in Old Testament "type" and New Testament "antitype" testified to a larger scheme of imaging directed towards God's glorification.

To summarize thus far, there were precedents for the figural reading of nature and history; the world was "slickt up in types." But to Edwards the whole of creation "imaged" the divinely-communicated spiritual substance, in which it found its "consummation." Material creation comprised a language of types, designed by God for his self-communication to his saints. The types that united the Testaments were but one example of the typical system that comprised creation. So rather than confine himself to specific correlations permitted by New Testament warrant, Edwards's metaphysical commitments demanded that he explore Scripture, creation and history, believing all to be pregnant with typological significance at every point, and this in a teleology aimed at God's glorification.

In what follows I will argue that Edwards is guided by Scripture in his typological exegesis to a degree hitherto unrecognized. Furthermore, once Scripture's role in Edwards's system is fully appreciated, the unitary nature of his typology throughout his *corpus* is apparent.

THE BIBLICAL GRAMMAR OF "A CERTAIN SORT OF LANGUAGE"

The Invitational Role of the Bible in Edwards's Typological Exegesis

In his methodological notebook, "Types," Edwards notes: "See pamphlet entitled, Creation, the Ground-work of Revelation, pp. 49–50."[88] The reference is to a short work by Andrew Wilson (1718–92), in which the author argues that God created the material world as a reflection of the superior spiritual world.[89] In addition God devised and gave humanity the Hebrew language to describe and explain this relationship. Wilson thus presents the Hebrew language as fundamental to the correct understanding of creation's typical language. He notes that "there is a mysterious harmony between this world and an invisible one; and the language of the Old Testament is the key to this mystery . . . The Hebrew language, by the perfection of its composition [is] fully adapted to convey divine discoveries, and

---

88. "Types," *WJE* 11:152.
89. Wilson, *Creation*.

disclose the relations between material operations and the divine procedure in a superior analogous dispensation..."[90]

Shalom Goldman claims that Edwards's typology "may owe something to the influence of Wilson."[91] Edwards's interest in the Hebrew language is beyond doubt.[92] He saw theological significance in it and began keeping a notebook of Hebrew idioms around the time of his composition of the "Types" notebook. In his letter to the trustees of the College of New Jersey in October 1757 in which he outlined his two projects, "A History of the Work of Redemption" and "The Harmony of the Old and New Testament," Edwards also expressed his desire to teach the Hebrew language in order to improve his own grasp of it.[93] However, while Ed-

90. Wilson, *Creation*, 24. Wilson's observations regarding the significance of material creation extends beyond discussion of the Hebrew language. Edwards copied a lengthy extract from Wilson's work into his own "Blank Bible" under Matt 2:23 ["And he came and dwelt in a city called Nazareth, that it might be fulfilled which was spoken by the prophets, He shall be called a Nazarene."] Wilson notes, "The deity, careful to obviate and rouse the inattention of mankind, ordinarily connected some analogous external circumstance, with the spiritual completion of the types and prophecies, in the person of the Messiah." "Blank Bible," *WJE* 24:828.

91. Goldman, *God's Sacred Tongue*, 84.

92. On Edwards's study of Hebrew as a student see, Morris, *Young Jonathan Edwards*, 64–65. As a tutor at Yale College in 1724 Edwards taught Hebrew. Furthermore, throughout his life his biblical notebooks are full of observations of theological significance in the construction of Hebrew words or phrases; see for example, Gen 2:22–23 in the "Blank Bible," *WJE* 24:135–36. At the same time a revival of Cabbalism, a discipline that sought to read mystical significance into the letters of Hebrew words, was part of the theological ether of the early eighteenth century. Its interest to Edwards was in its conception of language and reality which, Anderson notes, was similar to his own in its understanding that "word and idea were somehow unified in an epistemological, metaphysical and even ontological sense, and conveyed the larger underlying unity of God and creation." *WJE* 11:24–26 (26). Under the heading, "Books to be inquired for" in his catalogue of reading, Edwards writes, "the best that treats of the Cabalistical learning of the Jews." *WJE* 26:165. In his notes for the prophetic and typological sections of his projected "Harmony" ("Miscellanies," nos. 891, 922, 1067, 1069) he refers to Basnage, *History* which contains a lengthy description of Cabbala. However, in his study of Edwards as a Hebraist, Shalom Goldman argues that it would wrong to overemphasize Cabbalism's influence on Edwards's thought. Goldman, *God's Sacred Tongue*, 87.

93. Clyde A. Holbrook cites as another reason to improve his Hebrew, Edwards's engagement with the capable Hebraist, John Taylor (1694–1761), his principal opponent in *Original Sin* (1758). Holbrook, "Editor's Introduction," *WJE* 3:68–70. Edwards's competence in Hebrew is disputed, however. While John Smith argues that he was "well equipped to deal with the subtleties of Hebrew syntax," Goldman, suggests that he was no expert. Smith, *Jonathan Edwards*, 143; Goldman, *God's Sacred Tongue*, 77–79. Edwards's interest in the biblical languages extended to Greek. The fact that

wards was interested in the theological significance of Hebrew, Andrew Wilson could not have been important to the development of Edwards's typology as Goldman claims. Not only was Edwards's typology consonant with the metaphysical commitments he reached in the 1720s, but more significantly many of his interpretations of the types of the natural world in his "Images" notebook predate by more than twenty years the publication of Wilson's treatise in 1750.[94]

The importance of the Hebrew language as the key to explaining the relationship between material and spiritual worlds chimed with Edwards's belief in an ancient universal revelation—a tradition known as the *prisca theologia* (ancient theology). Associated with Clement of Alexandria, employed by the Apologists and revived during the Renaissance, the *prisca theologia* held that vestiges of biblical truths such as the Trinity, monotheism and the Fall of mankind were apparent in the philosophies and religions of the pagans, having been borrowed by Plato and other classical philosophers from the Jews and corrupted through the centuries as they were passed down.[95] Edwards frequently consulted *The Court of the Gentiles,* a work by English Nonconformist, Theophilus Gale (1628–78), whose declared aim was threefold: (1) to defend the authority of the

---

the New Testament was written in Greek aided the dissemination of the gospel and the fellowship between churches in the early centuries of the Apostolic church, according to Edwards. "Work of Redemption," *WJE* 9:273–74. He also comments in his notes for the unwritten "A History of the Work of Redemption," that Greek and Latin were "so much more fitted to express things speculative moral & divine than all other Languages." Jonathan Edwards, "A History of the Work of Redemption."

94. Furthermore, Edwards's reference to Wilson can be dated to ca. 1755–56, the handwriting being most similar to Edwards's entries in "Images," nos. 199–206. See the editorial "Note on the Manuscript of 'Types,'" *WJE* 11:145.

95. Edwards employed the *prisca theologia* in his confrontation with the Deists, arguing that any knowledge of God possessed by the heathen was not due to the light of nature, but to divine revelation. He made use of Gale, *Court of the Gentiles* in both his "Notes on Scripture" and his "Blank Bible." It is likely Edwards borrowed Gale's work from the library of the Hampshire Association of ministers in 1741. Edwards's search for allies in his battle with the Deists took him to unlikely sources, among them Cambridge Platonist, Cudworth's *Intellectual System*, the Jacobite, Ramsay's *Travels of Cyrus* and his *Philosophical Principles*. Edwards found in both Cudworth and Ramsay support for an ancient and universal revelation. Edwards copied extensively from Cudworth in his later "Miscellanies"; see for example, "Miscellanies," no. 1359, *WJE* 23:640–713. See [598., 650.] "Catalogues," *WJE* 26:273–74, 292. On the history of the *prisca theologia*, see Walker, *Ancient Theology*. On Edwards's interest in other religions and his use of *prisca theologia*, see McDermott, *Edwards Confronts the Gods*, 97–109. Fiering, *Moral Philosophy*, 15, suggests that Edwards may have been introduced to the *prisca theologia* by Samuel Johnson, his tutor at Yale.

Christian Scriptures by arguing on philological and historical grounds that the Jewish oracles were the source of the learning and literature of the ancient Gentiles; (2) to demonstrate Christ's grace to his church in that the ancient Greeks, who were esteemed the "eye of the world for human wisdom," should "come and light their Candles at this sacred fire, which was loged [sic] in the Jewish Church"; (3) to show the imperfection of nature's light, in that the best thoughts of the Gentile philosophers "were but some corrupt Derivations, or at best but broken Traditions, originally traduced from the Sacred Scriptures, and Jewish Church."[96] Gale argued that Hebrew was the first language, given by God and spoken in Eden. From Hebrew all other languages are derived. It was God who inspired Adam to give to the animals names "proportionable to their respective Natures and operations; so that the image, picture, and face of the thing, might be discovered in the name," words being how men represent objects to each other.[97] A similar argument is advanced by the Jacobite exile, Andrew Michael Ramsay (1686–1743). An unlikely source for the New England Reformed theologian, Edwards quotes from Chevaliler Ramsay in both his "Images" notebook and later "Miscellanies" in support of an ancient and universal divine revelation. In the passage Edwards copied into "Images," no. 206 in ca. 1754 Ramsay discusses hieroglyphs, arguing that "the first sages of the most remote antiquity made use of sensible signs . . . to represent intellectual and spiritual truths . . ." The basis of hieroglyphs, according to Ramsay, is "that great truth," namely that "the visible world is representative of the invisible; that the properties, forms and motions of the one were copies, images, and shadows of the attributes, qualities and laws of the other."[98] The attraction of this sentiment to Edwards is obvious, given the idealist metaphysics he had formulated as a young man. And almost immediately Edwards follows the quotation from Ramsay with three from Ralph Cudworth's *True Intellectual System of the Universe*, a work he had harvested for his scientific notebook, "The Mind," no. 40, some thirty years earlier.[99]

96. Gale, *Court of the Gentiles*, 5-6.

97. Ibid., 53.

98. Ramsay, *Philosophical Principles*, 2.11–12, quoted in "Images," no. 206, *WJE* 11:127–28. See also, for example, "Miscellanies," no. 1255, *WJE* 23:190–91.

99. Cudworth, *True Intellectual System*. The three references to Cudworth are: "Images," no. 208. "Our breath to support life, a representation of our dependence on the Spirit of God for spiritual life . . ."; no. 209. "The Sun a type of Christ . . ."; no. 210. "Simplicius acquaints us, that Empedocles made two worlds, the one intellectual, and the other sensible and the former of these to [be] the exemplar and archetype of the

Edwards drew support from a wide range of thinkers for his belief in an ancient universal revelation. Andrew Wilson stood among them. Thus while Goldman's claim for the significance of Wilson's influence on Edwards's typology is overstated, nevertheless, it is likely that Edwards found in Wilson a useful ally. Of particular interest to Edwards was Wilson's notion of types as a dynamic language. The part of Wilson's work that Edwards refers to in his "Types" notebook describes the Old and New Testaments as being related in the manner of a parable and its interpretation, or a fable and its moral: one gives the material representation, the other spiritual signification. As a result the task of Christ and the New Testament writers was not to explain exhaustively the Old Testament, but to "fulfil and display that true glory, which, when completely revealed, appeared the true original of what was prefigured of old."[100] In direct contrast to Samuel Mather, Andrew Wilson argues against those who warn of the dangers of interpreting anything in the Old Testament as a type of what is revealed in the New unless the New Testament gives express warrant for it: "I hope that it may, some time or other eventually be shown that the citations which are made from the Old Testament in the New, are so wisely chosen, as to serve as a general direction unto the proper application of these two revelations unto one another, which the most unskillful may be taught safely to that use..."[101]

According to Wilson, the saint is expected to be able to go beyond the examples of the New Testament's use of the Old Testament and learn how to read the harmony of the Testaments himself. Although the New Testament does not exhaustively explain all instances of Old Testament typology, the reader is expected to be able to learn the typological language and use it in his reading of Scripture. In the same way, Edwards, believed types to be a divinely-conceived language—"a certain sort of language in which God is wont to speak to us"—the understanding of which the spiritually-enlightened reader ought to be able to acquire and employ. Furthermore,

> there is, as it were, a certain idiom in that language which is to be learnt the same that the idiom of any language is, viz. by good acquaintance with the language, either by being naturally

---

latter." "Images," nos. 208–210, *WJE* 11:129. In his Stockbridge "Miscellanies" Edwards quotes at length from both Ramsay (for example, nos. 1351 and 1355, *WJE* 23:461–81 and 543–75 respectively) and Cudworth (notably, no. 1359, *WJE* 23:640–713). Edwards wrote "The Mind," no. 40, *WJE* 6:359 in ca. 1726, according to Anderson, "Note on 'The Mind'," *WJE* 6:327. See my discussion of Edwards's idealism above.

100. Wilson, *Creation*, 50.

101. Ibid., 49–50.

> trained up in it, learning it by education (but that is not the way in which corrupt mankind learned divine language), or by much use and acquaintance together with a good taste of judgment, by comparing one thing with another and having our senses as it were exercised to discern it (which is the way that adult person must come to speak any language, and in its true idiom, that is not their native tongue).[102]

As "a certain sort of language" typology's rudiments could be learned and through exercise and experience applied effectively in exegesis. Thus in Edwards's hands, the Bible on one level functioned much like a grammar book, teaching the rudiments of the language of typology with the expectation that the language would be used in the daily reading of Scripture and the wider world. To limit one's use of the language to its expressions in Scripture, as Samuel Mather had urged, would be merely to rehearse the exercises in the grammar book without ever attempting to use the language itself elsewhere.[103] Like Wilson, Edwards believes that the Bible presents a sufficient introduction to the language: "God han't expressly explained all the types of Scriptures, but has done so much as is sufficient to teach us the language."[104] And Scripture itself expects that we will grow familiar with the language of typology. In "Types" Edwards argues that Scripture's very silence speaks loudly of its expectations that its readers become competent interpreters of types. He gives as an example of Scripture's invitation to "typologize" the fact that the writer to the Hebrews does not explain the Temple's theology fully: "That many more particulars in the form of the sanctuary and its various parts, vessels and utensils, than are explained is evident by Heb. 9:5, 'And over it the cherubims of glory shadowing the mercy seat; of which we cannot now speak particularly' plainly intimating there [are] many particulars in those things representing heavenly things which he now thought it not expedient to explain."[105] With an insight into his similar approach to prophecy (the subject of the previous chapter), Edwards argues:

> To say that we must not say that such things are types of these and those things unless the Scripture has expressly taught us that they are so, is as unreasonable as to say that we are not to

---

102. "Types," *WJE* 11:150–51.

103. On the relationship between the Bible and natural revelation in Edwards's thought, see my discussion below.

104. "Types," *WJE* 11:151.

105. Ibid., 153.

interpret any prophecies of Scripture or apply them to these and those events, except we find them interpreted to our hand, and must interpret no more of the prophecies of David, etc. For by the Scriptures it is plain that innumerable other things are types that are not interpreted in Scriptures (all the ordinances of the Law are all shadows of good things to come), in like manner as it is plain by Scripture that these and those passages that are not actually interpreted are yet predictions of future events.[106]

Would the writer to the Hebrews not want us to explore what he had left silent? Edwards finds it inconceivable that he would not. But to limit one's biblical typological exegesis to the correspondences between the Testaments according to Mather's approach is wrong for a further reason, according to Edwards, a reason I will explore more fully in chapter 4: it means that the Old Testament saints were prevented from searching out the meaning of the overwhelming majority of types that were presented to them. "If we may use our own understanding and invention not at all in interpreting types, and must not conclude anything at all to be types but what is expressly said to be and explained in Scripture, then the church under the Old [Testament], when the types were given, were secluded from ever using their understanding to search into the meaning of the types given to 'em; for God did, when he gave 'em, give no interpretation."[107]

---

106. Ibid., 152. See also Edwards's comment at the end of "Miscellanies," no. 1069, *WJE* 11:323–24.

107. "Types," *WJE* 11:150. Wilson Kimnach misquotes this entry in his "Editor's Introduction," *WJE* 10:232, rendering the very opposite meaning from that intended by Edwards. Kimnach quotes Edwards thus: "If we may use our own understanding and imagination not at all in interpreting types, and must not conclude anything at all to be types but what is expressly said to be and [is] explained in Scripture, then the church is under the old [Dispensation]." In Kimnach's hands the text suggests the church of the Old Testament could not interpret the types presented to it. However, from *WJE* 11, which I quote above in the body of text and which is identical with the online volume at http://www.edwards.yale.edu, Edwards is arguing for his expanded typology by appealing to the example of the Old Testament church which *could* interpret types despite the fact that they were not expressly explained to her. Similarly, Edwards asks: "[H]ow could any of these types be of any manner of instruction to the Jews to whom they were given, if they might judge nothing without interpretation, for the interpretation of none was then given?" However, as with his understanding of prophecy, so Edwards argues that although the types were given to the Old Testament saints for their instruction, "yet they were given much more for our instruction under the New Testament; for they understood but little, but we are under vastly greater advantage to understand them than they. . . . 1 Cor. 9:9–10, 1 Cor. 10:6, 11." "Types," *WJE* 11:148–49. I will return to this notion of "epistemic progress" through redemption history in my concluding chapter.

I have noted already that to Edwards the examples of type and antitype in Scripture are but one part of the wider imaging network that comprises reality. He now appeals to the fact that the Old Testament saints were instructed in the faith, being presented with the gospel under shadows and types even though these shadows and types did not come with interpretation. Even conservative typological practitioners, like Samuel Mather, accepted this. But while Edwards notes elsewhere the greater clarity of revelation enjoyed by the New Testament saint, as I will explore in the following chapter, nevertheless in one sense the saint in Northampton stands in the same situation as the saint in ancient Israel. Both are presented with uninterpreted types of spiritual reality. And just as the saint in ancient Israel had the capacity to understand the types presented to him, so too does the saint in Northampton. Scripture not only demonstrates the typical nature of reality, according to Edwards. It also shows that typological interpretation is perfectly possible.

The Constraining Role of the Bible on Edwards's Typological Exegesis

In Edwards's system typological exploration of the Bible, nature and history is not only invited by Scripture. It is also constrained by Scripture. For this reason, Stephen Stein's depiction of Edwards's poetic "flights of exegetical fancy" must be rejected. Stein claims that Edwards was "unencumbered from the apparatus of critical scholarship," giving him room to "exercise his exegetical imagination without limit."[108] Edwards's relation to critical scholarship is beyond the bounds of the present enquiry and has been discussed elsewhere, but as regards an unrestrained imagination, in his methodological notebook, "Types," Edwards cautions against human ingenuity in the interpretation of types, arguing that there is "a medium between those that cry down all types, and those that are for turning all into nothing but allegory and not having it to be true history."[109] I have argued above that Edwards maintains the historical character of types, setting them within the teleological *schema* of God's glorification through

---

108. Stein, "Edwards and the Rainbow," 440.

109. On Edwards's relation to nascent biblical criticism see Brown, *Edwards and the Bible, passim*. "Types," *WJE* 11:151. Anderson sees Edwards's targets here as being, on the one hand the Deists and rationalists (like Anthony Collins whose critique of figurative readings of Scripture I addressed in the previous chapter), and on the other the Roman and High Church tendencies to dissolve all Scripture into non-historical allegory. Anderson, "Editor's Introduction," *WJE* 11:11–23.

self-communication.¹¹⁰ Yet aware of the dangers posed by this dynamic conception of the language of types, Edwards warns that readers ought to be careful not to give way to "wild fancy" and not to fix an interpretation "unless warranted by some hint in the New Testament of its being the true interpretation."¹¹¹ He cautions those who would employ the language to be "well and thoroughly acquainted" with it, or "we shall never understand [or] have a right notion of the idiom of the language.... If we go to interpret divine types without this, we shall be just like one that pretends to speak any language that hadn't thoroughly learnt it. We shall use many barbarous expressions that fail entirely of the proper beauty of the language, that are very harsh in the ears of those that are well versed in the language."¹¹²

The guiding role played by Scripture in Edwards's identification and interpretation of types has been neglected by both Stephen Stein and Mason Lowance. Lowance mistakenly depicts Edwards as following the approach of Samuel Mather in his approach to biblical types. At the same time by neglecting the constraining influence of Scripture on Edwards's typology, Lowance portrays the Northampton divine as "liberal" in his extension of typology to the natural world. Edwards's typology is presented as bifurcated. In seeking to demonstrate the error of this account, I will first consider how Scripture guides Edwards in his use of the language of types in the natural world. I will then do the same regarding Edwards's typological interpretation of the Bible. In each case I will argue that Edwards is guided in his interpretation of types by the grammar book of that language, the Bible.

The Grammar Employed: The Natural World

In 1948 Perry Miller claimed that Edwards exalted nature to "a level of authority co-equal with [special] revelation."¹¹³ Therefore, before considering the guiding role of Scripture in the interpretation of natural types, a brief comment on Edwards's relationship to natural revelation and natural

---

110. The second sub-heading of Edwards's "Images" notebook is: "The Language and Lessons of Nature," *WJE* 11:50 n. 2. Stephen Holmes notes that the dynamic nature of the typological language fits perfectly with Edwards's dynamic theology of history. See also Knight, "Learning the Language of God," *passim*.

111. "Types," *WJE* 11:148.

112. Ibid., 148–51.

113. Miller, "Introduction," *Images*, 28.

theology is necessary, mindful that he did not leave a definition of either term.[114] Issues of natural revelation and natural religion were brought sharply into focus in Edwards's own day in Matthew Tindal's *Christianity as Old as Creation* (London, 1730).[115] Tindal argued that, "too great a stress can't be laid on Natural Religion; which, as I take it, differs not from Reveal'd, but in the manner of its being communicated: The one being the Internal, as the other the External Revelation of the same unchangeable Will of a Being, who is alike at all times infinitely wise and good."[116] Since, according to Tindal, natural religion was delivered perfect, revealed religion adds nothing to it: "Can Revelation, I say, add any thing to a Religion thus absolutely perfect, universal and immutable?"[117] The answer in the Deist's mind is a firm negative.

I have noted above Edwards's belief that nature comprises a network of types, divinely designed to communicate spiritual reality. "Religion ... [is] the end of creation."[118] In "Miscellanies," nos. 1337 and no. 1340 Edwards addresses Tindal's arguments directly, agreeing that nature does indeed reveal spiritual truths.[119] The problem, according to Edwards, however, is Tindal's logic that the fact that the law of nature is perfect means that the light of nature is also sufficient: "What according to the nature of things is fittest and best may be most perfect, and yet our natural discerning and knowledge of this may be most imperfect."[120]

There is also a distinction, Edwards notes, between the duties of religion that we have as God's creatures and those we have as sinners, but in both instances natural revelation is insufficient. "As to the former, 'tis manifest from fact that nature alone is not sufficient for the discovery of the religion of nature. . . . And as to the latter, viz. the religion of a sinner, or the duties proper and necessary for us as depraved, guilty and offending creatures, 'tis most evident the light of nature cannot be sufficient for our

---

114. Further discussion may be found in: Gerstner, *Rational Biblical Theology*, 1.107–13; Holmes, *God of Grace*, 104ff; Moody, *Edwards and the Enlightenment*, 119–54; Nichols, *Absolute Sort of Certainty*, 21–45; Schweitzer, "Harmony of Reality," chapters 2-3; Stein, "Spirit and Word," 125.

115. Edwards responds to Tindal directly in "Miscellanies," no. 1340 "REASON AND REVELATION," *WJE* 23:359–76.

116. Tindal, *Christianity*, 2.

117. Ibid., 3.

118. "Miscellanies," no. gg, *WJE* 13:185.

119. "Miscellanies," no. 1337, *WJE* 23:342–45; "Miscellanies," no. 1340, *WJE* 23:359–76.

120. "Miscellanies," no. 1337, *WJE* 23:342.

information by any means, or in any sense whatsoever. . ."[121] That is, not only are we incompetent on our own to comprehend natural revelation, but on its own nature itself is insufficient to instruct us.

There is a further distinction to take account of in considering Edwards's estimation of natural revelation and it is here that Miller's claim may be qualified. Edwards distinguishes between the benefits of natural revelation for the unregenerate and for the regenerate. As regards the former Edwards follows Calvin and the mainstream Reformed tradition in believing that while natural revelation is insufficient to save humanity, it is nevertheless sufficient to condemn it.[122] As regard the regenerate, Edwards's account is more generous than that of his tradition. Those enlightened by the Holy Spirit, under the guidance of Scripture, can learn a divinely-designed dynamic language of types and thereby participate in God's self-glorification. Both nature and Scripture constitute God's revelation, but without the latter the former is an incomprehensible language. With this brief comment on natural revelation, I return to the governing role of Scripture in Edwards's typology.

In "Images," no. 156 Edwards is explicit that "the Book of Scripture is the interpreter of the book of nature" in two ways. First, Scripture declares the "spiritual mysteries" that are typified in nature. Despite the infinite number of natural types that present themselves for comparison and reflection, access to the significance of the types is found only in the Bible. Second, Scripture "in many instances" makes applications of those natural types of spiritual mysteries.[123] Among these many instances of worked examples that Edwards explores in his notebooks is "Images," no. 68 on the Lord's Supper. "As wheat is prepared to be our food, to refresh and nourish and strengthen us, by being threshed and then ground to powder and then baked in the oven, whereby it becomes a type of our spiritual food, even Christ the bread which comes down from heaven, which becomes our food by his sufferings, so the juice of the grape is a type of the blood of

---

121. "Miscellanies," no. 1337, *WJE* 23:344-45.

122. "Miscellanies," no. 1338, *WJE* 23:355. However, Gerald McDermott, argues controversially that Edwards's doctrine of natural types, his use of the *prisca theologia* and his adoption of a "dispositional soteriology" combine to offer the possibility of the salvation of the unevangelized. McDermott, "Possibility of Reconciliation," 173-202; McDermott, *Edwards Confronts the Gods,* 130-145. I contest McDermott's account of Edwards's soteriology (particularly in its application to the Old Testament saints) in chapter 4, below.

123. "Images," no. 156, *WJE* 11:106.

Christ as it is prepared to be our refreshing drink, to exhilarate our spirits and make us glad, by being pressed out in a winepress."[124]

Lowance argues that Edwards understood the value of the sacrament as a divinely-instituted presentation of Christ's sacrifice but also read into it allegorical significance so that other activities of nature (namely, the preparation of the wheat and grapes) also represent aspects of Christ's sufferings. While Lowance notices that Edwards applies the nomenclature of type-antitype to an imaging relationship between material creation and spiritual truth, he fails to take sufficient account of Edwards's sophisticated biblical literacy. Edwards's typology is not uncontrolled. Frequently, as in "Images" no. 68, his observations are richly permeated with biblical references and subtle allusions arising from detailed exegesis. As I have argued above the reason for this is to be found in Edwards's conception of typology as a language taught in Scripture, a language in which the careful practitioner can acquire fluency. What initially appears to modern eyes to be arbitrary or imaginative interpretations on the part of Edwards frequently on closer inspection betray signs of him struggling to interpret types by comparing Scripture with Scripture. "Images," no. 68, quoted above, is only one of several entries on grain, grapes and the preparation of bread and wine.[125] It was a subject on which Edwards meditated considerably. In "Images," no. 197, Edwards asserts that the baking of bread represents the sufferings of Christ. He does this first by referring to the Tabernacle shewbread, which was not burned as an offering but eaten by the priests, and yet is described as "most holy unto him of the offerings of the LORD made by fire"; Edwards interprets this to refer to the baking of the bread in fire which elsewhere he notes represents "the fire of God's wrath."[126] Second, Edwards sees all offerings as types of Christ: "'Tis evident the baking of bread is a type of the sufferings of Christ, because the shew bread is said to be 'an offering made by fire unto the Lord' (Lev. 24:7, 9); but it was an offering made by fire no otherwise than it was baked with fire. But all the offerings made by fire by the Mosaic law were types of Christ, undoubtedly, and their suffering the fire was also undoubtedly a type of Christ's suffering."[127] Scripture guides Edwards's typological interpretation. Edwards's typology

---

124. "Images," no. 68, *WJE* 11:73. Elsewhere Edwards notes that "natural things were ordered for types of spiritual things," citing the example of Christ's calling himself the "Bread of Life." "Images," no. 45, *WJE* 11:62–63.

125. See for example, "Images," nos. 45, 48, 149, 187, 189, 197, *WJE* 11.

126. "Images," no. 48, *WJE* 11:64.

127. "Images," no. 197, *WJE* 11:124.

Typology

is a principled typology. It is not arbitrary, however strange it may seem to modern sensibilities. The grammar of typology is taught in Scripture and Scripture therefore guides Edwards's use of it.

The Grammar Employed: The Bible and History

In contrast to a "liberal" typology employed of the natural world, Lowance depicts Edwards as adopting the "conservative" approach of Samuel Mather to biblical types. Yet, as I have argued above, Edwards does not employ two competing typological systems, nor does he seek to reconcile two approaches. Rather, he consistently employs his transformed typology under the guidance of Scripture. Lowance's failure to give due regard to the role of Edwards's exegesis of Scripture in his identification and interpretation of types may be for two reasons. First, in part this is the result of Lowance confining himself to the "The History of the Work of Redemption" sermons, Edwards's notebooks on types and his "Miscellanies," while not paying sufficient attention to Edwards's other biblical notes, principally the "Notes on Scripture" and the "Blank Bible," sources which have only recently been published.[128] Second, Lowance does not pay sufficient attention to the nature of the texts. It would not be surprising were Edwards to exhibit a more cautious application of typology in public, namely in his 1739 Redemption sermons, while in his private notebooks he might feel freer to explore his expansive typological system. Thus in what follows, Mason Lowance's conclusions, shared by John F. Wilson (the editor of the Yale edition of *The History of the Work of Redemption*) will need to be qualified as the 1739 sermons are read alongside Edwards's other biblical works. I will argue that while Edwards appears to pursue a conservative approach in the first part of *The History of the Work of Redemption*, this is not in fact the case. Rather, the apparently conservative results are delivered by Edwards's transformed typology operating in the familiar confines of the Old Testament. That is, the biblical nature of much of *The History of the Work of Redemption* masks the new operating system of types according to which Edwards works.

The History of the Work of Redemption is structured in three parts: (1) from the Fall of man to Christ's incarnation; (2) from Christ's incarnation

---

128. "Notes on Scripture," *WJE* 15 (1998) and "The Blank Bible," *WJE* 24 (2006) have only been published since Lowance's *Language of Canaan* (1980) and his introduction to "Types of the Messiah" in *WJE* 11 (1993).

till his resurrection; (3) from the Christ's resurrection till the end of the world.[129] I will treat each in turn.

John Wilson argues that Edwards's approach to typology in the first part of the work represents the familiar and well-worn path of the Christian appropriation of Jewish sacred history.[130] Edwards appears to pursue a conservative typology, much like that of Samuel Mather. The first part of the work is permeated with familiar types: Noah's ark was a type of Christ, "the true hiding place of the church."[131] The Exodus was typical: "the glorious Redeemer was he that redeemed the church out of Egypt from under the hand of Pharaoh, as Christ by his death and suffering redeemed his people from Satan, the spiritual Pharaoh."[132] God's election of the people of Israel was that "they might be a typical nation, and in them God might shadow forth and teach as under a veil all future glorious things of the gospel."[133] Many other examples from the first period of the discourse could be cited, but in each case Edwards appears to be pursuing a conservative typology.

A comparison with Edwards's other exegetical work, however, suggests that his public orthodoxy in these sermons hides a far greater willingness to explore the Old Testament for its types and draw more detailed doctrinal conclusions than his predecessors had. This willingness stems from, and indeed was demanded by, Edwards's conception of types as a divine language, consonant with his idealism that saw creation as inherently communicative, and being as inherently harmonious. To Edwards, biblical history is expressive of this universal typology.[134] An example will illustrate. In an entry in the "Blank Bible" on Exodus 34:1 Edwards argues that Moses' breaking the tablets of the Law portrayed to Israel the casting away of the covenant of works as an impossible and "useless" way of obtaining eternal life—a way being now "utterly and everlastingly to be despaired of." However, Israel received the tablets of the Law a second time through the ministration of Moses, a type of the gospel ministry: "God commanded that the second tables should be committed to the ark to preserve them,

---

129. "Work of Redemption," *WJE* 9:127.
130. Wilson, "Editor's Introduction," *WJE* 9:41.
131. "Work of Redemption," *WJE* 9:152.
132. Ibid., 175.
133. Ibid., 286–87.

134. See my discussions above of "Miscellanies," no. 362, *WJE* 13:434–35, and below of the opening paragraphs of "Miscellanies," no. 1069 ("Types of the Messiah"), *WJE* 11:191ff.

that they might not be broken as the first were (Compare Deut. 9:16–17 with 10:1–2). Thus the affair of the preservation of the hearts of God's people in holiness is committed to the keeping of Christ."[135] Edwards continues by suggesting that Moses' breaking the tablets of the Law signified not just the setting aside of the covenant of works, but the whole federal dispensation by which God was a husband to his people Israel, in favor of a new federal dispensation to be introduced, fulfilled and confirmed by Christ. It appears that Edwards is prepared to examine typologically the events of Old Testament history in a degree of detail alien to his tradition, and to draw detailed doctrinal conclusions in line with his own covenantal commitments.[136]

Many other instances of this could be given, innumerable as types were to Edwards. His exegesis of "Canticles" [Song of Solomon] in his various biblical notebooks shows how the grammatical-historical considerations of the text are evidence to Edwards that the subject of the song is not merely the love between Solomon and a wife, but portrays "the most excellent love" between Christ and his bride, the church.[137] For example, Edwards notes how the first persons singular and plural are used promiscuously in Song 1:4: "Draw *me*, *we* will run after thee. The king hath brought *me* into his chambers. *We* will be glad and rejoice in thee; *we* will remember thy love more than wine." He refers to Song 3:10 and chapter 6 in identifying the plural subjects as the virgin maidens who are invited to share in the delights of the lover and comments that "'tis evident that the spouse that is speaking, though one spouse, yet is more persons than one." Again, he draws attention to the last clause of Song 1:4 ("the upright love thee") and argues that "the same word is used all over the Old Testament to signify the saints." The virgins who rejoice in the king thus parallel the "sincerely godly . . . saints"; they are one and the same. "And how well does this agree with what we suppose, viz. that this song is intended as a song of love between Christ and the church, or the assembly of the saints." Finally, he notes that the bridegroom calls his beloved "my sister, my spouse" [Song 4:9–10, 12; 5:1]. He remembers that Jews were forbidden

---

135. Exod 34:1, "Blank Bible," *WJE* 24:246–47.

136. See also among Edwards's many typological observations in the "Twelfth Sign" of *Religious Affections*, his detailed exposition of how the glorious furnishings of the Temple typified the fruitful life of the church: "The golden bells on . . . [Aaron's] ephod, by their precious matter and pleasant sound, do well represent the good profession that the saints make; and the pomegranates, the fruit they bring forth." *Religious Affections, WJE* 2:400ff. (401).

137. "Notes on Scripture," no. 147, *WJE* 15:92.

to marry a near relative [Lev 18:9] and argues that for the same reason it would be unusual to compare a spouse with a sister. The relationship being describes must be that between Christ and his bride: "This well agrees with Christ's relation to believers, who is become our brother and near kinsman . . . and we are become his brethren also by the adoption of his Father."[138] In short, it appears that Edwards's typological approach to the Old Testament is far more innovative than appears in Lowance's and Wilson's depictions, once his wider biblical *corpus* is taken into account.

Turning to the second period in the *Work of Redemption*, that from the Incarnation to the Resurrection, Wilson echoes Lowance's contention that Edwards's biblical typology is thoroughly conservative. He describes Edwards's approach in this second period as being "no less traditional and orthodox."[139] However, a remark in the fifteenth sermon suggests that Edwards was in fact once again employing his transformed typology. Commenting on Christ's miracles, Edwards notes, "They were in general such works as were images of the great work he came to work on man's heart."[140] The comment is similar to one Edwards makes in his private "Blank Bible," namely, "the facts related in the history of Christ in the New Testament are typical or mystical, as well as the facts of the history of the Old Testament."[141] To Edwards types are not simply Old Testament prefigurations of things concerning the Messiah, but are images of spiritual substance. As such they are not confined to the Old Testament. So in a note on John 9:6-7, Christ's healing of the man born blind, Edwards comments: "As Christ spit on the ground, so he puts the word and spirit of his mouth into earth, into ministers that are but clay, and with them opens men's eyes."[142] The comment initially sounds surprising and yet perhaps Edwards's conclusion is not as arbitrary as appears. He has drawn the parallel between the man's physical blindness and his spiritual blindness, which appears to have been John's intention (John 9:3-4, 39-41). He has then noted that spiritual blindness in every age is cured through the application of God's Word and Spirit. His innovation is to extrapolate further in drawing a lesson for ministers. Is Edwards here *typologizing* or

138. Song 1:4, "Blank Bible," *WJE* 24:609-10; "Notes on Scripture," no. 336, *WJE* 15:322.

139. Wilson, "Editor's Introduction," *WJE* 9:41.

140. "Work of Redemption," *WJE* 9:317.

141. John 9:7, "Blank Bible," *WJE* 24:945. Similarly, in "Types of the Messiah" Edwards comments that, "The external works of Christ were typical of his spiritual works." "Miscellanies," no. 1069, *WJE* 11:192.

142. John 9:6-7, "Blank Bible," *WJE* 24:944.

merely *illustrating* a prior doctrinal commitment? His exegesis of the Johannine sign suggests that, though Edwards does not refer to the incident as a "type," he is treating it as such. This apparently looser definition of a "type," as representing a spiritual truth fits perfectly Edwards's metaphysical commitments outlined above. Nature does not merely illustrate spiritual truths in the hands of the creative exegete; it is a network of images and shadows that are divinely designed to communicate to perceiving minds their spiritual substance. In the scheme of God-glorifying redemption history, types shadow forth spiritual substance in a relationship thought of by God. Therefore, Old and New Testaments may both contain examples of types and antitypes.

One further example of Edwards's extension of the typological method into the gospels shows the similarly detailed conclusions he was prepared to draw from the narratives. In "Miscellanies," no. 694 Edwards argues that water baptism in the gospels was a type of the Spirit-baptism of Pentecost. It was "most probable" that John the Baptist baptized by "affusion, and not by dipping or plunging," there being a greater agreement and conjunction between type and antitype and therefore in eighteenth-century Northampton the practice of pouring water on the person to be baptized is preferable to baptism by immersion.[143] This last example links biblical type and contemporary practice: baptism in the New Testament and baptism in New England. Both share a temporal plane and typify a spiritual reality by God's designation. Thus in interpreting not only the Old Testament but also the New Testament typologically Edwards is innovative. *Contra* Lowance and Wilson, Edwards does not pursue Mather's approach when interpreting Scripture and depart from it only in his exegesis of the natural world and history. Rather Edwards's exegesis of the Bible operates according to a new typology, of one piece with his typological explorations of nature and history. This will be more apparent in the final part of the present chapter, in which I consider Edwards's notes, "Types of the Messiah."

Returning to *The History of the Work of Redemption,* Wilson argues that it is only in the third section, that concerning the period from Christ's Resurrection to the end of the world (when Edwards moves beyond Apostolic history), that he departs from the typological tradition he inherited. According to Wilson, by identifying patterns throughout history that

---

143. "Miscellanies," no. 694, *WJE* 18:276. Edwards's awareness of the Anabaptist argument for baptism by immersion is shown in his treatment of Paul's burial/baptism analogy in Rom 6:4, "Blank Bible," *WJE* 24:1001, as Stein notes in his "Editor's Introduction," *WJE* 24:53.

constrained the elect and reprobate, Edwards "moved... decisively beyond a conservative typological hermeneutic."[144] Edwards's willingness to interpret the historical events typologically is well-documented. Constantine's revolution and "the destruction of the heathen Roman empire" was "a lively image and type of . . . Christ's coming to the final judgment."[145] And in "Images" Edwards notes that America's exports to the world functions as a "type and forerunner" of the future time "when the world shall be supplied with spiritual treasures from America."[146]

The step-change in Edwards's typological approach between the second and third parts of the *Work of Redemption* that is demanded by Wilson's account is however, mistaken. As I have argued, Edwards's typology is a unitary approach agreeable to his metaphysical commitments and guided by Scripture. He employs this approach in exegeting the biblical history depicted in the first two parts of the *Work of Redemption*, as examination of his wider biblical *corpus* has suggested. However, the canonical character of the first two periods masks the new typology by which Edwards arrives at familiar conclusions. It is only in the "post-Apostolic history" of the third part, in which it is impossible that Old Testament type/New Testament antitype can be Edwards's interpretive paradigm, that his innovative typology is apparent. It is this new *clarity* that Wilson mistakes for a new methodology. But the "step change" in Edwards's typology according to Wilson's account is mistaken for a further reason. While the typology that links the Testaments is but one part of the larger typological world, to Edwards the Christian Bible also "contains" the whole world within its narrative. Thus Edwards does not require a different typological method for the third period of redemption history because to him the Bible does not simply record the "prophetic" and "Apostolic" eras, but

---

144. Wilson, "Editor's Introduction," *WJE* 9:49.

145. "Work of Redemption," *WJE* 9:351. See also *WJE* 9:394. For an overview of the structure of this third period of Redemption history, see Wilson's comments in, "Editor's Introduction," *WJE* 9:53–56.

146. "Images," no. 147, *WJE* 11:101. In 1739, the year in which he preached the thirty Redemption sermons, Edwards comments in his "Personal Narrative" that the study of history could prove delightful when attention was paid to Scripture's promises and prophecies of Christ's kingdom. "Personal Narrative," *WJE* 16:800. Three years later, following the Awakening in Northampton, Edwards records his belief that the recent work of God's Spirit made it likely that New England was to be the site of "the dawning, or . . . prelude of that glorious work of God, so often foretold in Scripture." *Some Thoughts Concerning the Present Revival of Religion in New England*, *WJE* 4:353, 358. For a survey of the literature surrounding Edwards's conception of America's role in history heading towards the millennium, see above, n. 22.

encompasses all of history: from creation to the consummation of God's Kingdom on earth. In this third period of redemption history Edwards maintains the approach of the linear/eschatological typology of Christ's work of redemption. All of history is redemption history aimed at God's self-glorification through his self-communication. All of history and creation finds its existence and purpose in Jesus Christ and stands in relation to Him. This relationship is expressed in the very fabric of creation at every moment throughout history. Therefore, Edwards employs his typology to understand the third period of the *Work of Redemption* just as he has for the previous two periods. Strange though it sounds to modern ears, it is no anomaly for Edwards to interpret Constantine's revolution and "the destruction of the heathen Roman empire" as "a lively image and type of . . . Christ's coming to the final judgment."[147] For Edwards, the return of Christ and His millennial rule on earth are events on the plane of redemption history every bit as much as Old Testament history, the incarnate life of Christ or the Apostolic era. Where Samuel Mather limited the identification of typology to cases expressly warranted in Scripture, Edwards's teleological view of creation as the vehicle of God's communication demands that, under the guidance of Scripture, he interprets nature and history as well as Scripture in a typological manner.

To summarize thus far: I have argued that, consonant with his philosophical commitments, Edwards transforms the typology he has inherited from a tool that unites the Old and New Testaments into a language of spiritual imaging capable of reading Scripture, history and the natural world. Yet Edwards's typology is a principled one. The grammar of the language of types is taught in Scripture and by careful attention to its idiom there, those in possession of the new spiritual sense can employ it to discover God's self-revelation in other arenas. But what happens when Edwards uses this universal language of images to answer the narrower question of the relationship of Old and New Testaments? In the final part of this chapter I consider this question by looking at "Miscellanies," no. 1069, Edwards's observations for the typological part of his projected "Harmony."

---

147. "Work of Redemption," *WJE* 9:351.

Jonathan Edwards's Bible

THE "HARMONY": "MISCELLANIES," NO. 1069, "TYPES OF THE MESSIAH"

The Role of the "Preface"

As I have noted already Mason Lowance places Edwards's typological writings on a spectrum of conservative-liberal typology: "Images" represents the liberal typology of vertical imaging; the 1739 sermons broadly represent the conservative typology of historical adumbration; the "Miscellanies" represent Edwards's attempts to fuse the previous two approaches. Therefore, in their introduction to the Yale edition of "Miscellanies," no. 1069 ("Types of the Messiah"), Edwards's notes for the typological part of his "Harmony," Mason Lowance and David Watters note that "while the body of the doctrinal treatise follows closely an orthodox and conservative schema that Edwards derived from Samuel Mather's *Figures or Types of the Old Testament*, the arguments of the last sections suggest an expanded and broadened typology which would permit allegorizing of the world of nature in a Platonic fashion."[148]

Lowance and Watters support their argument, that Edwards intended to pursue a typological *via media* in "Types of the Messiah," by noting an addition Edwards made once the body of the treatise was completed in ca. 1749. Sometime during the years in Stockbridge the missionary-theologian composed three further paragraphs which he indicated should be inserted at the head of the work, functioning as its preface.[149] Given the importance of this "preface" to the discussion that follows, I quote the second of these paragraphs in full:

> This may be observed concerning types in general, that not only the things of the Old Testament are typical; for this is but one part of the typical world. The system of created things may be divided into two parts, the typical world and the antitypical world. The inferior and carnal, i.e. the more external and

---

148. Lowance and Watters, "Editors' Introduction," *WJE* 11:173. The title of a subsection of their introduction, ("Problems of Interpretation in 'Types of the Messiah,'") expresses the tension they perceive in Edwards's "reconciliation" of the two approaches.

149. In addition it appears that Edwards revised the manuscript and added several more entries sometime after 1747. For the dating of the composition of the work according to Thomas Schafer's study of handwriting and inks see Lowance and Watters, "Editors' Introduction," *WJE* 11:165; "Note on the Manuscript of 'Types of the Messiah,'" *WJE* 11:183–86.

transitory part of the universe, that part of it which is inchoative, imperfect and subservient, is typical of the superior, more spiritual, perfect and durable part of it, which is the end and as it were the substance and consummation of the other. Thus the material and natural world is typical of the moral, spiritual and intelligent world, or the City of God. And many things in the world of mankind, as to their external and worldly parts, are typical of things pertaining to the City and kingdom of God, as many things in the state of the ancient Greeks and Romans, etc. And those things belonging to the City of God, which belong to its more imperfect, carnal, inchoative, transient and preparatory state, are typical of those things which belong to its more spiritual, perfect and durable state, as things belonging to the state of the church under the Old Testament were typical of things belonging to the church and kingdom of God under the New Testament. The external works of Christ were typical of his spiritual works. The ordinances of the external worship of the Christian church are typical of things belonging to its heavenly state. Here see "Miscellanies," bk. 9, pp. 82, [first column].[150]

Lowance and Watters argue that Edwards's new "preface" has a transformative effect on the whole work. It "changes the reader's perspective on the main body of the 'Types of the Messiah'. . . . The restrictive, conservative patterns outlined in the early pages . . . were broadened and modified by the preface."[151] That is, the familiar conservative biblical typology of Mather is now transformed as it is subsumed within an altogether different approach. Yet in this chapter I have argued that Lowance's account is mistaken and that Edwards is consistent throughout his *corpus* in employing a typological approach of spiritual imaging, an approach consonant with his philosophical commitments and one that is both invited and constrained by the practice of Scripture. As evidence of this I have drawn examples from Edwards's "Images" notebook, 1739 Redemption sermons and his hitherto-neglected biblical notebooks. Within my account of Edwards's typology his "Miscellanies" do not represent a "special case"—the fusion of two typological approaches employed elsewhere. Rather they are consistent with Edwards's practice elsewhere. For this reason the new preface to "Miscellanies," no. 1069 cannot be said to transform the treatise as

150. "Miscellanies," no. 1069, WJE 11:191–92. Edwards's cross-reference at the end is to the conclusion of "Miscellanies," no. 1307 and the whole of no. 1308. I discuss these when I examine the relationship between prophecy and types in the previous chapter of this work.

151. Lowance and Watters, "Editors' Introduction," WJE 11:174–75, 181.

a whole into something it was not already. Rather it simply makes explicit at the outset Edwards's typological approach employed throughout the treatise and indeed throughout his entire *corpus*.

Edwards was certainly aware of the novelty of his typology and the reactions it might provoke, as shown by a comment in his methodological "Types" notebook: "I expect by very ridicule to be called a man of a very fruitful brain and copious fancy..."[152] But the general observations Edwards makes regarding the fitness of types as a method of instruction underscores the fact that the purpose of the new "preface" to "Miscellanies," no. 1069 is as an explanatory introduction to the approach that drives the entire work. Edwards argues that the principles of human nature render types a fit method of instruction. Types "enlighten and illustrate... convey instruction with impression, conviction and pleasure" and are memorable. This is consonant with man's innate delight in the arts.[153] Furthermore, other methodological paragraphs conclude "Types of the Messiah" in which Edwards raises the objection of the "abuse that will be made of this doctrine of types" that he has employed. His response is that biblical types are not more abused than the "visionary representations" of the book of Revelation, yet no-one object to attempts to interpret them.[154]

A comparison of the "preface" to "Types of the Messiah" (composed sometime after 1751) with "Miscellanies," no. 362 (ca. 1728), quoted earlier, further reveals the unitary nature of Edwards's typology. Edwards appears to have forged his typology early in his career and not departed from it. In both "Miscellanies" Edwards expresses his typology in dynamic terms, consonant with his theology of God's self-glorification. The type is: inferior, shadowy ("Miscellanies," no. 362); inferior, carnal, transient, external, imperfect, subservient, material, natural ("Miscellanies," no. 1069). The antitype is: the crown and glory, the head and soul, the very end, the alpha and omega of all other works, the highest and most excellent end ("Miscellanies," no. 362); superior, more spiritual, perfect, durable, the end, the substance, the consummation ("Miscellanies," no. 1069). In both "Miscellanies" Edwards appeals to the example of Scripture's types, which are but one part of the typical world that takes in also history and nature. In both "Miscellanies" Scripture functions simultaneously to invite and

---

152. "Types," *WJE* 11:152.

153. "Miscellanies," no. 1069, *WJE* 11:191.

154. The book of Revelation functions for Edwards as evidence of what I have described above as "the invitational role of the Bible" in the interpretation of types; its images of spiritual reality suggest to Edwards that this is God's manner of communication and that we are expected to interpret it.

constrain typological interpretation both of itself and of the wider world. The unitary nature of his typology is further underlined when it is noted that just as Edwards prefaces "Types of the Messiah" from the Old Testament with an explication of his notion of types, so before his first entry in "Images" he notes, "Under the head of Creation, vid. 'Miscellanies' [no.] 362."[155] Edwards introduces his typological exegeses of the Old Testament and the natural world with the same conception of typology: in one case expressing it with the new "preface"; in another case with "Miscellanies," no. 362. It seems likely therefore, that the new "preface" to "Types of the Messiah" does not broaden or modify "restrictive, conservative patterns" in the early part of the work, as Lowance and Watters claim. Rather it functions as an explication of the typology that Edwards formulated early in his career and employed consistently.

Although "Types of the Messiah" delivers results that in places look very much like those of Mather's account of the biblical material, the operating system on which Edwards runs his exegesis is once again his expanded conception of types and shadows. This is why throughout the body of the treatise, completed some two years before Edwards composed the "preface," types that would be familiar to Mather are found interspersed with many other unfamiliar types, as I will show below. Indeed, "Types of the Messiah" re-iterates Edwards's early conviction that "almost everything that was said or done, that we have recorded in Scripture from Adam to Christ, was typical of gospel things. Persons were typical persons; their actions were typical actions . . . their land was typical land; God's providences toward them were typical providences; their worship was typical worship . . . and indeed the world was a typical world."[156]

Edwards's Argument in "Types of the Messiah"

In the previous chapter I noted Edwards's strategy of confining himself to the text of the Old Testament in an attempt to undercut the criticisms voiced by Anthony Collins regarding the New Testament's claim to prophetic fulfillment of the Old Testament Scriptures. I argued that Edwards seeks to defend the nature of predictive prophecy by indicating instances within the Old Testament itself of both prophecy and fulfillment. Having established this phenomenon to his satisfaction he then painstakingly argues for the coherence of all Old Testament prophecy in the person,

---

155. "Images," *WJE* 11:51.
156. "Miscellanies," no. 362, *WJE* 13:435.

work and kingdom of the Messiah. His argument is that since prophecy is integral to the unity of the Old Testament, it is not surprising for it to be integral to the relationship of the Old and New Testaments.

In the second part of his "Harmony" Edwards now takes the same approach. Again his strategy is to appeal to the discrete witness of the Old Testament, as the full title of "Miscellanies," no. 1069 indicates: "That the things of the Old Testament are types of things appertaining to the Messiah and his kingdom and salvation, *made manifest from the Old Testament itself.*"[157] Just as Edwards sought to defend the nature of predictive prophecy from within the Old Testament, so now he begins his consideration of the typological relationship of the Testaments with a defense of typology from within the Old Testament: "We find that it was God's manner throughout the ages of the Old Testament to typify future things, not only as he signified them by symbolical and typical representations in those visions and prophecies in which they were revealed, but also as he made use of those things that had an actual existence, to typify them either by events that he brought to pass by his special providence to that end, or by things that he appointed and commanded be done for that end."[158] The direction of his argument is itself evidence that he is employing a different typology from that of Samuel Mather. As the new "preface" makes explicit, for Edwards it is not definitive of a type that it finds its antitype in the New Testament. Rather a type is defined by its imperfection and transience in relation to its consummation and spiritual substance. Therefore, just as the New Testament contains types, so also the Old Testament is full of antitypes. Edwards is able to cite numerous examples of Old Testament types of events and things that found their antitype *within* the Old Testament: Moses' preservation and being drawn out of the Nile functions as a type of the preservation and deliverance of the children of Israel, of whom he was head; Joash's striking the ground three times in 2 Kings 13:18–19 is a type of his defeating his Assyrian enemies three times. And as Edwards notes above, God also sometimes orders men in the Old Testament to act in ways that would "typify future events." So, Abijah's tearing Jeroboam's garment into twelve pieces and giving him ten in 1 Kings 11:30–31, was intended to typify to Jeroboam the division of the kingdom of Israel and his receiving ten tribes. And among many instances in the lives of the

---

157. "Miscellanies," no. 1069, *WJE* 11:191. Emphasis added. Furthermore, the phrase "'tis apparent by the Old Testament" peppers the entire entry, betraying once again Edwards's strategy of arguing from the discrete witness of the Old Testament.

158. Ibid., 194.

Typology

prophets that Edwards cites, Isaiah was commanded to go naked and barefoot to typify the Egyptians and Ethiopians going naked and barefoot in their captivity (Isa 20), while Hosea was commanded to typify God's relationship with adulterous Israel by taking to himself an adulterous wife (Hos 1).[159] According to Edwards it was God's manner throughout the Old Testament to "represent divine things by outward signs, types and symbolical representations and especially thus to typify and prefigure future events that he revealed by his Spirit and foretold by the prophets."[160]

Edwards continues that since it is clear from the Old Testament that it has always been God's practice to employ types in communicating spiritual truths to his people, it would be unlikely if the *greatest* concern of the Old Testament, things concerning the Messiah, his kingdom and redemption, were not also typified therein. At this point Edwards begins to build on his conclusions from the first part of the "Harmony," as he explores the relationship between prophecies and types: "The remarkable similitude there is between many of the events in the Old Testament, both miraculous and others, and the prophetical descriptions of events relating to the Messiah, is an argument that the former were designed resemblances of the latter. God's causing light to shine out of darkness, as Moses gives us an account of it in the history of the creation, has a great similitude with what is foretold to come to pass in the Messiah's times. Is.42:16, 'I will make darkness light before 'em'. Is. 9:2 . . . Is. 29:18 . . ."[161]

His argument that it is reasonable that the things of the Messiah would be typified in the Old Testament develops in a number of steps. First, he recalls his conclusion to the first part of his "Harmony," namely that the things of the Messiah are "the main subject of the prophecies of the Old Testament."[162] Second, the coming of the Messiah was the event which the people of God were always most concerned in.[163] Third, since from God's call of Abram in Genesis 12 the very being of God's people was ordered for the coming of the Messiah, it would be likely that many things ordered among them would be typical of things concerning the Messiah. Fourth, Edwards argues that many lesser redemptions in the Old Testament are typified. For example, the promise of Hezekiah's healing and going up into Temple on the third day (2 Kgs 20:1–11) is typified

159. Ibid., 194–202.
160. Ibid., 202.
161. Ibid., 219–20.
162. Ibid., 202ff.
163. Ibid., 204.

by the sun going back ten degrees. Yet such redemptions are "as nothing in comparison of the salvation and victory of the Messiah."[164] Fifth, Edwards argues that it is reasonable to suppose that types of the Messiah should keep pace with prophecies of the Messiah throughout the Old Testament, since type and prophecy have gone together since the beginning. (In Genesis 3:15 mankind's enmity toward snakes functions as a type of the enmity between the Seed of the woman and Satan, Edwards argues).[165] Sixth, the Old Testament suggests that not only were particular events among the Jews typical of the Messiah, but "their way of living in many things was typical," as indicated by the example of Jonadab's family, who were commanded to live in tents so that they might "live many days in the land where ye be strangers" (Jer 35:6–8).[166] Again, this echoes Edwards's conviction, expressed in "Miscellanies," no. 362, that the Old Testament world was typical in the smallest detail.[167] Seventh, building on his conclusions from the previous part of the "Harmony" that the prophecies of the Old Testament have respect chiefly to the Messiah, Edwards argues that the Old Testament itself speaks of events in Israel's history as representations of the Messiah, his redemption and kingdom. Among many examples that Edwards cites are: Isaiah 51:9–11 where Pharaoh's destruction

---

164. Ibid., 205.

165. Ibid., 206–7.

166. Ibid., 208.

167. See my discussion of "Miscellanies," no. 362, above. In *WJE* 11:208 Edwards cites Basnage, *History*, 367. Lowance, *WJE* 11:208 n. 2, notes that Edwards is referring to the opening part of Basnage's chapter entitled, "Of the Helps which the Jewish Church had in the Time of Christ to know the Messiah." Basnage comments, "They as yet admitted the Maxim of St. *Paul*, that all things had happened to the Fathers in Types and Figures of the *Messiah*. And therefore they apply'd to him part of the Histories, and Events of the Old Testament." Edwards also cites Kidder, *Demonstration of the Messias*. Unfortunately, Lowance wrongly identifies the edition Edwards used as being the first edition [London, 1684], whereas it was in fact the second [London, 1726]. The result is that the excerpt from Kidder that Lowance quotes has nothing to do with Edwards's argument on the didactic significance of types. Lowance writes: "JE cited pp. 73–74, but meant pp. 74–75, in which place Kidder begins his discussion of those Old Testament texts which show that the Jews anticipated Jesus' appearance: 'I shall begin, and shew what the time was in which the Messias was to come according to the predictions of the old Testament . . .'" In fact Edwards *did* intend pages 73–74, but of the *second* edition. Correctly identified, Edwards's use of Kidder at this point fits perfectly his own argument that the "ancient Jews" themselves understood their religious life and history as typical of the Messiah. On pages 73–74 Kidder argues that the death of Jesus was typified in the lifting up of the brazen serpent in the wilderness (Num 21): "And in its first institution it was intended for a sign or symbol of some future good."

in the Red Sea is spoken of as "a type of the Messiah's bruising the head of the old serpent, or dragon"; and Hosea 2:15 in which Israel's rejoicing at her redemption from Egypt is spoken of as a resemblance of the joy of God's people at a future redemption by the Messiah.[168] The "remarkable similitude" between Old Testament events and prophecies of the Messiah suggests to Edwards that the former events are "designed resemblances" of the latter.[169] In short, Edwards's argument is far more breathtaking than simply re-asserting, like Samuel Mather before him, the notion that there are types of the Messiah in the Old Testament, finite instances of Messianic foreshadowing. Rather just as he argued in "Miscellanies," no. 1347 that promises and prophecies of the Messiah are so intertwined with Old Testament narrative (especially in the Pentateuch) as to be inextricable, so by identifying Old Testament history as typological Edwards portrays the Old Testament as a single, vast presentation of the Messiah in prophecy and history, in word and event.[170] Founded upon his notion of types as a network imaging spiritual reality, and guided by Scripture, Edwards transforms the typology he inherits beyond the explicit co-ordination of Old Testament type and New Testament antitype. Old and New Testament are related typologically not at finite specific points, but at every moment in their presentation of the Messiah, his redemption and kingdom.

Edwards's next move is to demonstrate his claim for the typological nature of the Old Testament by launching into a survey of redemption history, organized around such events and figures as the Flood, Joseph, Moses, Joshua, the Judges (of particular interest: Deborah, Gideon and Samson), David, Solomon and the return of the Jews from captivity.[171] Once again Edwards treats each according to his threefold scheme of the Messiah, his redemption and kingdom. As I have already indicated, Edwards's thorough interspersion of conservative types with novel ones indicates once again that when he exegetes Scripture he is not following the conservative lead of Samuel Mather, but is making use of his notion of types as a network of images of spiritual reality. Employing in the Old Testament this notion of typology as a universal language communicating

---

168. "Miscellanies," no. 1069, *WJE* 11:212. See also Edwards's lengthy analysis of the Flood as typological of things concerning the Messiah, through comparison with Old Testament prophecies. "Miscellanies," no. 1069, *WJE* 11:221–25.

169. Ibid., 219–20.

170. See for example Edwards's comment, "There is yet a more remarkable, manifest and manifold agreement between the things said of David in his history and the things said of the Messiah in the prophecies." "Miscellanies," no. 1069, *WJE* 11:259.

171. "Miscellanies," no. 1069, *WJE* 11:221–98.

spiritual truths, Edwards is able to present the relationship of the Old and New Testaments as typological of things concerning the Messiah at every moment and in the smallest detail.

Frequently, an individual is introduced with a comment about his or her name, indicating their identity as a type of the Messiah.[172] For example, Edwards notes that Joshua is first called "Oshea" (Num 13:8, 16) "which signifies 'savior'" as the Messiah is called savior in various places. Edwards further notes that in Numbers 13:16 Moses changes Oshea's name to "Jehoshua," which he translates as "the Lord the Savior or Jehovah our Savior." He comments that this makes Joshua's name "still more agreeable to the name and nature of the Messiah."[173] Then following consideration of the person of the Messiah typified in each individual, Edwards moves in each case to consider how they typify the Messiah's redemption and kingdom. Again Edwards does this in great detail. For example, he identifies twenty-six ways in which Joseph's life typifies things concerning the Messiah.[174] In David's life Edwards highlights fifty-six typological features, while his study of Solomon's life runs to seventy paragraphs, each of which is concerned with a distinct aspect of Solomon's typological character.[175]

---

172. Edwards comments in "Miscellanies," no. 1069, WJE 11:298–99: "With respect to some of the principal persons spoken of in the Old Testament, there is this evidence that they were types of the Messiah, viz. that the Messiah in the prophecies is called by their names." He cites as examples, "Israel" (Isa 49:3); "David" (Jer 30:9); "Solomon" (Cant 3:7); "Zerubbabel" (Hag 2:3). On the typological significance of names Edwards notes, "The Holy Ghost intends to teach divine mysteries by the signification of persons' names that were given accidentally, i.e. without any special command from God or any such design in them who gave the name. This seems to be manifest by Heb. 7:2." See also, "Images," no. 30, WJE 11:58 and Edwards's note on the "Permutation of Names" in "Types," WJE 11:150. But for Edwards it is not just personal names that have a designed typological significance. Places and events share this characteristic. The prophets speak of the destruction of the Messiah's enemies as "the destruction of the old world, of Sodom and Gomorrah, or the Egyptians and Canaanites. . . as has been observed before." See also Edwards's argument that the Old Testament sacrifice of atonement is so named, not because of any efficacy it had in itself, but because of its relationship to its antitype, the rule being that God calls the shadow by the name of the substance. "Miscellanies," no. 1069, WJE 11:302–3, 308–13. In chapter 4 I will explore further the role of types in Edwards's understanding of salvation in the Old Testament.

173. "Miscellanies," no. 1069, WJE 11:241–42.

174. Among them, the fact that the sun, moon and stars bow down to Joseph in his dream of Gen 37 is a type of creation's rejoicing in the Messiah's rule in Pss 50:6; 69:34; 96:11–13; 97:6; Isa 44:23; 49:13. "Miscellanies," no. 1069, WJE 11:228–37 (229–30).

175. "Miscellanies," no. 1069, WJE 11:259–76 and 276–94 respectively; compare this with Mather's brief treatment of the typological significance of David and Solomon in Mather, *Figures or Types*, 106–7 and 107–9 respectively.

Typology

Operating according to his expanded typological imaging system under the guidance of Scripture's prophecies, Edwards plumbs Solomon's life for all its typological worth. A selection of Edwards's observations concerning Solomon give a flavor of his approach. He follows his usual practice of beginning his study of Solomon's life with a comment on his name. He notes God's giving Solomon a name that "signifies 'peace' or 'peaceable', which is agreeable to the Messiah's title of 'Prince of Peace'" (Isa 9:6). He moves on to points in Solomon's life, commenting for example that just as the glorious reign of Solomon is introduced by the pleadings and petitions of his mother, Bathsheba with his father, David (1 Kgs 1:15–21), "so the prophecies often represent that the glorious peace and prosperity of the Messiah's reign shall be given in answer to the earnest and importunate prayers of the church. Ezek. 36:37 . . . (Jer. 29:11–14, Cant. 2:14, Zech. 12:10)." Solomon's offering of sacrifices, unrivalled in the Old Testament, is agreeable to what the prophets represent of the Messiah's sacrifice of greater worth than "thousands of rams and ten thousands of rivers of oil" [Mic 6:7]. And Solomon's building of the Temple represents the Messiah's building a glorious dwelling place for God, according to Zech 6:12–13.[176] Many other examples could be cited but the above are sufficient to demonstrate Edwards's general approach. In contrast to Lowance's depiction of Edwards's typology, the New England theologian is not pursuing the familiar conservative approach of Samuel Mather when he exegetes Scripture. Rather, he is employing in his exegesis of the Old Testament as in his exegesis of nature and history, his transformed typology, consonant with his metaphysical commitments outlined above. Edwards's interpretation of this language of types is closely constrained by Scripture, however, in this instance the prophecies of the Old Testament, so that he sees the characters and events of the Old Testament as typological of the Messiah to a degree unequalled by his predecessors.

Edwards ends his argument by identifying the Messiah from the types of the Old Testament. When treating prophecy in the "Harmony" Edwards first established the coherence of Old Testament prophecies in the things of the Messiah, before identifying the Messiah as Jesus of Nazareth by the numerous agreements between the prophecies and the events of Jesus' life. Now when considering types he does the same. He concludes: "*Corol.* Seeing it is thus abundantly evident by the Old Testament itself that the things of the Old Testament were typical of the Messiah and things appertaining to him, hence a great and most convincing argument

---

176. "Miscellanies," no. 1069, *WJE* 11:277, 276, 279, 285–86.

may be drawn that Jesus is the Messiah, seeing there is so wonderful a correspondence and evident, manifold and great agreement between him and his gospel and these types of the Old Testament."[177] In this, the second part of his "Harmony" Edwards employs once again the single typological approach used throughout his *corpus*. Despite the biblical nature of the "Harmony," it is apparent that even here Edwards's typology is radically different from that of Samuel Mather.

Conclusion

In this chapter I have argued that the biblical typology Edwards inherited was an interpretative tool that linked Old and New Testaments together in a limited and explicit relationship of temporal Christological prefiguring and fulfillment. In his hands this tool underwent a transformation, consonant with his philosophical commitments. Typology became for Edwards a language that expressed the metaphysical relationship between imaging type and spiritual substance, within created history, to the end of God's self-glorification. The grammar of this language was found in Scripture, which both invited and constrained Edwards's typology to a degree hitherto unrecognized. When Edwards turned his conception of typology to the question of the connection of Old and New Testaments it delivered a Christological relationship manifest not only at finite specific points, but at every moment. To Edwards the Old Testament in every detail shadowed forth the "more excellent" end and spiritual substance. In short, Edwards was able to bind the Testaments more tightly together with his typology than his predecessors had been able to with theirs.

I have argued that Mason Lowance's account of Edwards's typology is fatally weakened by the insufficient attention he pays to the role of Scripture in Edwards's interpretation of types. Nevertheless, Lowance's account inadvertently draws attention to a significant weakness inherent in Edwards's typology. There seems to be no guarantee that Edwards's interpretation of the language of types could be reproduced by another saint. Even allowing for the guiding role of Scripture, as a dynamic language, Edwards's typology seems too open-ended. Even for Edwards a single type may have multiple referents. For example, Edwards notes that water

---

177. Ibid., 321. Lowance and Watters, "Editors' Introduction," *WJE* 11:322 n. 6, note that the remainder of the "Miscellanies," no. 1069 manuscript is in a later hand, possibly dating to the Stockbridge years, suggestive that the corollary initially concluded the entire entry.

"commonly signifies misery, especially that which is occasioned by the wrath of God."[178] Yet a few entries later he describes it as being "a type of sin or the corruption of man" in its flattering, harmless appearance.[179] In short, Edwards may have a principled typology consonant with his metaphysics, yet it is on such a grand design and so tortuous in its construction that it is difficult to escape the conclusion that it is an immense piece of theological solipsism. By paying closer attention to the hitherto neglected role of Scripture in Edwards's typology specific instances of it can be explicated, yet it would seem impossible that another saint might replicate it to any practical effect.

---

178. "Images," no. 64, *WJE* 11:72. See also "Images," no. 27, *WJE* 11:58 in which Edwards cites various texts from the Psalms in support of his interpretation.

179. "Images," no. 117, *WJE* 11:94.

3

"Doctrine and Precept"

Introduction

In CHAPTER 1 I argued that Edwards holds all Scripture prophecy to be coherent only when its referent is Messianic; all prophecy speaks of some aspect of the Messiah's person, redemption or kingdom. In chapter 2 I argued that Edwards's typology renders all sensible reality typical of spiritual substance, thus turning the Old Testament into a vast phenomenal presentation of the Messiah's person, work and kingdom. In this chapter I will consider the third aspect of Testamental harmony that Edwards outlines to the New Jersey trustees: a harmony in "doctrine and precept." As before, I will first explore this concept in Edwards's wider *corpus* before examining in more detail his notes for the "Harmony." I will argue that redemption history and a covenantal system, apparent in his wider *corpus*, provide the unseen framework to Edwards's "Harmony" when he considers doctrine and practice. I will further argue that Edwards's confidence in both prophecy and typology to present the Messiah, his redemption and kingdom yields a detailed harmony in doctrine and precept, ultimately stressing the substantial continuity of the covenant of grace over against its administrative differences in Old and New Testaments.

The Work of Redemption

Eighteenth-century moral philosophers had placed man's happiness as the central concern of God's governance of the world.[1] God ruled over creation

---

1. Alexander Pope's famous lines express the prevailing mood: "God in nature of each being, founds, Its proper bliss, and sets its proper bounds: But as he fram'd the

in such a way as to maximize human happiness; humanity stood at the center of creation's purpose. At the same time, Deist thinkers painted God as distant from and disinterested in the daily affairs of his creation. Edwards responds to both by claiming that God has always been intimately involved the life of creation, directing all of history to just one end: not man's happiness as an end in itself, but his own divine glory.[2] Edwards argues that it was not that God was lacking in some way prior to creation, or that creation added anything to him. Rather, as a community of perfect goodness and love, God wished to extend his love and share his goodness with others. Indeed there was in God "a disposition ... as an original property of his nature, to an emanation of his own infinite fullness, [which] excited him to create the world."[3] His perfection and glory emanated from him like beams of light from the sun, and man's greatest happiness was to be found in sharing this relationship and reflecting back God's perfect self-knowledge and love. Man's happiness could not be considered apart from this sharing in God's glory. "The beams of glory come from God, and are something of God, and are refunded back again to their original. So

---

Whole, the Whole to bless, On mutual Wants built mutual Happiness: So from the first, eternal order ran, And creature link'd to creature, man to man." Pope, *Essay on Man*, Epistle 3, 2.109–14, 103. For a brief overview of the prevailing philosophies, see Marsden, *Jonathan Edwards*, 460–62. The assumption is displayed also as Matthew Tindal introduces chapter 9 of *Christianity* with the following synopsis: "Human Happiness being the ultimate Design, and End of all Traditional, as well as Original Revelation, they must both prescribe the same Means; since those Means which, at one time, promote human Happiness, equally promote it all Times."

2. Edwards ultimately expresses his thoughts on divine self-glorification in the first of his "Two Dissertations," *Concerning the End for which God Created the World* (*WJE* 8:405–536) published posthumously in 1765, though he gathered thoughts on the subject throughout his career in his "Miscellanies." The relationship between God and creation has proved controversial in recent Edwardsean scholarship. Prof. Sang Hyun Lee has argued that in his metaphysics Edwards replaced an Aristotelian conception of substance with a dispositional one. In this novel scheme creation is portrayed as a dynamic expression of the divine disposition to self-enlargement. For the fullest account of Lee's position see, Lee, *Philosophical Theology*. Lee's position is not without its critics, as I will show when I explore this important topic in the next chapter. Stephen Holmes's account of *End of Creation* paints God's chief end in redemptive terms; Holmes, *God of Grace*, 44–59, 131 n. 21. However, as Oliver Crisp argues, this seems to be a confusion of "ultimate" ends and the "chief" end in Edwards's thought at this point; Crisp, *Metaphysics*, 5–24. Edwards comments: "In the creature's knowing, esteeming, loving, rejoicing in, and praising God [i.e. ultimate ends definitive of the saint's conversion], the glory is both exhibited and acknowledged [i.e. the chief end, God's glory]." *End of Creation*, *WJE* 8:531. (Crisp's argument that this crucially affects the logical order of the divine decrees is beyond the scope of the present enquiry).

3. *End of Creation*, *WJE* 8:435.

that the whole is of God, and in God, and to God, and God is the beginning, middle and end in this affair.... God's respect to the creature's good, and his respect to himself is not a divided respect; but both are united in one, as the happiness of the creature aimed at is happiness in union with himself."[4] Creation's goal was the glory of God through participation in the love of the Trinity.[5] Man's greatest happiness, therefore, was to be found in a God-centered life, in which God's glory was man's chief concern. So central was this to Edwards's entire system that Marsden notes that *End of Creation* functions as a sort of prolegomenon to all he wrote, and had he completed his projected "History of the Work of Redemption," the treatise would likely have formed its point of departure.[6]

If God's glory underlay the very existence of creation and was the goal towards which creation was heading, the affairs of the world could only be understood in the light of God's glory. The affairs of the world were not abandoned to laws of nature, but were directed in a grand scheme towards this glorious goal. It is this grand scheme that Edwards wished to expound in his sermon series of 1739, published posthumously in 1774 as *A History of the Work of Redemption*. The text of the entire thirty-sermon series, Isaiah 51:8 ["For the moth shall eat them up like a garment, and the worm shall eat them like wool: but my righteousness shall be for ever, and my salvation from generation to generation"] expressed the future hope of God's kingdom and the ultimate defeat of his enemies. The sermons expounded this in a narrative of redemption history from the Fall of man to the second coming of Christ.

Early in his first sermon Edwards notes that the work of redemption may be understood in two respects:

> 1. With respect to the effect wrought on the souls of the redeemed, which is common to all ages from the fall of man <to the end of the world>. This effect that I here speak [of] is the application of redemption with respect to the souls of particular

---

4. *End of Creation*, WJE 8:531–33.

5. In chapter 2, under "Being and Knowing," I discussed Edwards's belief that God is the space that contains all other reality, that he is the only substance and that nothing has existence but in his consciousness. In this way Edwards seems to advocate a form of panentheism, though not of the kind proposed by Sang Hyun Lee. (See my discussion in chapter 4, below). See also Cooper, *Panentheism*, 74–77. Edwards's discussion here and elsewhere regarding the relationship between God and the saint has led some scholars to attribute to Edwards some form of *theosis*. This too will be discussed in the following chapter, a case study in the harmony of the Testaments in soteriology.

6. Marsden, *Jonathan Edwards*, 460.

persons in converting, justifying, sanctifying and glorifying of them. By these things the souls of particular persons are actually redeemed—do receive the benefit of the Work of Redemption in its effect in their souls.[7]

2. . . . with respect to the grand design in general as it relates to the universal subject and end of it, is carried on from the fall . . . in a different manner, not merely by the repeating and renewing the same effect on the different subjects of it, but by many successive works and dispensations of God, all tending to one great end and effect, all united as the several parts of a scheme, and altogether making up one great work.[8]

Since I will examine the first of these aspects of the work of redemption in detail in the following chapter I will discuss it only briefly below. Before doing that, however, I will concentrate my discussion on Edwards's chief concern in his "Redemption sermons": God's grand design.

The Grand Design of Redemption

It is this sense of the work of redemption as God's grand scheme of self-glorification worked through history that chiefly occupied Edwards in his sermon series. His aim was to help his congregation understand their place within God's sovereign plan—in the words of a recent biographer, to enable them to rise above the "pettiness and self-absorption that went with their low horizons, which hardly reached to the next town."[9] In particular Edwards hoped that he could ameliorate the controversies surrounding the recent awakening in Northampton by helping his town to see the revival both as part of, and as illustrative of, the great universal conflict between Christ and Satan.

To paint God's grand scheme of redemption Edwards employs four images. First, Edwards likens it to a building work in which "first the workmen are sent forth, then the materials are gathered, then the ground fitted, then the foundation is laid, then the superstructure erected one part after another, till at length the topstone is laid. And all is finished. Now the Work of Redemption in that large sense . . . may be compared to such a

---

7. "Work of Redemption," *WJE* 9:120. (Angle brackets indicate text absent from Edwards's own notes but supplied by Yale editor, John F. Wilson based on the context and rhetorical structure of these sermons. See his "Editor's Introduction," *WJE* 9:106).

8. Ibid., 121.

9. Marsden, *Jonathan Edwards*, 194.

building that is carrying on from the fall of man to the end of the world."[10] In this image the emphasis is not only on the gradual, purposeful work of redemption, but on the Spirit-led nature of that work. In this excerpt Edwards seems to be drawing on the picture of the Temple in Zechariah 4, one that he returns to much later in the sermon series. In sermon twenty-six the rebuilding of the Temple stands for the revival and propagation of the gospel by the power of God's Holy Spirit. Edwards quotes Zechariah 4:6–7 to point to the Spirit-inspired work of redemption reaching its completion: "'Not by might, nor by power, but by my spirit', saith the Lord of hosts. 'Who art thou, O great mountain? Before Zerubbabel thou shalt become a plain': and he shall bring forth the headstone thereof with shoutings, crying, 'Grace, grace unto it.'"[11] For Edwards the motor of redemption history is the effusive Holy Spirit whose awakenings throughout history, and recently in Northampton, drives history ever onwards to its climax of the saints' union with God.[12] In terms of Christ's incarnation and second coming the Old Testament was like the preparatory work in a building project. The progress of the great building project, the work of redemption, is exemplified in one of Israel's own buildings, the Temple. In the tenth sermon in the series Edwards explains how the Jewish exile and the destruction of the Temple in Jerusalem prepared for the coming of the Messiah: "In order to introduce the glorious dispensation of the gospel the external glory of the Jewish church must be diminished. . . . Again, by this captivity the glory and magnificence of the temple was taken away, and the temple that was built afterwards was nothing in comparison of it. Thus it was meet that when the time drew nigh that the glorious antitype of the temple should appear that the typical temple should have its glory withdrawn."[13]

The 1739 sermon series was not intended to be an examination of the relationship between the two Testaments. Its purpose is much wider: to trace the whole work of redemption beyond the historical borders of the Bible. To Edwards, both Old and New Testament eras formed one

10. "Work of Redemption," *WJE* 9:121.

11. Ibid., 460.

12. The role of the Holy Spirit in God's self-glorification through the communication of his internal fullness *ad extra* will be discussed in the following chapter on soteriology.

13. "Work of Redemption," *WJE* 9:252–53. In "Types of the Messiah" Edwards argues that Jesus' Messianic identity is shown not only by the correspondence between type and antitype, but also by the fact that the typical state of things ended with his coming. "Miscellanies," no. 1069, *WJE* 11:321–22.

continuum of building towards the final coming of Christ and the establishment of his kingdom.[14] His understanding of all history as the progress of God's self-glorification encapsulated within the covers of his Bible encouraged him to exegete post-Apostolic history. The significance he gave to the destruction of Jerusalem and the conversion of the Roman Empire under Constantine are the most celebrated examples of this.

The second image Edwards employs to describe the work of redemption is a river's course: "We began at the head of the stream of divine providence, and we have followed it and traced it through its various windings and turnings till we are come to the end of it, and we see where it issues: as it began in God, so it ends in God. God is the infinite ocean into which it empties itself."[15] The aim of this image is to capture the complexity of redemption's course through history. Despite its apparent meanderings it has one source and one end. Edwards's notebook, "Images or Shadows of Divine Things," provides important background to the use of these pictures of God's grand scheme of redemption. A number of entries, dated to late 1737 or early 1738, show that Edwards had been considering God's grand providential scheme before the sermon series itself. They suggest also that Edwards is not merely looking in creation for illustrations of divine providence. Rather in his expanded conception of typology Edwards sees the images he chooses as created types of God's providence, as I have argued in chapter 2. In "Images," no. 77, for example Edwards notes that, "There is a wonderful analogy between what is seen in RIVERS... The innumerable streams of which great rivers are constituted, running in such infinitely various and contrary courses, livelily represent the various dispensations of divine providence: some of them beginning at the greatest distance from the common mouth, others nearer to it, multitudes of them meeting first to constitute certain main branches of the river before they empty themselves into the main river and so into the ocean."[16]

A third image of God's providential scheme of redemption is that of an imperial army, with the Roman triumph as "a remarkable type of Christ's ascension."[17] With this image Edwards portrays history in terms of the enmity between the seeds of the woman and of Satan in Genesis 3:15.

---

14. On Edwards's understanding of history against the background of Augustinian and Reformation historiography, see Zakai, *Jonathan Edwards's Philosophy of History*, 131–271.

15. "Work of Redemption," *WJE* 9:517.

16. "Images," no. 77, *WJE* 11:77–80.

17. "Images," no. 81, *WJE* 11:82–84.

The final crushing of Satan would be achieved fully at Christ's second coming, but the struggle was both apparent in, and typified by, many struggles throughout history: "The glorious Redeemer was he that redeemed the church out of Egypt from under the hand of Pharaoh, as Christ by his death and suffering redeemed his people from Satan, the spiritual Pharaoh. He redeemed them from hard service and cruel bondage, as Christ redeems his people from the cruel slavery of sin and Satan."[18] In this, as in other examples, the one event functions in numerous ways simultaneously. The exodus is at the same time a rescue of the church by the Redeemer, a type and presentation of Christ's redemption of the church, and a historical preparation for the incarnation of that Redeemer. In Edwards's redemption history Christ was in every way the central character of the grand design.

Finally, the fourth image Edwards employs of redemption's grand scheme is that of a tree, an image that he explores elsewhere in his notebooks. He does this in two ways. First, in a "Miscellanies" entry Edwards uses the image to describe the progress of the work of redemption in mankind as a whole.[19] Some of the branches of the tree have "holy seed" in them, which stands for the elect church, those who would trust in Christ whether in the present, or many generations ahead in the future. These branches are therefore preserved until that seed appears. Meanwhile other branches of the human race that possess no holy seed are cut off, for example the nation of the Amalekites though descended from Abraham, and the nations of Canaan. God frequently employs pagan political powers in cutting off dead branches from the tree, most dreadfully in the Jewish-Roman war when Jerusalem was destroyed. The greatest pruning was yet to come, however, according to Revelation 19.17–21, to prepare the way for the planting of God's elect seed in the new age.[20] Second, Edwards uses the image of a tree to describe God's providential dispensations since the incarnation.[21] In this sense the centrality of Christ is even more evident. Edwards likens the resurrected Christ to a tree trunk rising out of the ground, the apostles being its branches of whom Paul was a chief branch. The tree grows and fills the whole earth. In this picture Edwards seems to combine the image of Jesus the vine in John 15 with the parable of the mustard seed in Mark 4. In this same entry in his "Images" notebook

---

18. "Work of Redemption," *WJE* 9:175.
19. "Miscellanies," no. 991, *WJE* 20:315–20.
20. Ibid.
21. "Images," no. 78, *WJE* 11:80–81.

"Doctrine and Precept"

Edwards combined the tree and river images of God's scheme of redemption to unite pre- and post-incarnation dispensations in the person of Christ:

> [T]he course of the sap of the tree, from its beginning in the extremities of the roots to its end in the extremity of the branches, is an emblem of the whole series and scheme of divine providence, both before and after Christ, from the beginning to the end of the world. The sap in the roots is like the water of a river gathering from small branches into a common body, and this, as was said before, represents the course of divine providence during the times of the Old Testament, when the designs of providence as they related to Christ and the work of redemption, which is as it were the summary comprehension of all God's works of providence, was hid as it were underground. All was under a veil and the scheme of redemption was a mystery kept secret from the foundation of the world; but after this, the mystery was removed, and the scheme of providence was, like a tree above ground, gradually displayed as the branches successively put forth themselves. Hence we may observe that God's calling of Abraham and anointing of David was, as it were, the planting the root whence the tree should grow, and Abraham and David were main roots whence the tree grows, but Christ himself is the sprout or branch from these roots which becomes the tree whence all other branches proceed.[22]

As this last note demonstrates most clearly, Edwards employs these images to represent the grand scheme of God's glorification through redemption. Christ's incarnate work of redemption, treated so briefly in the sermon series, is the crux of history. It is the event in the light of which centuries of Old Testament history is preparatory and prospective, and in the light of which the saints of centuries after look back for the ground of their faith. History is a grand scheme divinely directed to God's own glory through the redemption of Christ.

Individual Redemption

As I noted above, in addition to the grand scheme of redemption Edwards recognizes another sense in which the work of redemption could be understood: the application of Christ's salvation to individual souls. He notes that the progress of the grand work of redemption is "very much after the

22. Ibid.

same manner as the carrying on of the same work and the same light in a particular soul" from conversion to glorified perfection.[23] I will examine the application of redemption to the individual saint in greater detail in the following chapter which functions as a case study of soteriological harmony in the Old and New Testaments. Therefore only a brief mention will be made here.

According to Edwards, Christ's work of redeeming his elect began immediately after the Fall, with the salvation of Adam and Eve who were "earnests of the future harvest" and whose salvations were "forerunners of the great salvation Christ was to work out when he came."[24] To Edwards the individual application of redemption is common to all ages and will continue until the return of Christ: "The way that the Work of Redemption with respect to these effects of it respecting the souls of the redeemed is carried on from the fall <of man to the end of the world> is by repeating after continually working the same work over again, though in different persons from age to age."[25]

In summary, Edwards sees the work of redemption as two-fold. It encompasses both the grand scheme of history directed to God's glory, and the application of salvation to individuals common throughout history. The relationship of these two aspects of the work of redemption is the key to understanding the doctrinal harmony of the Testaments in Edwards's theology. Here another image helps, an image Edwards employs in numerous places, and one that links for Edwards the two senses of redemption that he outlines in his 1739 sermons: that of a wheel. "Providence is like a mighty wheel whose ring or circumference is so high that it is dreadful with the glory of the God of Israel above upon it, as 'tis represented in Ezekiel's vision. We have seen the revolution of this wheel, and how that as it was from God so its return has been to God again."[26] The image of the wheel, and particularly of wheels within wheels, was one that Edwards apparently finds particularly appropriate. It appears in his "Images" notebook several times.[27] Each time he employs it to present the complex, even apparently contradictory, workings of God's providence towards one

---

23. "Work of Redemption," *WJE* 9:144–45. Westra, "Divinity's Design," 131–57, argues that Edwards's 1739 sermon series follows the method God takes with the world: first to reveal his justice and then to reveal his grace. For discussion of Edwards's approach to the doctrine of preparation, see chapter 4 of the present work.

24. "Work of Redemption," *WJE* 9:128–29.

25. Ibid., 121.

26. Ibid., 517–18.

27. "Images," nos. 89, 154, 178, 389, 394, *WJE* 11.

divinely-directed end. In one of these entries one great wheel represents "the entire series of events in the course of things through the age of the visible universe."[28] It performs one great revolution. Inside this great wheel is a lesser wheel that performs two revolutions to its one. Inside these are further wheels, each smaller than the previous. Within them all and smallest of all, man's life is depicted as a wheel that rises from the nakedness of his mother's womb and returns to the dust of the earth. The grand scheme of redemption and the individual human life are connected in this depiction of God's providence.

In "Miscellanies," no. 1353, ("The Two Dispensation Compared, That Under Moses and That Under Christ") Edwards hints at the relationship between the two senses of redemption. The long entry begins with a list of nine ways in which the two dispensations agree. In the seventh point Edwards notes that, "Not only were these things, mentioned under the last head, in some sort *exhibited and represented* under both dispensations, but also were in some degree *made known and revealed* under both."[29] Though Edwards uses the terms "exhibited"/"represented" and "made known"/"revealed" rather fluidly in the rest of the entry, it is nevertheless apparent that he sees a distinction between gospel things represented and exhibited in the Old Testament for the Christian church that would follow, and gospel things made known and revealed to those who lived in the Mosaic dispensation. As I have argued in the previous two chapters of this work, the prophecies and types of the Old Testament not only possessed a historical integrity of their own in the grand scheme of redemption, speaking to the New Testament church of some aspect of Christ and his work of redemption. But to Edwards they were also didactic and prophetic, proclaiming to the Old Testament saints the coming Messiah, his kingdom and redemption. Enoch's translation in Genesis 4:5 serves to illustrate. First, Edwards sees the event as an historical one itself, part of the grand scheme of redemption: "Now this translation of Enoch was the first instance that ever there was of restoring the ruins of the fall with respect to the body."[30] At the same time, however, Edwards argues that the event spoke to Enoch's contemporaries of the gospel: "[T]he church of God in this instance was favored with an instance of it [the life and immortality brought to light by the gospel (2 Tim 1.10)] set before their eyes, in that one of their brethren was actually taken up to heaven without

---

28. "Notes on Scripture," no. 389, *WJE* 15:375.
29. "Miscellanies," no. 1353, *WJE* 23:494. Emphasis added.
30. "Work of Redemption," *WJE* 9:145.

dying; which we have all reason to think the church of God was knowing in the time of it as they were afterwards of Elijah's translation."[31]

The Messianic character and didactic nature of prophecies and types is central to understanding the doctrinal harmony Edwards observes in Scripture. The gospel was revealed in the Old Testament era through prophecies and types, but in the New Testament era it is revealed directly. According to Edwards, the faithful, whether in Old or New Testament are members of the one church. An examination of "covenants" in Edwards's theology will throw light on this.

COVENANTS

Although Edwards did not write a systematic account of the covenants, they are, as Carl Bogue noted, "very much alive throughout his work on both an explicit and implicit level."[32] Though Edwards nowhere mentions the covenants in his "Harmony" notebooks they are the unseen beams upon which he constructs his work. Arising from Calvin, Edwards follows a continental Reformed tradition in assuming both the substantial continuity and administrative differences of the covenant of grace through redemption history. When coupled with his commitments to the Messianic nature of prophecy and the nexus of Messianic types in the Old Testament, this enables Edwards to identify and explicate in more detail than his teachers had, the "Harmony" of faith and practice of the saints in Old and New Testaments.

When Edwards commenced his studies at the Collegiate School in Wethersfield, Connecticut (soon to be part of Yale College) in 1716 the "covenant" was a vital part of the theological furniture. In 1701 the trustees of the school had insisted that the rector of the college must use only those systems and synopses approved by the trustees for the instruction of his students in theology. They named the *Westminster Shorter Catechism* and the works of William Ames as the systems "most Conducive to their Establishment in the Principles of the Christian protestant Religion."[33] They considered Ames' *Medulla Theologiae* (*The Marrow of Theology*) to be the best presentation of Reformed orthodoxy; it was also required reading at

---

31. Ibid., 146.

32. Bogue, *Covenant*, 97.

33. Quoted in Warch, *School of the Prophets*, 234; see pp. 226–49 for an account of the theological curriculum at Yale. On Edwards's Yale education, see Morris, *Young Jonathan Edwards*, passim.

"Doctrine and Precept"

Harvard. Two years before Edwards arrived at the college Johannes Wollebius' *Compendium Theologiae Christiannae* (*The Abridgment of Christian Divinity*) joined Ames on the curriculum. [34] And as I noted in chapter 1 Edwards was also familiar with the works of Peter van Mastricht and "the great Turretine."[35] Turretin has a major section on covenants in his *Institutio Theologiae Elencticae* (*The Institutes of Elenctic Theology*), while van Mastricht's *Theoretico-practica theologia* devotes "Book VIII" to tracing the covenant of grace through history. [36]

The term "covenant theology" is perhaps an unhelpful one, suggesting wrongly the existence of theological homogeneity across two centuries and two continents.[37] Yet despite the imprecision of the term, some attempt

34. John Eusden notes that no-one analyzed the covenant of grace with the acuteness of Ames, though others, for example Johannes Cocceius (1603–69) and John Cotton (1584–1652) added greater detail and structure. Eusden, "Editor's Introduction," *Marrow*, 51. In his study of the early influences on Jonathan Edwards, Morris describes Edwards as "mastering Ames," though not "following him slavishly." Morris, *Young Jonathan Edwards*, 72. On the covenants in Edwards's *curriculum*, see especially, Ames, *Marrow*, 1.10, 24, 32, 38, 39; Wollebius, *Abridgment*, 1.8, 15, 21.

35. *Religious Affections*, *WJE* 2:289 n. 4.

36. Ramsey, Appendix 4, *WJE* 8:742 n. 9 notes that in "Miscellanies," no. 292 (ca. 1727) written when Edwards was twenty-five, there is a reference to both "Turretinus" and "Mastricht." He comments that Edwards may have studied the two theologians at Yale, but certainly he had done so by the time he was tutor there. For discussion of the covenants in Turretin and Mastricht, see Bogue, *Covenant*, 61-67. Turretin, *Institutes* 12.1–12; Mastricht, *Theoretico-practica theologia*, Bk. VIII, ch. 1, '*De Dispensatione sub Patriarchis*"; ch. 2, '*De Dispensatione sub Mose*"; ch. 3, '*De Dispensatione sub Christo*"; ch. 4, '*De Dispensatione sub aeternitate*." See Aza Goudriaan's discussion of Mastricht's view of history in Goudriaan, *Reformed Orthodoxy*, 212-31. Goudriaan, *Reformed Orthodoxy*, 15, n. 84, comments that recent research has begun to note Mastricht's debt to Williams Ames, whose *Marrow* was used for theological education in Utrecht, where Mastricht studied. Adriaan Neele highlighted the similarities between the structure of Mastricht's *Theoretico-practica theologia*, Bk. VIII and Edwards's own proposed "A History of the Work of Redemption" in his paper, "Petrus Van Masstricht: Exchanges in Scotland, the Netherlands, and America," delivered at the 'Jonathan Edwards and Scotland' conference, Glasgow University, 30–31 March 2009. See also Neele, *Living to God, passim*; *Petrus van Mastricht*, esp. Appendix 7.

37. Stephen Holmes notes the sterility of the question of whether Edwards can properly be called a "covenant theologian," since it depends more on the definition of the term than on any insight into Edwards's theology. Holmes, *God of Grace*, 147, n. 69. An overview of Reformed accounts of the covenants is to be found in Heppe, *Reformed Dogmatics*, 133–49, 281–447. On the relationship between Continental Reformed and Puritan theologies of the covenant see, Bogue, *Covenant*, 53–76. De Jong, *Covenant Idea*, 30, argues that the parallel development of covenant theology on both sides of the English Channel suggests that "a type of Federal theology is a universal phenomenon wherever Reformed theology is seriously pursued." See also

at an explication must be made. Conrad Cherry notes that at its heart the doctrine of the covenant represented "a history of the manner in which God dealt with his people."[38] An eternal covenant of redemption between the Divine Persons preceded God's covenant of works with pre-lapsarian Adam in which God promised salvation to humanity on the condition of perfect obedience. Following man's disobedience and Fall God graciously entered into another covenant with him, one that did not depend on man fulfilling certain legal conditions. This covenant of grace was, in Turretin's words, "a gratuitous pact entered into in Christ between God offended and man offending, in which God promises remission of sins and salvation to man gratuitously on account of Christ, man, however, relying upon the same grace promises faith and obedience."[39]

This covenant of grace was conceived as running through both Old and New Testaments. Though its substance was constant throughout its temporal expressions, it differed in administration.[40] In the infancy of the church the grace was veiled, the covenant being administered through promises, prophecies, sacrifices and other types all "fore-signifying Christ to come: which were, for that time, sufficient and efficacious, through the operation of the Spirit, to instruct and build up the elect in faith in the promised Messiah . . . ; and is called the Old Testament."[41] When Christ

---

Miller, *New England Mind: The Seventeenth Century*, 92. By contrast George Marsden, "Perry Miller's Rehabilitation of the Puritans," 91–105, esp. 99–100, argues that the parallel and independent development of covenant doctrine is due to "a recovery of biblical teaching." A recent account of the rhetoric of New England covenant theology and its relations to Puritan traditions in England and Holland is to be found in Knight, *Orthodoxies in Massachusetts*, esp. 88–108.

38. Cherry, *Theology of Jonathan Edwards*, 108.

39. Turretin, *Institutes*, 12.2.5.

40. Calvin argues that the covenant made with all the patriarchs is "so much like ours in substance and reality that the two are actually one and the same. Yet they differ in the mode of dispensation." Calvin, *Institutes*, 2.10–11 (2.10.2). The distinction between substance and administration is a familiar one in Continental Reformed theology. See for example Turretin, *Institutes*, 12.5.1–45; 12.8.1–25. Heppe, *Reformed Dogmatics*, 371–409. See also the *Westminster Confession*, 7.6. The thorny question of the relationship between Calvin and covenantal theology is beyond the scope of the present enquiry. For an introduction to this see for example, Møller, "The Beginnings of Puritan Covenant Theology," 46–67; Rolston, "Responsible Man in Reformed Theology," 129–56; von Rohr, *The Covenant of Grace*; Emerson, "Calvin and Covenant Theology," 136–44; Kendall, *Calvin and English Calvinism*; Helm, *Calvin and the Calvinists*; Muller, *Christ and the Decree*.

41. *Westminster Confession*, 7.5. Edwards's opinion of the Westminster Confession is revealed in his response to an enquiry by John Erskine as to whether he might accept

came in the flesh the administration of the covenant changed, the signs and shadows being rendered obsolete by the arrival of the reality. It is this new administration of the covenant that defines the New Testament. Thus according to the *Westminster Confession*, "there are not ... two covenants of grace, differing in substance, but one and the same, under various dispensations."[42] However, the question of Edwards's relationship to covenantal theology has had a turbulent recent history.

In 1949 Perry Miller, father of the Edwardsean renaissance, argued that Edwards threw out the entire covenantal scheme that obligated God in his relationship with humanity and instead preached the free and sovereign grace of God, in which man may make no claims on God but simply depend on him for salvation.[43] Miller claimed that Edwards returned to the doctrine from whence the covenant tradition had started, namely Calvin, becoming "the first consistent and authentic Calvinist in New England."[44] The reason for this, according to Miller was Edwards's detection of Arminian tendencies latent in New England covenant theology, particularly in the doctrine of preparation and the conditionality of the covenant of grace. First, to Miller, "preparation" was preached in early eighteenth-century New England as something that a sinner might do to predispose himself for grace.[45] Second, according to Miller, the covenant of grace and the conditionality of faith had grown out of man's need for assurance of salvation from Calvin's inscrutable God. The covenant of grace obligated God to the saint by replacing predestination and the divine decrees (from the saint's viewpoint) with the assurance of God's love and acceptance,

---

a pastorate in Scotland. Edwards writes, "As to my subscribing to the substance of the Westminster Confession, there would be no difficulty." Letter no. 117, "To the Reverend John Erskine," 5 July 1750, *WJE* 16:355.

42. *Westminster Confession*, 7.6. William Ames, *Marrow*, 1.24, compares the covenant of works with Adam (which he calls "the old covenant") with the covenant of grace (which he prefers to call the "testament," indicating God's freely given word of salvation). Wollebius, *Abridgment*, 1.21.2, uses the same nomenclature: "Therefore the covenant of Grace is called a Testament or Disposition; because, by this God hath appointed to his sons an heavenly inheritance, to be obtained by the mediation of his own Son's death." He argues it is wrong to identify the Old Testament with the covenant of works, and the New Testament with the covenant of grace.

43. Miller, *Jonathan Edwards*, 30-32, 76–78; *New England Mind: The Seventeenth Century, passim*; *Errand*, 98.

44. Miller, *Errand*, 98. On the relation between Calvin and "covenant theology," see above, n. 40.

45. Miller, "'Preparation for Salvation,'" 253–86. I discuss preparation in more detail in the following chapter.

based on the saint's fulfillment of the condition of faith. He writes, "No grounds for moral . . . individual assurance could be devised so long as God was held to act in a way that utterly disregarded human necessities or human logic. In order to know that God will unquestionably save him . . . man must know that God is in reality the sort of being who would, or even who will have to, abide by these conditions."[46] It was this obligating of God in his relationship with humanity that aroused Edwards's hostility, according to Miller. Both preparationism and the covenant of grace represented the granting of meritorious action to the elect, according to Miller, a significant departure from Calvin and an expression of crypto-Arminianism that prompted Edwards's rejection of covenant theology in its entirety.

Acknowledging the long reception of Miller's thesis, Michael McClenahan has recently argued that it was nevertheless based on a misunderstanding of Reformed theology that not only set Calvin against his heirs, but mistakenly employed the nineteenth-century "central dogma theory" (of predestination) to Calvin's thought.[47] First, McClenahan argues that as regards "preparationism" Miller failed to take seriously the important distinction between meritorious and non-meritorious causes of salvation. The doctrine of preparation did not hold that man might prepare *himself* for conversion, but that *God* might prepare him. Second, as regards the covenant of grace McClenahan points out that Miller overlooked Calvin's own commitment to the covenant and its conditionality as later New England theology expressed it, an observation already noted by Carl Bogue.

Bogue rejects Miller's account, arguing that while the covenant of grace is not an organizing principle of Calvin's *Institutes*, its essentials are "definitely present."[48] Calvin uses the covenant to show the essential unity of God's gracious dealings with his people in the Old and New Testaments and argues that "as God binds himself to keep the promise given to us, so the consent of faith and obedience is demanded from us."[49] Therefore, according to Bogue, it is not true that Edwards needed to embrace the one (Calvin) at the expense of the other (the covenant of grace).[50] Analyzing Edwards's sermons and "Miscellanies," Bogue contends that the covenant

46. Miller, *Errand*, 51.
47. McClenahan, "Justification," 60–75.
48. Bogue, *Covenant*, 56.
49. "The covenant made with all the patriarchs is so much like ours in substance and reality that the two are actually one and the same." Calvin, *Institutes*, 2.10.2; *Genesis*, 451–52, quoted in Bogue, *Covenant*, 57.
50. Bogue, *Covenant*, 77–92. On the relationship between Calvin and covenantal theology, see above n. 40.

was foundational to Edwards's theology. Consequently, he rejects Peter De Jong's depiction of the 1739 sermon series, namely that "Edwards consistently used covenant terminology without making the idea truly determinative. . . . [demonstrating] that at the time the covenant idea was not yet forgotten."[51] Instead Bogue argues that so significant was the "covenant" to Edwards that the sermon series might well have been entitled, "A History of the Covenant of Grace."[52]

Though Conrad Cherry follows Miller in depicting the history of the covenant of grace in New England as the history of the attempt to "chain" the transcendent God of Calvin in pursuit of personal assurance, he rejects the latter's account of Edwards's position. Like Bogue, Cherry argues that the eighteenth-century theologian constantly employed the covenantal categories in his expression of God's dealings with his people.[53] On the conditional nature of the covenant of grace Cherry finds Edwards wrestling with two co-existent motifs. First, God had condescended to be bound to humanity in covenant and as a result placed himself in debt such that man could "sue" him in faith for salvation. And second, man's faith, itself a gift from God, was the necessary instrument and condition of enjoying God's covenantal relationship. Cherry argues that Edwards never satisfactorily resolved the tension between the two. In his better moments, Cherry concedes, Edwards saw faith as the reception of covenant blessings, a gift received as God himself consummates the covenant.[54]

Cherry's "concession" does indeed seem to represent Edwards's position.[55] Edwards follows Calvin and Ames in believing that faith is a conditional response that is "binding," but it is itself part of the promise and thus a gift of God. In "Miscellanies," no. 2 Edwards notes that making faith a condition of the covenant of grace is to reduce it to a covenant of works on man's part, and is "doubtless the foundation of Arminianism and neonomianism." He comments that disagreements over the conditional nature of faith are due to a wrong distinction between the covenants of grace and redemption. The covenant of works was made with Adam and his seed in him, and was conditional on the obedience of its federal head. Similarly, the covenant that was made with Christ (the covenant of redemption) was

---

51. De Jong, *Covenant Idea*, 122.

52. Bogue, *Covenant*, 115–24 (117).

53. Cherry, "Puritan Notion of the Covenant," 328–41; *Theology of Jonathan Edwards, passim*.

54. Cherry, *Theology of Jonathan Edwards*, 122.

55. See my discussion in chapter 4.

made with his seed in him, and was to his seed similarly conditional upon the obedience of its federal head. "Christ has performed the condition of the new covenant." Therefore, in the covenant of grace between Christ and his spouse, "We have nothing to do, upon the account of which we are to be saved; we are to do nothing but only to receive Christ and what he has done already... This taking and receiving is faith.... Faith can't be called the condition of receiving, for it is the receiving itself.... 'Tis true, those that don't believe are not saved, and all that do believe are saved: that is, all that do receive Christ and salvation, they receive it; and all that will not receive salvation, never do receive it and never have it."[56] Edwards elaborates this in "Miscellanies," no. 617 in which he compares the covenants of redemption and grace and argues that though they are not entirely different, they must not be confounded. Both are conditional, but the conditions in the one are the promises in the other. Regeneration, faith, means of grace, justification and perseverance are Christ's reward from the Father in the covenant of redemption, but are conditions of the covenant of grace. Similarly, the incarnation, sufferings and death of Christ are promises in the covenant of grace, but conditions of the covenant of redemption.[57]

Cherry contends that, far from throwing out covenant theology as Miller argues, Edwards was dependent on its categories to the extent that "he had difficulty freeing himself from [them] ... even at the points where he discerned their shortcomings."[58] However, in the following chapter I will explore Edwards's use of covenantal categories in the context of soteriology and will argue that, far from trying to free himself from them, they were indispensable to him, being crucial to his rooting a doctrine of justification by faith alone in both Testaments.

In New England the notion of "covenant" encompassed more than questions of individual election, preparation and assurance; it had ecclesial, public and political dimensions.[59] Harry Stout argues that Jonathan Edwards was every bit the covenantal theologian that his predecessors were, his covenantal theology being worked out in the daily life of his churches and local communities. Stout supports this claim through a

56. "Miscellanies," no. 2, *WJE* 13:197–99.
57. "Miscellanies," no. 617, *WJE* 18:148–51.
58. Cherry, *Theology of Jonathan Edwards*, 123.
59. For a discussion of the notion of national election in seventeenth-century America, see Weir, *New England, passim*; Bercovitch, *Puritan Origins*, 72–108; Stoever, "A Faire and Easie Way to Heaven." On the infamous Halfway Covenant of 1662 and Edwards's change of practice of admission to church membership, see, Hall, "Editor's Introduction," *Ecclesiastical Writings*, *WJE* 12:17–42; Holifield, *Covenant Sealed, passim*; Morgan, *Visible Saints*, 113–38; Marsden, *Jonathan Edwards*, 345–54.

study of previously unpublished fast sermons, sermons Edwards preached at times of local and national testing, such as the Great Earthquake of November 1727 and the French wars of the 1740s and late 1750s. He shows that, rather than renouncing the notion of the national covenant, Edwards preached the peculiar relation between God and New England that his own father and theological ancestors had, incorporating this into his conception of God's history of redemption.[60] Granted this recent turbulent scholarship, what light does Edwards's covenant theology throw on his relating of Old and New Testaments in terms of doctrine and precept?

To Edwards God's decision to glorify himself in the work of redemption led the Persons of the Trinity to confederate themselves in an eternal covenant of redemption.[61] In "Miscellanies," no. 1062 ("Economy of the Trinity and Covenant of Redemption") Edwards explores how the covenant of redemption is fitting to the order of subsisting of the divine persons. Edwards seeks to guard the equality of the divine persons, while asserting the Father's priority. Consequently he constructs three "levels" of Trinitarian relationship and activity: (i) ontological; (ii) "economical" (though strictly speaking Edwards is still dealing with the immanent Trinity); (iii) covenantal. He argues that "it is fit that the order of the acting of the persons of the Trinity should be agreeable to the order of their subsisting" and that this order is distinct from and prior to the covenant of redemption. In "pitching" upon the covenant of redemption, however, both the ontological relation of the persons and their economical order of acting is respected. The humiliation of the Son below his economical dignity had to be freely undertaken in order (i) to maintain the ontological equality of the Son, and (ii) to be meritorious. Therefore, a covenant was required. It is for this reason that Edwards assumes that strictly speaking only the Father and Son were covenanting parties in the covenant of redemption because only between them did a "new kind of subordination and mutual obligation" obtain. A covenant was required because in the work of redemption the Father's relationship with the Son was characterized by "a new right of headship and authority over the

---

60. Stout, "Puritans and Edwards," 142–59. Gerald McDermott contests Stout's reading of Edwards as "optimistic" regarding the national covenant. McDermott argues instead that Edwards held a more pessimistic view of America's status and destiny, fearing that God would transfer his covenant to another people should New England persist in her sin. McDermott, *Holy and Happy Society*, 11–36. Whether optimistic or pessimistic, Stout and McDermott are agreed that the notion of "covenant," in public life at least, was central to Edwards's thought, *contra* Miller's account.

61. See for example, the first sermon in the 1739 redemption discourse, *WJE* 9:118.

Son" in which the Father had the authority to prescribe what is needed to glorify himself through the work. On the Son's side, the Son willingly submitted to the Father in the work of redemption, a work far below his "excellency" and "dignity." Furthermore, the Son obtained a (temporary) new rule and authority with respect to creation, an authority he did not possess in the eternal economy of the Trinity. The Son also received the Holy Spirit "to dispense of it as he pleased to the redeemed." The Holy Spirit's subjection to the Son in the work of redemption is expressed in two ways. First, because of the Son's new (temporary) role as Lord and judge over creation, the Spirit is (temporarily) subject to him with the subjection that is economically due to the Father. And second, the Spirit is subject to the Son who is now the God-man, the eternal head and bridegroom of the church, who eternally communicates the Holy Spirit to his spouse. In both cases, however, the Holy Spirit's subjection to the Son does not constitute a mode of relating to him that differs from that of their eternal "economic" relationship. The subjection of the Holy Spirit to the Son in the covenant of redemption is only *circumstantially* new; it does not involve the Spirit's humiliation below his proper eternal "economical" character. For this reason, on Edwards's account, the Holy Spirit, though an interested party is not a covenantal partner in the covenant of redemption.[62] It is worth noting that Edwards is not departing from the *opera trinitatis ad extra sunt indivisa* principle here because he does not deny the role of the Holy Spirit in the work of redemption. He is simply arguing that a covenant of redemption is required where a new mode of relating between the divine Persons obtains.

To recapitulate, God's desire to glorify himself in the work of redemption was in the covenant of redemption fitting to the internal Trinitarian relations, so that the Son was elected as Mediator.[63] Strictly speaking the

---

62. "Miscellanies," no. 1062, *WJE* 20:430-43.

63. In "Miscellanies," no. 614, "Wisdom of God in the Work of Redemption," written sometime in early 1733, Edwards explores an economic reason for the election of the Son as Mediator: that a Mediator was needed between the Father and the Holy Spirit. The reason for the Son's election to this role, according to Edwards, is "upon a like account as it was necessary that [the Mediator] should be neither God the Father nor one of fallen men but a middle person between them." Edwards argues that the Father "sustained the rights of the Godhead and was the person offended and to be appeased by a mediator," while the Holy Spirit is the indwelling "principle of life and action" in the saint. In being Mediator between the Father and the saints, the Son is also Mediator between the Father and the Holy Spirit. "Miscellanies," no. 614, *WJE* 18:146-47. See also, "Miscellanies," nos. 73 and 781, *WJE* 18:359 and 450-52 respectively on the same theme.

covenant was one between Father and Son, with the Spirit an interested (though not covenanting) partner. At the same time, the covenant of redemption was one between the Father and elect humanity not yet in existence. Edwards notes that the Father's promises of blessing to the Son in the covenant of redemption were made to Christ mystical:

> [A]nd though the whole of Christ mystical was not yet in being, only the head of the body as yet is in being, and the members only existing in God's decree. And as in process of time the members, one after another, come into being, and then the same promises that were virtually made to 'em before are expressly revealed to 'em, and directed to 'em. Yet this does not make the promises, as revealed and directly made to the members, a different covenant from the promises that were before made to the head, that existed before 'em and stood for 'em.[64]

That is, Edwards argues that the covenants of grace between the Father and the elect through the mediation of the Son that were made at successive points in history were actually different expressions of the one covenant, temporal expressions of the covenant of redemption.[65] In "Miscellanies," no. 2 Edwards notes that much confusion surrounding the role of faith as a condition of the covenant arises from a wrong distinction between the covenants of redemption and grace.[66] He argues that just as the covenant of works was made with Adam and his seed in him, so the covenant of grace was made with Christ and his seed in him. (Edwards usually terms the latter the "covenant of redemption"). There is not one covenant between the Father and Christ (the covenant of redemption) and another with his seed (the covenants of grace considered conditional upon faith). Edwards argues that the only true condition of both the covenants of works and of grace is the standing of their heads, Adam and Christ.[67] In this sense both the covenant of works with Adam and the covenant of grace after the Fall exhibit a "works" character, their conditions requiring meritorious work to be performed, the difference between them being the identity of the one who performs the work. Consequently, faith is no

---

64. "Miscellanies," no. 1091, *WJE* 20:475.
65. "Jesus Christ, the Same Yesterday, Today and For Ever," *WJE BoT*, 2.950.
66. "Miscellanies," no. 2, *WJE* 13:197–99.
67. Edwards's innovative treatment of the imputation of Adam's sin is beyond the scope of the present enquiry, but see for example, *Original Sin*, *WJE* 3:389–412 and Clyde Holbrook's "Editor's Introduction" to that volume, esp. 41–60.

meritorious work, according to Edwards, but is simply the accepting of the covenant of grace performed by Christ.[68]

A distinctive contribution of Edwards to covenant thought is his description of the union between Christ and his bride as a "covenant of grace." According to Edwards, the covenant that Christ makes with his bride is "properly a different covenant" in two respects from the covenants of redemption and grace that involve the Father. First, unlike them, the covenant of grace between Christ and his bride is a direct one, not requiring a mediator. Second, while the covenant of redemption is without conditions to be performed by the elect—its condition is the perfect righteousness of Christ—Christ's covenant with his bride is conditional in the sense that that it requires her to yield to his offer of union.[69]

The covenants of grace made by the Father at successive points in redemption history were temporal expressions of the covenant of redemption, and in his redemption sermon series of 1739 Edwards portrays five examples of these in the Old Testament, those with: Adam and Eve after the Fall; Noah; the Patriarchs; Israel at Sinai; and David. Each was a different expression of the one covenant that punctuated the history of redemption. Edwards illustrates the relationship of the covenants of redemption

---

68. See for example, "Miscellanies," no. 299, *WJE* 13:386. A hint of the complexity and differing conceptions of "covenant theology" is glimpsed in "Miscellanies," no. 1091 as Edwards tries to reconcile two distinct positions: "The due consideration of these things may perhaps reconcile the difference between those divines that think [the covenant of redemption] and the covenant of grace the same, and those that think 'em different." "Miscellanies," no. 1091, *WJE* 20:477. Bogue speculates that as regards the former position Edwards may have in view here Boston, *Covenant of Grace*, a work Edwards had read. Boston, *Covenant of Grace*, 32, asserted that the covenants of redemption and grace "are not two distinct covenants, but one and the same" (cited in Bogue, *Covenant*, 110). Regarding the condition of the covenant of grace Boston argued that "Receiving is not the thing, upon which the buyer's right and title to the commodity... is founded: therefore, though it may be called a condition of connexion in the respective covenants, yet it cannot, in any propriety of speech, be called the condition of them." Rather, "The condition of the covenant of Grace, properly so called is, Christ in the form of a bond-servant, as last Adam." Boston, *Covenant of Grace*, 84. Given that Edwards also describes the covenant between Christ and the believer as the covenant of grace, to speak of Christ as the *condition* of the covenant, is nonsensical to him. Bogue, *Covenant*, 110–11. See also Edwards's letter to the Rev. Thomas Gillespie (4th September 1747) in which he confesses, regarding Boston's *Covenant of Grace*, that he "did not understand his scheme delivered in that book." Letter, no. 78, *WJE* 16:224–35 (235). On the importance to Edwards of distinguishing between the covenants of redemption and grace for the question of justification, see my discussion in the next chapter.

69. "Miscellanies," no. 1091, *WJE* 20:475–79.

and grace by recourse to the example of Abram. God's promises to Abram and his seed in Genesis 12 were the same as the covenants God made afterwards with Abraham's seed in the wilderness: "'Tis no more than a revelation of part of a covenant made already, and renewing of the same promises over again."[70] In the same way the historical covenants of grace with the elect were substantially the same as the eternal covenant between the Father and the elect in Christ, the Son. In chapter 4 I will explore the relationship between the covenants of redemption and grace in more detail and note that although Edwards does not consider the covenants of redemption and grace to be entirely different, he insists that they must not be confounded; the covenant of grace is the temporal "realization" of the covenant of redemption.

In *The Marrow* Ames analyses the administration of the covenant of grace before the coming of Christ, noting that "although the free, saving covenant of God has been one and the same from the beginning, the manner of the application of Christ or the administration of the new covenant has not always been so . . . [but has] varied according to the times during which the church has been in process of being gathered."[71] To prove this Ames examines three dispensations: Adam to Abraham; Abraham to Moses; Moses to Christ. In each dispensation he identifies familiar stages of the application of grace in the life of the saint. In the first period, for example, he notes: God's *calling*—evident in the distinction between the seed of the serpent and of the woman, and between the sons of God and sons of men (Gen 6:2); *justification*—set forth by expiatory sacrifices for sins; *adoption*; *sanctification*; and *glorification*—"publicly sealed by the example of Enoch and saving of Noah." In the period from Abraham to Moses "the benefits of the new covenant were all more clearly and distinctly witnessed to than before." Ames sees God's *election*—set forth in the examples of Isaac and Jacob, Ishmael and Esau; *redemption*; *calling*; *justification*; *adoption*; *sanctification* and *glorification*. Finally, in the period from Moses to Christ the same things are "further adumbrated." *Redemption* is typified in the exodus from Egypt; *justification* is set forth in the Passover as well as in the legal sacrifices and ablutions; *adoption* is portrayed in the dedication of the firstborn to God; *sanctification* is set forth; and finally, *glorification*—"shown in the inheritance of the promised land and the communion which they had with God in the holy of holies."[72]

---

70. "Miscellanies," no. 919, *WJE* 20:167.
71. Ames, *Marrow*, 1.38.
72. Ibid., 1.38.14–35.

Edwards similarly maintains the substantial continuity of the covenant of grace through redemption history. He argues that the covenant of grace established in the New Testament is not substantially different from that which God entered into with Israel, any more than "that the covenant that God entered into with Israel at Mt. Sinai was specifically diverse from that which he entered into on the plains of Moab, because that is spoken of as another covenant (Deut. 29:1)."[73] Comparing the dispensations under Moses and Christ Edwards notes that first, the same salvation in substance is given under both: sinners are by nature objects of divine wrath; they are alike called, justified, adopted and sanctified. Second, the medium of salvation in each dispensation is the same: the elect are saved by the same Mediator's suffering and satisfaction of divine justice. Third, the same Holy Spirit applies redemption. Fourth, the method of bestowing salvation is the same, the grand qualification for justification being faith. Fifth, the external means of applying the benefits of salvation are the same: principally, the word of God. Sixth, the previous five characteristics are represented under each dispensation, though the nature of this revelation differs. Seventh, these same things are not only "in some sort exhibited or represented" to the later church, but were "in some degree made known and revealed" to the church in each dispensation. Eighth, with the revelation comes promise of fulfillment and right to enjoyment of those things revealed.[74]

Though the covenant was substantially the same throughout redemption history, Edwards assumes that its administration differed. The covenant of grace at Sinai was given under the cortex of the Law. Consequently, the life of faith differed in its outward expression. Comparing the dispensations under Moses and Christ, Edwards notes that "the same exercises of faith were then required as are now, but there was a difference, answerable to the difference of the revelation in which the Mediator and his salvation is exhibited."[75] Among the outward expressions in which the life of faith of the Old Testament church differed from that of the New Testament one Edwards highlights "the degree and manner of weanedness from the world, self-denial, spirituality of worship, heavenly-mindedness, love to men, the degree and manner of our loving them, forgiveness of injuries, love to enemies, love to the wicked, love to all mankind, etc. According to the more particular and full revelation of the grounds of these

---

73. "Miscellanies," no. 1118, *WJE* 20:493.
74. "Miscellanies," no. 1353, *WJE* 23:492–506.
75. Ibid., 503. See also "Miscellanies," no. 439, *WJE* 13:488.

duties, and the new obligations laid upon us to them, evangelical duties, with their grounds, were not so fully revealed, so particularly prescribed, nor so much insisted on."[76]

The plainness of God's revelation was dependent on the administration of the covenant. In the Old Testament, the gospel is exhibited under a veil. In the New Testament that veil is removed and the gospel displayed plainly. The Son's incarnate work at the same time linked and distinguished the Old and New Testament expressions of the covenant of grace. With the Son's incarnate work came the reality which had cast the earlier shadows of the gospel into the Old Testament. With it also the earlier anticipatory expressions of the covenant of grace were fulfilled and consequently their shadowy forms were rendered obsolete. Therefore the title Edwards chooses for his second "great work" is not incidental: "The Harmony of the Old and New Testament" (note the singular "Testament") expresses both continuity and discontinuity, the substance and administration of the covenant of grace. Nevertheless, as Edwards develops the complexity of the Old Testament "veil," expanding the category of types and the Messianic nature and interconnectedness of prophecy whose meaning is made available to those in possession of the "new sense," so he inevitably emphasizes the substantial similarity between Old and New Testament expressions of the covenant of grace, as I will demonstrate below. Edwards's notebook for the third part of his "Harmony" reveals a willingness to find parallels in doctrine and precept that go beyond the familiar categories employed by Ames. It is his detailed analysis of the life and faith of the Old Testament saint in his "Harmony" notebook that is the subject of the following section.

The "Harmony": "Doctrine and Precept"

With Christ's redemption the great theme of the whole Bible, it was inevitable also that "the moral rules and precept of it are all given in subordination to him."[77] In the previous section I noted that the witness of the Old and New Testaments to Christ differed, not in content, but in form. Once again Edwards's dialectics of spirit-letter and kernel-husk are helpful in understanding the unity of gospel precept he observed in the Bible. The husk in which the gospel was presented to the church differed according to the church's place in redemption history, but the gospel kernel was

---

76. "Miscellanies," no. 1353, *WJE* 23:503.
77. "Work of Redemption," *WJE* 9:290.

constant. And just as the spirit of the gospel was the same with each new expression of the covenant, so the spirit of the *response* to that gospel was the same. In "Miscellanies," no. 439 Edwards records that the conditions of God's covenant with Israel were the same as the new covenant as to their general nature: "the exercise of the same spirit of holiness, and gracious respect to God in faith, and a sincere and universal obedience."[78] Again, prefacing the circumstantial differences which resulted from the different forms of the old and new covenants, Edwards maintains the essential unity of the covenant faith both in its content and in the response it elicited from the faithful: "The spirit or principle of faith in the heart was the same; and the person who is the object of faith is the same, viz. the Son of God, as Mediator. The same spirit of repentance and humiliation belonged to it then as does now."[79]

According to his letter to the college trustees in New Jersey, Edwards intended addressing the relationship of the Old and New Testaments in terms of faith and practice in the final third of his "Harmony." Robert E. Brown, one of the few scholars to have studied Edwards's critical engagement with the Bible, argues that the notebook, "The Harmony of the Genius, Spirit, Doctrines and Rules of the Old Testament and the New" represents Edwards's *first* attempt at the entire "Harmony."[80] He suggests that it was completed around the time of Edwards's separation from Northampton (1750) and that it is consequently "almost mono-thematically devoted to the problem of 'affliction.'"[81] Brown comments, "Thus while these notes may prove to be illuminating of the emotional anguish that Edwards experienced at his dismissal, they reveal little of his actual plans for the 'Harmony' as he subsequently outlined it in the letter to the Princeton trustees."[82] He argues that by the late 1750s Edwards had reorganized the project considerably, such that it would have "no doubt depended heavily on material from the 'Miscellanies' and 'Notes on Scripture.'"[83]

There are however, a number of problems with Brown's account as I will seek to demonstrate. First, Brown's thesis does not easily fit the chronology of the relevant manuscripts. Amy Plantinga Pauw, following

---

78. "Miscellanies," no. 439, *WJE* 13:488.

79. "Miscellanies," no. 1353, *WJE* 23:502.

80. Beinecke Library, Edwards Papers, f.33. For a description of the manuscript see Minkema, "Great Work," 61.

81. Brown, *Edwards and the Bible*, 165, 259. n. 5.

82. Ibid., 165.

83. Ibid.

Thomas Schafer's extensive study of paper, inks and Edwards's handwriting, dates "Miscellanies," nos. 1067–68 ("Prophecies of the Messiah" and "The Fulfillment of The Prophecies of the Messiah") to ca. 1743–44, and "Miscellanies," no. 1069 ("Types of the Messiah") to ca. 1744–49.[84] This suggests that Edwards had the "Harmony" project in mind four or five years before he began his "Genius, Spirit, Doctrine and Rules" notebook in 1748. Therefore, *contra* Brown, the latter notebook can hardly be considered a "first attempt" at the project. Rather than being an early version of the whole "Harmony," it is more likely that the "Genius, Spirit, Doctrine and Rules" notebook represents an early version of the final third of the entire project, and that Edwards began this notebook after he had already written substantial notes for the first two parts of the "Harmony."

Second, it is true that Edwards's observations for the third part of his "Harmony" appear relatively provisional when compared with his equivalent notes on prophecy and typology, but this need not be evidence of an abandoned first attempt at the "Harmony" as a whole. An equally plausible explanation is simply that Edwards's work on the final third of the "Harmony" had not advanced as far as the first two thirds. Though Edwards compiled the notebook following a lifetime of biblical scholarship expressed in his sermons, "Miscellanies," "Notes on Scripture" and the "Blank Bible," the present notebook makes scant reference to his notes elsewhere. It is instead a catalogue of shorthand, half-sentences, phrases, words and references that clearly would have triggered thoughts and links in the mind of the author, but whose full meaning is perhaps beyond recovery today. For example, Edwards's comment on Genesis 15:6 is simply, "Justification by faith." Edwards does not even make reference to Paul's use of this verse in Romans 4:3, 22 and Galatians 3:6. There was more that could be said, but Edwards felt no need to note it down. In compiling this notebook Edwards's intention does not appear to be to exegete Old Testament passages, as he has done in other notebooks. Many times in this notebook he does not even note all the places in the New Testament where a particular Old Testament text is cited. Similarly, he does not note things he has recorded elsewhere, however significant a use he might have made of them elsewhere. Rather, his aim in this notebook is to record one aspect only of the harmony of the Old and New Testaments and readers

84. Pauw, "Editor's Introduction," *WJE* 20:36–37. References to secondary works in "Miscellanies," nos. 1021 and 1073 locate these entries as having been written after 1742. Furthermore, "Miscellanies," no. 1069 ("Types of the Messiah") was begun in 1744 and contains numerous references to "Miscellanies," nos. 1067–68. On Schafer's dating of "Miscellanies," no. 1069, see Lowance and Watters, "Editors' Introduction," *WJE* 11:165.

must beware both of constructing too much from what was essentially a private notebook and of expecting more from the notebook than Edwards himself intended.

Third, as I will elaborate below, far from being clouded by the "emotional anguish" of the departure from Northampton as Brown contends, this third part of the project is recognizably of a piece with his earlier observations on prophecy and typology. Edwards is here continuing to pursue the "Harmony" project that he had begun at least four years earlier.

Fourth and finally, *contra* Brown, there is no need to suppose that by the late 1750s Edwards had "refined and reorganized the project substantially" along the lines described in his letter to the trustees, because the "Genius, Spirit, Doctrine and Rules" notebook *already* fits that description of the "Harmony" project. In short, it is likely that the notebook expresses Edwards's intentions for the final third of the "Harmony" project, a project he had begun some years earlier while still in Northampton.

The "Genius, Spirit, Doctrine and Rules" notebook may be divided into two parts. The first (brief) section has no title. Instead it comprises a collection of nine headings supported mainly by Old Testament texts not listed in canonical order. Edwards cites and frequently quotes Scripture in support of these claims. The list of nine is as follows:

> FAITH IN GOD THE GRAND DESIGN OF GOD'S SALVATION, PROTECTION, DELIVERANCE ETC.
>
> FAITH IN A MEDIATOR, IN THE SON OF GOD, IN THE MESSIAH
>
> IMMORTALITY AND A FUTURE STATE
>
> LOVE TO ENEMIES, FORGIVING INJURIES, DOING GOOD FOR EVIL ETC.
>
> HUMILITY TOWARDS MEN
>
> SELLING ALL FOR CHRIST
>
> WEEPING WITH THOSE THAT WEEP
>
> A BEING WITHOUT ANXIETY OR CAREFULNESS
>
> NOT HOARDING UP TREASURE FOR FUTURE TIME IN THIS WORLD, BUT LAYING OUT WHAT WE HAVE TO SPARE FOR PIOUS AND CHARITABLE PURPOSES

"Doctrine and Precept"

In response to Brown's contention that the notebook reveals little of Edwards's plans for the "Harmony" as he outlined it to the trustees at New Jersey, I suggest that there is in fact a clear similarity between the two. In his letter Edwards describes the third part of his project as a harmony in "doctrine and precept." Though Edwards does not intend the present notebook nor the eventual "Harmony" to function as a handbook of theology, like Mastricht's *Theoretico-practica theologia*, Ames' *Marrow* or Wollebius' *Abridgment*, nevertheless as he begins this notebook he seems to have in mind the fundamental Reformed distinction between doctrine and practice, or theoretical and practical theology, though he treats the two together.[85] In the list of nine headings above, it is likely that Edwards intends the first three to refer to doctrine and the following six to precept. The first four headings are supported solely by Old Testament texts. In this way Edwards continues the approach he employs in the first two parts of his "Harmony." Both there and here Edwards seeks to establish the discrete witness of the Old Testament without reference to the New Testament text. I will pass over the significance of the first three (doctrinal) point of harmony that Edwards identifies here, since the question of the object and content of faith will be considered in detail in the following chapter, a case study in soteriological harmony. I turn instead to the remaining six points of harmony in precept.

A close observation suggests that the unifying factor of the notes thus far is not to be found in Edwards's own reaction to his dismissal from Northampton as Brown contends, but in something more significant to Edwards's intentions. Four of the six precepts Edwards cites above bear striking resemblance to parts of the "Sermon on the Mount."[86] Given

---

85. Ames, *Marrow*, 1.1.1, divides divinity, or "the doctrine of living to God" into: "faith" and "observance"; Wollebius divides *Abridgment* into: Book 1, "Concerning the Knowledge of God," and Book 2, "Concerning the Worship of God." Of the two major theological works Edwards recommends to Bellamy in 1746/7 the first, Mastricht, *Theoretico-practica theologia*, as the title suggests, is a manual of systematic and practical theology. See Neele, *Living to God, passim*. In the *Institutes* Turretin considers the question of whether theology is theoretical or practical. He affirms that it is "mixed," since the essence of true religion demands the knowledge and worship of God which are connected together inseparably: "That knowledge of God [cannot] be true unless attended by practice.... Nor can that practice be right and saving which is not directed by knowledge." Turretin, *Institutes*, 1.8.1–15.

86. Of the other two, "Selling all for Christ" is possibly a reference to Jesus' command: "If thou wilt be perfect, go and sell that thou hast, and give to the poor, and thou shalt have treasure in heaven: and come and follow me [Matt 19:21]," while "Weeping With Those That Weep," echoes "Rejoice with them that do rejoice, and weep with them that weep [Rom 12:15]."

Edwards's identification of a threefold theme that unifies the Old and New Testaments (the Messiah, his kingdom and redemption) Christ's sermon represents to Edwards the natural place to begin consideration of the spiritual substance of life in this kingdom in old and new dispensations. Indeed Edwards seems to have been thinking along these lines five or six years earlier when he wrote "Miscellanies," no. 1030. Following a discussion of how the covenants of works and grace were delivered in the Ten Commandments at Mount Sinai, Edwards notes Jesus' words in Matthew 5:17 ["Think not that I am come to destroy the law, or the prophets: I am not come to destroy, but to fulfil"]. He comments, "'Tis evident, by the following part of the same sermon of Christ, that it was his fulfilling the law in this respect that he had especially in view, viz. teaching and leading and influencing his disciples to a true, sincere and real fulfillment of the duties of the law of God, as understood in its *spiritual and true meaning*..."[87] The final phrase brings to mind not only the full title of Edwards's notebook for this third part of his "Harmony" but also his commitment to the paradigm of substance and administration, in which the saint is dependent on the Holy Spirit to take him beyond the shell to the gospel kernel of revelation. By this means Edwards accounts for the similarities and differences between Old and New Testament. In a context that increasingly sought to separate the literal sense of a text from any other sense, as I noted in chapter 1, Edwards's concern is to defend the notion that the spiritual sense of the biblical text is rooted in the literal one, and he does this by seeking to demonstrate the coherence and unity of the Old Testament in this Spirit-given sense. In his "Blank Bible" Edwards comments in similar vein on the opening verses of the "Sermon on the Mount": "By these verses it is evident that the religion, and virtues, and duties that Christ taught were the same that was taught in the Old Testament; and the spirit of the gospel, and temper of the Christian church, is the same with the spirit that God's church was of under the old testament, for most of these beatitudes are taken from the Old Testament."[88] He continues by arguing that in Matthew 5:1–11 Christ's design was to correct the "corrupt notions [of] the

---

87. "Miscellanies," no. 1030, *WJE* 20:367–69. Emphasis added.

88. Matt 5:1–11, "Blank Bible," *WJE* 24:831. Commenting in his "Blank Bible" on Matt 5:6ff. ["Blessed are they which do hunger and thirst after righteousness: for they shall be filled"] Edwards illustrates this by quoting a litany of Old Testament prophecies, among them: Zech 9:15, Isa 55:2; and Ps 132:15. Given the nature of the text, dating the 5,000 entries in the "Blank Bible" is notoriously difficult. Nevertheless, following this entry a separate paragraph refers to "Fulfillment of Prophecies of the Messiah [ca. 1744]."

"Doctrine and Precept"

Jews," whose expectations of the Messiah's kingdom concerned a "worldly manifestation" rather than its spiritual character.[89] This worldly expectation is, on Edwards's line of thinking, evidence of the absence of the Spirit's enlightening of the Jews.

I argued in chapter 1 that Edwards devotes the first part of his "Harmony" to interpreting Old Testament prophecies, arguing that they cohere when their literal sense is taken to concern the spiritual (not the literalistic) character of things of the Messiah. He follows the same approach when considering types, as I argued in chapter 2. Transforming the typology he inherited, Edwards does not deny the historical reality of types, but sees them as images divinely designed to communicate a spiritual substance that is in some sense "more real" than the historical types themselves. Now in the third part of his "Harmony" Edwards illustrates the spiritual character of the life of the saint in each dispensation.

The significant influence of the Sermon on the Mount on this portion of Edwards's "Harmony" also reflects one of Edwards's chief concerns. Of abiding interest to the witness of Northampton's revivals were the authenticating marks of true religion.[90] To Edwards, these authenticating marks of a genuine work of the Spirit are plainly expressed in Christ's sermon which describes the character and behavior of members of his kingdom. I noted above that four of the six precepts Edwards cites in the "Harmony" are drawn from Matthew 5–7, while one is from Romans 12. Edwards's choice of texts brings to mind a passage in *Religious Affections*, written two years earlier in 1746. There Edwards concludes his analysis of "true religion" in *Religious Affections* with the twelfth sign: that "gracious and holy affections have their exercise and fruit in Christian practice."[91] "But there may be great positive appearances of holiness in men's visible behaviour: their life may appear to be a life of the service of God: they may appear to follow the examples of Jesus Christ, and come up in a great measure to those excellent rules in the 5th, 6th, and 7th chapters of Matthew, and

---

89. Matt 5:1–11, "Blank Bible," *WJE* 24:831–33.

90. In addition to *Distinguishing Marks of the Work of the Spirit of God*, *WJE* 4:215–88 and *Religious Affections*, *WJE* 2, see also Edwards's notebook, "Signs of Godliness," *WJE* 21:471–510, composed ca. 1728–40s. Minkema, "Great Work," 61, observes the "sign" character of the second part of the manuscript, but overlooks it in this first part.

91. *Religious Affections*, *WJE* 2:383. For an analysis of the work as well as its historical background, see Smith, "Editor's Introduction," *WJE* 2:1–83; Marsden, *Jonathan Edwards*, 268–90; Holmes, "*Religious Affections* by Jonathan Edwards (1703–58)," 285–97.

12th of Romans, and many other parts of the New Testament."[92] Although to Edwards no outward sign ultimately offers infallible evidence of grace, nevertheless Christian practice is "the most proper evidence of... gracious sincerity," both to oneself and to others.[93] Similarly, according to Edwards, "If you feel Christ's Sermon upon the Mount engraven on the fleshly tables of your hearts, you are truly sanctified."[94] In short, the "Sermon on the Mount" declares the essence of all the precepts of the Old Testament. It is the summation of true religion and as such it is a natural departure point for Edwards to demonstrate the harmony of the Old and New Testaments in precept.

Returning to the first part of the notebook, another characteristic of Edwards's presentation of both doctrine and precept is his frequent habit of quoting from the books of Psalms and Proverbs. Indeed quotations from either book or both appear in support of each of the nine subsections listed above, sometimes several under one heading. Of the seventeen references listed under "Love To Enemies, Forgiving Injuries, Doing Good For Evil Etc." no less than seven are from Proverbs. Stephen Stein explains Edwards's fascination with the Bible's Wisdom literature in terms of the way it challenged his religious imagination and provided "certain striking parallels to his own life experience."[95] In my discussion of Edwards's typology in chapter 2 I contested Stein's depiction of Edwards's "flights of exegetical fancy," the exercise of an unrestrained imagination. However, Stein is right to note that the book of Psalms resonated with Edwards's own experience, insofar as Edwards believed the Psalter, the hymnbook of the ancient church, expressed the spiritual experience of the saints in every age. To Edwards the Psalms were either prophetic of Christ, or were the words of Christ or Christ mystical. In his notebook on the "Prophecies of the Messiah," considered in chapter 1, Edwards comments, "In the book of Psalms in general, the Psalmist speaks either in the name of Christ, or in the name of the church.... and even in some of those psalms that seem to be the most direct and plain prophecies of Christ, some parts... are most

---

92. *Religious Affections*, WJE 2:418–19.

93. Ibid., 443.

94. "The Way of Holiness," WJE 10:473. Edwards makes this assertion while claiming that holiness is a conformity to God's law and commands, noting, "By God's law I mean all his precepts and commands, especially as they are delivered to us in the gospel, which is the fulfillment of the law of God."

95. "Blank Bible," WJE 24:33. Edwards's notes on the Wisdom literature comprise the largest of all sections in his "Blank Bible": 1,142 entries compared with the second largest body of entries: 915 entries for the Epistles.

"Doctrine and Precept"

applicable to the head or Christ, some parts ... are most applicable to the body or the church."[96]

In summary, the first part of Edwards's notebook presents the familiar Reformed distinction between doctrine and precept. And in treating these Edwards assumes the further distinction between outward form and inner substance.

At this point in the manuscript it looks as if Edwards begins the project again. The second (and longer) part of the notebook appears to mark a change of approach on the part of Edwards as he abandons the thematic approach outlined above for a canonical one. In the second part of the notebook Edwards proceeds canonically through the Old Testament Scriptures, sometimes quoting a text in full, more often simply citing a reference.[97] Next to each is a summary of the doctrine, precept or rule that he sees there, occasionally with cross-references to other Scriptures or to his other notebooks. For example, on Genesis 2:24 Edwards comments, "Against divorces." He assumes New Testament doctrine, but does not reference it. Christ's mention of Genesis 2:24 in Matthew 19:4–6 and Mark 10:5–9 are not noted, nor is the Apostle Paul's use of the verse in 1 Corinthians 6:16 or Ephesians 5:31–32, though the marriage of Christ and his bride is one Edwards frequently refers to elsewhere.[98] The notebook stands as an expression of Edwards's belief that just as the Old and New Testaments are united in their revelation of the covenant of grace, so they are both full of examples of believers who lived in response to that revelation.

A change in structure does not necessarily indicate a change in methodology. Indeed Edwards's change from a thematic structure to a canonical one in this notebook may only represent a return to the broadly

---

96. "Miscellanies," no. 1067, § 60, Yale transcript, 53. Similarly, to Edwards the book of Proverbs presents Christ, the Wisdom of God and rule for the believer's life of faith. "Blank Bible," *WJE* 24:33–34. Elsewhere Edwards notes the necessity that the church should have "such books of moral instructions relating to the affairs and state of mankind, and the concerns of human life, containing rules of true wisdom and prudence for our comfort in all circumstances, as we have in Proverbs and Ecclesiastes." "Work of Redemption," *WJE* 9:288.

97. The notebook covers only the books of Genesis to Psalms. If there was another notebook that continued Edwards's observations to the end of the Old Testament it no longer exists.

98. For example, "Images," nos. 5, 9, 12, 56, *WJE* 11:52, 53–54, 67; "Notes on Scripture," no. 232, *WJE* 15:181–82; Eph 5:30–32; 32–33, "Blank Bible," *WJE* 24:1104; "Apocalyptic Writings," *WJE* 5:131–32, 343ff. The theme is common to Edwards's sermons. Amongst many possible examples, see: *WJE* 10:155; *WJE* 14:143, 288–90, 533; *WJE* 19:566; *WJE* 22:227.

canonical structure he employs in "Types of the Messiah," within which his trinity of the Messiah's person, redemption and kingdom fits, as I noted in chapter 2. Of more significance, however, is that Edwards entitles this second section of the present notebook, "Particular Texts In The Old Testament, Which Harmonize With Ye Doctrines, Precepts, Etc., Of The New." Kenneth Minkema comments, "Thus this biblical exercise becomes for Edwards a means of illustrating the central features of his theology, particularly his interest in Christian behavior as the primary 'mark' or 'sign' of true sainthood."[99] However, as I have argued above Minkema's observation applies equally to the first part of Edwards's "doctrine and precept" notebook. Furthermore, Minkema arguably misses a crucial point. He identifies as the change of approach merely the switch from a thematic to a canonical structure, but the title Edwards chooses for this "second attempt" appears to suggest a far more profound *methodological* change. Hitherto in his treatment of prophecies and types Edwards has sought to establish the distinct witness of the Old Testament before comparing it with the New Testament in a demonstration of harmony, thus defending the integrity of the Christian Bible. Now Edwards appears to abandon that approach and instead looks in the Old Testament for examples—texts, narratives, prophecies, etc.—that harmonize with his New Testament referents. It seems unlikely that in the final third of his Harmony, someone as fastidious as Edwards would abruptly abandon without good reason the approach that he has employed thus far so religiously. It may well be, of course, that the difference in Edwards's approach is really no difference at all and that it can best be accounted for in remembering that this notebook is just that: a notebook. As such its contents should be viewed to a degree as provisional. Certainly, of all Edwards's surviving notes for the "Harmony," the final third is the least developed, showing greatest evidence of being a work in progress. That said, the problem remains of the title Edwards has chosen for this part of his "Harmony," with its implication of a new methodology.

At times in this third part of his "Harmony" Edwards appears to follow the same approach as he has when treating "prophecies" and "types." He confines himself to the Old Testament text, refusing to offer a New Testament referent and instead simply comments on the passage in question. So, against Ruth 2 he writes, "Ruth, though a Gentile and a Moabitess, when converted was without difficulty received among God's people, to all intents."[100] On almost as many occasions however, Edwards begins his

---

99. Minkema, "Great Work," 61.
100. Ruth 2, "Harmony of Doctrines and Rules," Yale transcript, 103.

comment with a New Testament citation or quotation, as in his notes on Genesis 22:1–12, Abraham's offering of Isaac; here he simply quotes Matthew 10:37 ["He that loveth son or daughter more than me is not worthy of me"] and Luke 14:26 ["If any man come unto me, and hate not . . . his children . . ."].[101] The frequency of explicit citation and quotation of New Testament texts marks this third part of the "Harmony" as methodologically distinct from the previous two parts. Whether or not Edwards cites a New Testament referent, the Old Testament text is playing the same role: that of illustrating the doctrine or precept in Edwards's mind—in the case of Ruth 2, presumably the inclusion of the Gentiles into the people of God in the New Testament. In short Edwards *does* appear to follow a new approach when considering the harmony in doctrine and precept.

Perhaps this "new approach" may be explained by reference again to Edwards's letter to the trustees at the college in New Jersey. Edwards describes the harmony in doctrine and precept as the "third and great part" of the "Harmony." Given the amount of material Edwards amassed for the previous two parts, his description suggests that this third part would have been lengthy indeed had it been completed. And it is possible that, important though they were, Edwards conceived of the previous two sections as in some sense preparatory to this, the climax of the "Harmony." The harmony in doctrine and precept presupposes the discrete witness of the Old Testament that Edwards has argued for in the previous two sections of his "Harmony." Having established that the Old Testament is coherent as a witness to the coming Messiah, his redemption and kingdom, Edwards is now free to explore the implications of this for the faith and practice of the Old Testament saints by explicit comparison with the New Testament.

Conclusion

In this chapter I have argued that the way Edwards relates Old and New Testaments lies within his governing theological categories of redemption history and covenant relationship. Edwards grounds this third aspect his "Harmony" in the results delivered in the first two parts (concerning prophecies and types). His confidence in both prophecies and in types to present the Messiah, his redemption and kingdom to the saints of the Old Testament yields a more detailed harmony in doctrine and precept than his teachers had granted. Ultimately, Edwards stresses the substantial continuity of the covenant of grace over against its administrative differences.

101. Gen 12:3, "Harmony of Doctrines and Rules," Yale transcript, 12.

4

Case Study

A Harmony in Soteriology

Introduction

THE PREVIOUS THREE CHAPTERS of this work have explored the forms of Testamental harmony that Jonathan Edwards outlined in his letter to the trustees of the college at New Jersey: prophecy and fulfillment; types; doctrine and precept. The present chapter functions as a case-study of that harmony by looking at Edwards's soteriology.

Many of the debates surrounding Edwards's soteriology are beyond the scope of this chapter. My limited concern here is with Edwards's understanding of the salvation of the Old Testament saints. In order to provide a framework for this study, the present chapter will seek to engage with the thesis of dispositional soteriology advanced by Anri Morimoto, a thesis that has established itself as foundational to much of the subsequent scholarship on Edwards's soteriology.[1] In his work Morimoto built on that of his

---

1. Morimoto, *Catholic Vision*. His basic thesis appears also in his "Salvation as Fulfillment of Being," 13–23. In *Edwards Confronts the Gods*, McDermott builds on Morimoto's conclusions, arguing that in addition to a dispositional soteriology Edwards employs both the *prisca theologia* and the pedagogical role of types in heathen religions to open the possibility of the salvation of non-Christians. McDermott's thesis is also summarized in: "Possibility of Reconciliation," 173–202; "Edwards, Newman and non-Christian Religions," 127–37. McDermott, "Jonathan Edwards on Justification by Faith," 92–111, qualifies Morimoto's conclusions regarding created grace yet presents Edwards as a rallying point for ecumenism and one whose mature views on justification pre-empted N. T. Wright's "New Perspective" theology. Studebaker, "Pneumatological Concept of Grace," 324–39, claims that the absence of Christological

doctoral supervisor, Sang Hyun Lee, applying the latter's thesis of dispositional ontology to Edwards's doctrine of salvation.[2] Lee sees in Edwards a revolutionary move away from a metaphysic of substance and accidents, to one of habit and dispositions. He portrays Edwards's theology as one that conceives of the divine essence as dispositional and the created world as the dynamic expression of God's continual self-enlargement. In accepting Lee's thesis Morimoto understands Edwards's salvation to be part of God's process of emanation. In effect, salvation involves a *theosis*. Morimoto argues that God communicates himself to human beings, creating in them a mediating platform of activity, "the new disposition." In an Edwardsean soteriology directed towards *theosis* possession of this new habit is salvific. There is no ultimate need for the disposition to be actualized or realized (through conversion) as it would be if it encountered the right conditions, namely hearing the gospel. Mere possession of this "virtual reality" is the necessary and sufficient ground for salvation. Morimoto sees significance in Edwards's comment in "Miscellanies," no. 27b that "the disposition is all that can be absolutely necessary. 'Tis the disposition and principle is the thing God looks at. . . . Supposing a man dies suddenly and not in the actual exercise of faith, 'tis his disposition that saves him."[3] He looks too to "Miscellanies," no. 303, in which Edwards claims that "a person according to the gospel may be in a state of salvation, before a distinct and express act of faith in the sufficiency and suitableness of Christ as Savior. Persons are justified upon the first appearance of a principle of faith in the soul by any of the soul's acts."[4] The significance of these extracts for the present enquiry is the conclusion Morimoto draws. Morimoto argues that Edwards's dispositional soteriology offers "a definitive answer to the age-long question of the salvation of the Old Testament faithful."[5] The Old Testament

---

specificity in Edwards's soteriology encourages belief that the Spirit can be communicated without the need to hear the message of Christ. For a discussion of dispositional soteriology set within a critique of modern evangelical responses to the salvation of the unevangelized, see Strange, *Possibility of Salvation*, Appendix 1, 313–16.

2. Lee, *Philosophical Theology, passim*. Lee does not accept his former student's account entirely. He notes that the Holy Spirit does not "turn into" a disposition of the regenerate person, but neither does he produce an intermediary principle logically distinguishable from the Holy Spirit himself. Rather the indwelling Spirit acts directly but in accordance with an abiding law that he acts after the manner of a human principle of action. Lee, "Grace and Justification by Faith Alone," 130–46; "Editor's Introduction," *WJE* 21:1–106 (esp. 46–86). See also below, n. 31.

3. "Miscellanies," no. 27b, *WJE* 13:213–15 (214). Morimoto, *Catholic Vision*, 63–64.

4. "Miscellanies," no. 393, *WJE* 13:455–59 (458). Morimoto, *Catholic Vision*, 62.

5. Morimoto, *Catholic Vision*, 63–64.

elect were given the saving disposition, but their temporal situation meant that it was not "realized" in conscious faith in Christ.

This chapter is not intended as a systematic response to either Lee's dispositional ontology or Morimoto's dispositional soteriology, though at times it will challenge their accounts.[6] I will first argue that Morimoto has misunderstood what Edwards means by the term, "the new disposition," and will suggest that the term refers to the immediate active presence of the indwelling Holy Spirit. In the rest of the chapter I will demonstrate how this understanding of the "new disposition" is both fundamental to the harmony in soteriology that Edwards sees between the Old and New Testaments, and is more in line with Edwards's theological tradition than in Morimoto's account. At the same time, by bringing together the three aspects of biblical harmony that I have considered in this work—namely, prophecy, types, and doctrine and precept—I will suggest that Edwards exceeds the bounds of his tradition in the content of faith he permits the Old Testament saints.

THE NEW DISPOSITION

Even a brief reading of Edwards is sufficient to show that Morimoto is right to identify the notion of the "new disposition" as central to Edwards's soteriology; the phrase punctuates his discussion of conversion and his analysis of religious experience. But as I will argue below, although Morimoto is also right to trace the notion of "disposition" in Edwards's thought back to his conception of God, he errs in adopting Lee's dispositional ontology as an adequate account of God's being.

Edwards offers an *a priori* account of the Trinity that is Augustinian in shape.[7] He explains the begetting of the Son in terms of God's self-regard: "God perpetually and eternally has a most perfect idea of himself." This idea, being perfect, is substantial and is exactly like him in every respect.[8] The procession of the Holy Spirit occurs upon this divine act of self-reflection:

---

6. Although a lengthy rebuttal to Lee has not yet appeared, his thesis is not universally accepted. See above, ch. 2, n. 54. See also Bombaro, "Vision of Salvation," 45–67.

7. Thomas Schafer, in a footnote to "Miscellanies," no. 94, *WJE* 13:256, n. 1, suggests that Edwards's source for his Augustinian analogy may have been a similar passage in Mather, *Blessed Union*, 46–48.

8. The concern that Edwards's explanation delivers too much, namely a second *theos*, is noted in Helm's editorial introduction to Edwards's *Treatise on Grace*, 20–21 (following B. B. Warfield's discussion of "The Biblical Doctrine of the Trinity," in

[T]here proceeds a most pure act, and an infinitely holy and sweet energy arises between the Father and the Son: for their love and joy is mutual, in mutually loving and delighting in each other.... This is the eternal and most perfect and essential act of the divine nature, wherein the Godhead acts to an infinite degree and in the most perfect manner possible. The Deity becomes all act ... So that the Godhead therein stands forth in yet another manner of subsistence, and there proceeds the third person in the Trinity, the Holy Spirit, viz. the Deity in act: for there is no other act but the act of the will.[9]

Similarly, in his earliest account of the Trinity, written seven years earlier in ca. 1723, Edwards notes, "The Holy Spirit is the act of God between the Father and the Son, infinitely loving and delighting in each other." This act of mutual rejoicing by the Father and Son "is distinct from each of the other two, and yet it is God; for the pure and perfect act of God is God, because God is a pure act. It appears that this is God, because that which acts perfectly is all act, and nothing but act."[10] Rather than introduce the concept of dispositional ontology, Edwards appears to hold firmly to *actus purus* as an account of God's being.[11] This is underlined by Edwards's observations on the Holy Spirit in his "Discourse on the Trinity." To Edwards the very title of the third Person "naturally expresses the divine nature as subsisting in pure act and perfect energy, and as flowing out and breathing forth in infinitely sweet and vigorous affection."[12] The reason for this is twofold. First, it is confirmed by his being called the Spirit, since the word "spirit" in Scripture when used concerning minds "when it is not put [for] the spiritual substance or mind itself, is put for the disposition, inclination or temper of the mind.... So I suppose when we read of the Spirit of God, who we are told is a spirit, it is to be understood of the disposition,

---

Warfield, *Biblical Doctrines*, 137–38). Crisp, "Jonathan Edwards's God," 90, goes further, noting that if God's infinite delight in his perfect idea of himself is another divine person then since there are no unrealized possibilities in the divine mind the problem is not simply the existence of two *theoi*, but of infinitely-begetting *theoi*.

9. "Discourse on the Trinity," WJE 21:121. See also Edwards's discussion of the immanent relations in his sermon, "Heaven is a World of Love," *Charity and Its Fruits*, WJE 8:125–397 (373–74).

10. "Miscellanies," no. 94, WJE 13:260.

11. For a critique of Lee's dispositional ontology and further discussion of Edwards's commitment to *actus purus*, see Holmes, "Dispositional Ontology?" *passim*; Crisp, "Jonathan Edwards on Divine Simplicity," *passim*.

12. "Discourse on the Trinity," WJE 21:122.

temper or affection of the divine mind."[13] Second, it is confirmed by his being called "holy." According to Edwards, while both Father and Son are infinitely holy, it is the Spirit who is denominated "Holy" because "it is in the temper or disposition of a mind and its exercise that holiness is immediately seated."[14] God's holiness consists in his infinite love of himself and delight in the excellence of his nature. In short, Edwards is unequivocal that God is a pure act realized in the love for himself that is the Holy Spirit.

This has important implications both for understanding God's purpose in creation and his relationship to it, implications that Edwards expounds in his *Dissertation Concerning the End for Which God Created the World*.[15] If God is *actus purus* then there is no unrealized potentiality in God, as there is according to Lee's dispositional account of the divine nature. Consequently, creation is not another manifestation of the divine disposition to self-enlargement that Lee argues it is. Rather God's being is one of eternal self-regard and self-love. Edwards explains God's creation *ad extra* in terms of divine glory. As a Being of infinite perfection it is fitting and morally right that God should be infinitely regarded and loved by himself and others.[16] To this end central to Edwards's project is his concern in *End of Creation* that God's perfections include "a propensity of nature to diffuse of his own fullness" and that it is not "possible for [God] to be hindered in the exercise of his goodness and his other perfections in their proper effect."[17] God "must" create in order to display his glory, which he defines as "the emanation and true external expression of God's internal glory and fullness."[18] God's fullness consists in his understand-

---

13. Ibid.

14. Ibid., 123.

15. This is the first of the "Two Dissertations," the other being *The Nature of True Virtue*. They were first published posthumously in 1765 and now appear in *WJE* 8.

16. Paul Ramsey, *WJE* 8:433, n.5, notes Edwards's use of "communication" and "emanation" and raises the question of which term governs the other. If "communication" governs "emanation," then the dissertation is more biblical—communication expressing an action, disposition or will in God. If "emanation" is the governing term, the result is a more Neoplatonic conception of procession of or from God. It seems likely that Edwards intends the former. Throughout the dissertation he ties the notion of disposition to the perfection and infinite value of God who is worthy of infinite regard. He does not draw a link between disposition and an extension of God's being. The divine disposition is to a communication of good and his perfect happiness, not to an enlargement of the divine self.

17. *End of Creation*, *WJE* 8:447.

18. Ibid., 527. Furthermore, since God always does what is most fitting and best Edwards seems committed to the notion that it is *this* world that God must create. The

ing and his happiness—his self-knowledge and self-love—and so his glory consists in the communication of these to his creatures: "The fullness of the Godhead is the fullness of his understanding, consisting in his knowledge, and the fullness of his will, consisting in his virtue and happiness. And therefore the external glory of God consists in the communication of these ... God communicates himself to the understanding of the creature, in giving him the knowledge of his glory; and to the will of the creature, in giving him holiness consisting primarily in the love of God: and in giving the creature happiness, chiefly consisting in joy in God."[19] In creating it is therefore fitting to one infinite in perfections that he should create intelligent creatures capable of knowing and loving him—capable of sharing his disposition to self-regard and self-love ... and this in infinitely increasing measure.[20] Thus God's glory, in the communication of his fullness in creation, comprises both "the manifestation of his internal glory to created understandings" and "the creature's high esteem of God, love to God, and complacence and joy in God; and the proper exercises and expressions of these."[21] Edwards summarizes: "In the creature's knowing, esteeming, loving, rejoicing in, and praising God, the glory of God is both exhibited and acknowledged; his fullness is received and returned. Here is both an *emanation* and *remanation*. The refulgence shines upon and into the creature, and is reflected back to the luminary ... So that the whole is *of* God, and *in* God and *to* God; and God is the beginning, middle and end in this affair."[22]

---

notion that God must create *this* world is beyond the scope of the present enquiry, but discussion may be found in Wainwright, "Necessity of Creation," 119–33.

19. *End of Creation*, WJE 8:528–29. Since intelligent creatures possess understanding and will, the perception of God's glory involves the response of the affections.

20. Edwards expounds this theme of the saints' eternally increasing love of God and each other in his sermon, "Heaven is a World of Love," *Charity and Its Fruits*, WJE 8:366–97. While heaven is a world of love, Edwards warns his congregation that "hell is a world of hatred." Between the two is the present intermediate world, "a world where good and bad, love and hatred are mixed together; a sure sign that the world is not to continue." WJE 8:390. That Edwards planned to structure his unwritten "A History of the Work of Redemption" in an identical triple-decker way only further underlines that the divine disposition to self-knowledge and love was paradigmatic for Edwards's entire thought. On God's creation of "intelligent creatures capable of being ... the willing active subjects or means of God's glory," see "Miscellanies," no. 1218, WJE 23:153.

21. *End of Creation*, WJE 8:527.

22. Ibid., 531. Emphasis original.

God's activity *ad extra* is agreeable to the "twofold subsistences which proceed from him *ad intra*, which is the Son and the Holy Spirit."[23] Once again, however, it is important to note that it is not God's being that is "extended" in creation, but his glory which is communicated. God's activity *ad extra* is not an *extension* of the divine life *ad intra*, the further expression of a divine disposition to self-enlargement that Lee proposes, since Edwards is committed to an *actus purus* account of God's being, as I have argued above. Rather God's activity *ad extra* is the ultimate example of Edwards's notion of harmony in the things of God: the *ad extra* activity is "fitting" to the divine life *ad intra*.

What are the implications of all this for understanding the new disposition? The answer to this lies in what happens then when the Holy Spirit is infused. According to Morimoto's thesis the Edwardsean account of salvation involves a participation in God's own nature by humanity, a *theosis*, implying an ontological change in which saints are not just *counted* righteous, but are *made* righteous.[24] As evidence of this Morimoto cites Edwards's comment that "grace in the soul is as much from Christ, as light in a glass, held out in the sunbeams, is from the sun." Crucial for Morimoto's account is Edwards's qualification that the analogy fails because the glass "remains as it was, the nature of it not being at all changed, it is as much without any lightsomeness in its nature as ever." Instead, to Edwards the light of the Sun of Righteousness is so communicated to the saints that they shine also "and become little images of that Sun."[25] According to Morimoto, the saints' luminosity is evidence of their possessing a created gracious principle, the new disposition, distinct from the infused uncreated grace, the Holy Spirit. Morimoto argues that, following Thomas Aquinas, Edwards contends that an unmediated exercise of the Holy Spirit in the human heart, such as Peter Lombard had urged, would destroy human spontaneity and responsibility.[26] Any act of charity would cease to

---

23. "Miscellanies," no. 1218, *WJE* 23:153. Similarly, "[The] twofold way of the Deity's flowing forth *ad extra* answers to the twofold way of the Deity's proceeding *ad intra* . . . and indeed is only a kind of second proceeding of the same persons, their going forth *ad extra*, as before they proceeded *ad intra*." "Miscellanies," no. 1082, *WJE* 20:466.

24. Morimoto, *Catholic Vision*, 5, 28–30, 150–56, 161. This claim is echoed by, for example, Chamberlain, "Editor's Introduction," *WJE* 18:39; Pauw, *Supreme Harmony*, 141–42.

25. *Religious Affections*, *WJE* 2:342–43, 200–201. Morimoto, *Catholic Vision*, 47. See my discussion of this image below.

26. Lombard, *Sentences*, 88–91, 94–100. In *Summa Theologica*, 3.2.2.23, Article 2, "Whether Charity is Something Created in the Soul," Aquinas argues, "If the will is

be a voluntary act. He suggests that, following Aquinas, Edwards believes that the infused Holy Spirit (*gratia increata*) produces an intermediary habit (*gratia creata*) through which he operates. It is this created grace that is the new disposition in the heart of the saint. Just as the Holy Spirit does not operate independently of this new disposition so, according to Morimoto, the new disposition depends continually on the Holy Spirit for its existence.[27] In this way Morimoto presents Edwards as mediating the (essentially Lombardian) "Protestant concern" for the continual divine influence on the human subject, with the (essentially Thomist) "Catholic concern" for the ontological reality of the new creation. Considered within a framework of dispositional ontology the new disposition does not need to be exercised in order to be ontologically real. It is a virtual reality, possession of which marks out an individual as saved, irrespective of whether that individual ever exercises faith.

In his "Treatise on Grace," however, Edwards explicitly counters those (like Morimoto) who deny the immediate work of the Holy Spirit in men's hearts: "Indeed there seems to be a strong disposition in men to disbelieve and oppose the doctrine of true disposition, to disbelieve and oppose the doctrine of immediate influence of the Spirit of God in the hearts of men, or to diminish and make it as small and remote a matter as possible, and put it as far out of sight as may be."[28] Examination of Edwards's "Blank Bible" demonstrates that Edwards does not hold a view of *gratia creata*. The principle of action in the heart of the regenerate person is nothing other than the Holy Spirit himself. In a note on Galatians 5:17 Edwards asserts that "grace in the heart is no other than the Spirit of God dwelling in the heart, and becoming a principle of life and action there, acting and exerting its nature in the exercise of man's faculties . . ."[29] The new disposition is the Spirit's manner of existing and acting within the human heart. Again in his "Blank Bible" Edwards's identification of the new

---

moved to love by the Holy Spirit, it must itself perform the act of love. . . . It is especially necessary for charity . . . that there should be in us some habitual form superadded to our natural power, inclining it to act with charity, and causing it to do so readily and joyfully." Edwards *may* have had access to Thomas' thought through the library of his grandfather, Solomon Stoddard, but his own "Catalogue" of reading makes no mention of Thomas. Furthermore, Peter Thuesen notes that when Edwards invokes Aquinas he does so disparagingly. Thuesen, "Editor's Introduction," *WJE* 26:63-64.

27. Morimoto, *Catholic Vision*, 60.

28. "Treatise on Grace," *WJE* 21:177.

29. Gal 5:17, "Blank Bible," *WJE* 24:1085-90 (1085). Bombaro, "Vision of Salvation," 53.

disposition with the Holy Spirit is clear in his discussion of flesh and Spirit in Galatians 5. The "spiritual principles" of love to God and relish of divine beauty have never been part of human nature *in se*, according to Edwards: "Man can be man without 'em." Even before Adam's Fall these "spiritual principles" did not flow from anything in man's nature, but from the Spirit of God dwelling in him and "exerting itself by man's faculties as a principle of action." When Adam fell the Holy Spirit left him "and so all his spiritual nature or spiritual principles [left him]; and then only the flesh was left, or merely the principles of human nature in its animal state."[30] From this it appears that in contrast to Morimoto's account, Edwards does not consider that the Spirit needs to create a mediating platform of activity to safeguard the integrity of the human act. He is unequivocal that the Spirit acts immediately in the hearts of men as a principle of life and action.

To Edwards the immediately active presence of the Holy Spirit is not inconsistent with talking about his creation or infusion of "spiritual principles," as the above excerpts from Edwards's "Blank Bible" show.[31] But these infused spiritual principles do not constitute Morimoto's conception of a mediating platform of the Spirit's work. For Edwards to talk of the

---

30. Gal 5:17, "Blank Bible," *WJE* 24:1085–86. On Edwards's distinction between "spiritual" or "moral" principles and "natural principles" in God and humanity see *Religious Affections*, *WJE* 2:256; *Original Sin*, *WJE* 3:380–83. Briefly, Edwards argues that God has two kind of attributes: "moral" attributes, which are summed up in his holiness; and "natural" attributes, of strength, knowledge, etc. In Adam, the spiritual principles of love to God governed the natural principles. At the Fall, the superior principles left mankind, abandoning him to self-love and enmity to God. Edwards employs this argument in *Original Sin*, *WJE* 3:380–88, to explain how God can permit sin without being its Author. Edwards sees a difference between the Spirit's indwelling of Adam before the Fall and his indwelling of the elect soul afterwards: the difference is found in his novel conception of Christ's purchase of the Spirit from the Father under the terms of the covenant of redemption. This is a move through which Edwards seeks to establish the equality of the divine Persons in the economy of redemption. The Spirit, purchased for the elect soul, belongs to him/her and cannot be taken away. "On the Equality of the Persons of the Trinity," *WJE* 21:146–47; "Treatise on Grace," *WJE* 21:189–91; "Miscellanies," no. 755, *WJE* 18:403–4. The implications of this for Edwards's position in terms of eternal justification will be explored below.

31. See also for example, *Religious Affections*, *WJE* 2:207: "[T]he Spirit of God in his spiritual influences on the hearts of his saints operates by infusing or exercising new divine and supernatural principles; principles which are indeed a new and supernatural nature"; "Treatise on Grace," *WJE* 21:176: "[T]his holy and divine principle . . . which does radically and summarily consist in divine love, comes into existence in the soul by the power of God in the influences of the Holy Spirit." Lee, "Grace and Justification," 130–36, argues that for this reason Edwards's position regarding the nature of grace is inconsistent.

immediacy of the Spirit's influence in the saint's actions is to refer to the absence of other formal causes of those gracious acts, not the absence of gracious principles. To Edwards the term, "principle of nature," whether natural or supernatural, refers to the abiding manner of an agent's activity, the foundation laid in the soul that governs a continued course of the subject's behavior.[32] So, "the Spirit of God, united to human faculties, acts very much after the manner of a natural principle or habit, so that one act makes way for another; and as it were settles the soul in a disposition to holy acts; but that it does so is by grace and covenant, and not from any natural necessity."[33] The existence of spiritual principles in no way subverts the immediacy of the indwelling Spirit. To Edwards the spiritual principles and habits of grace have no ontological reality distinct from the Holy Spirit and are only "abiding" insofar as they are expressions of the Spirit's activity, whose abiding is rooted in the covenant.[34]

The "created grace" account is not the only account offered of Edwardsean *theosis*, however. A second approach emphasizes Edwards's language of participation. In *End of Creation* Edwards strongly implies the saints' participation in the life of God. God communicates the fullness of himself to his creatures and is glorified as they know and love him. His acting for their sake is one with making himself his last end, so that the saints' knowledge and love of God is nothing less than a participation in God's own self-knowledge and self-love, "as much as 'tis possible for that to be, which is infinitely less in degree."[35] As God's self-communication continues eternally, so too the degree of union between the creature and God increases, approaching the "strictness and perfection of union" between the Father and Son. Likewise, Edwards comments in *Religious Affections* that the infusion of the Holy Spirit into the saint is unique as a work of God in that there is no other work in which "God does so much communicate himself" and in which the creature has "in so high a sense, a participation of God."[36] But what does "participation of God" mean to Edwards?

---

32. *Religious Affections*, WJE 2:206.

33. "Treatise on Grace," WJE 21:196.

34. Ibid., 192–97. See McClenahan's discussion of the nature of grace in the context of Edwards's confrontation with Arminian accounts of natural man's ability to produce gracious acts. McClenahan, "Justification," 281–93.

35. *End of Creation*, WJE 8:428-35, 436–44 (441–42).

36. *Religious Affections*, WJE 2:203.

Edwards is clear that participating in the divine nature does not mean a participation in the divine essence. He insists that the essential distinction between God and creature is preserved: "Not that the saints are made partakers of the essence of God, and so are 'Godded' with God, and 'Christed' with Christ, according to the abominable and blasphemous language and notions of some heretics; but to use the Scripture phrase, they are made partakers of God's fullness (Eph. 3:17–19; John 1:16), that is, of God's spiritual beauty and happiness." This partaking is effected by the Holy Spirit "communicating itself in *its own proper nature*."[37] Following an apparent objection to this very claim, Edwards clarifies for an unnamed correspondent what he means. After noting the imprecision of the term, "nature" he offers as a definition: "That property which is natural to anyone and is eminently his character, I think, is, without abuse of language or going cross to the common use of it, called his proper nature, though [it] is not just the same with his essence. Thus we say concerning an exceeding good-natured man, that ingenuity is his very nature."[38] According to Edwards, holiness is the proper nature of the Holy Spirit as "his peculiar beauty and glory," as brightness is the peculiar nature of the sun and sweetness the peculiar nature of honey. But second, holiness is the nature of the Spirit that he especially manifests and exercises economically. Thus by "nature" Edwards seems to have in mind a subject's disposition

---

37. Ibid. Emphasis added.

38. Letter no. 66, "To an Unknown Correspondent," [after 13 March 1745/6], *WJE* 16:199–203 (202). McClymond, "Salvation as Divinization," 139–55, notes the similarity in Edwards's distinction between "essence" and "nature" to that between "essence" and "divine energies" in the thought of Gregory Palamas (ca. 1296–1359). There is, however, no evidence that Edwards had read Palamas. More in the line of Edwards's theological heritage is Calvin's comment on 2 Pet 1:4: "The end of the gospel is to rend us eventually conformable to God, and, if we may so speak, to deify us. . . . But the word *nature* is not here essence but quality." Having noted those "fanatics" who, like the Manicheans before them, imagine that God "swallows up our nature," Calvin asserts that the Apostle is referring to the saints' divesting themselves of the corruptions of the flesh, those "vicious and depraved affections," so as to be "as it were one with God as far as our capacities will allow." Calvin, *Second Epistle of Peter*, 371–72. Here there is a striking similarity to Edwards's distinction between the self-love of the flesh ("natural principles") and the divine love ("supernatural principles"), in which the latter conforms the saint to the [spiritual] image of Christ. See also Calvin's comment in the *Institutes*, 3.25.10 that to partake of the divine nature is for God to share his glory, power and righteousness with the elect and give himself to be *enjoyed* by them, and "somehow make them to become one with himself."

Case Study

or the character of their activity, rather than ontological concepts of their being or essence.[39]

In my discussion above on his "Discourse on the Trinity" I noted that Edwards conceives of the Holy Spirit as the temper or disposition of the Godhead, being the mutual love of Father and Son. Thus concerning the Godhead a*d intra* there is no distinction between the Holy Spirit's essence and principle of nature. The Spirit "*is* divine love substantialized and personalized."[40] But it appears that *ad extra* Edwards does conceive of a distinction between essence and nature, such that the Spirit, operating in the saint after a principle of nature communicates to the saint his own proper nature, namely divine love or "holiness," but he does not communicate his essence: "[T]he Spirit of God in the souls of his saints exerts his own proper nature; that is to say, it communicates and exerts itself in the soul in those acts which are its proper, natural and essential acts in itself *ad intra*, or within the Deity from all eternity. The proper nature of the Spirit of God, the act which is its nature and wherein its being consists, is . . . divine love."[41] Again, in the letter to an unknown correspondent quoted above: "the saints are made partakers of [the Holy Spirit's] holiness, as the Scripture expressly declares (Heb. 12:10), and that without imparting to them his essence."[42] Thus despite his language of participation in *End of Creation* it appears to be Edwards's argument that *ad extra* God can communicate his nature to the creature in a mysterious way that does not blur the divine-creature distinction. "God thus 'exists' *ad extra* only in his communicated nature, not in an enlargement or extension of his essence," *contra* Lee's account outlined above.[43]

A final way of shedding light on Edwards's doctrine of *theosis* is, as Caldwell does, to consider the nature of the union between the Holy Spirit and the saint in terms of the subjectivity of action.[44] That is, given the Spirit's indwelling of the saint after the manner of a principle of nature, whose holy acts are they? Since the gracious actions arise immediately from the Spirit, perhaps they are properly to be understood as the Spirit's. But if

---

39. In this I follow Caldwell, *Communion*, 111ff.

40. Ibid., 112. Emphasis original.

41. "Miscellanies," no. 471, *WJE* 13:513.

42. Letter no. 66, "To an Unknown Correspondent" [after 13 March 1745/46], *WJE* 16:203.

43. Caldwell, *Communion*, 113. Nevertheless, it is true that for Edwards, God "must" create a world, the best of all possible worlds since God is essentially communicative.

44. Ibid., 111ff.

the saint acts according to a supernatural principle of nature in his soul, are those gracious acts not truly his? In answering this question both the "created grace" and "essential participation" accounts outlined above are further shown to be inadequate. First, Morimoto's "created grace" account appears promising. The Holy Spirit indwells the saint and he infuses into the saint a created grace; this infused grace safeguards the saint's "ownership" of the gracious acts. But Edwards argues that the saints are made partakers of God's holiness "not only as they partake of holiness that God gives, but [as they] partake of that holiness by which he himself is holy."[45] There is one holiness of both God and the saint. Second, an account of *theosis* that blurs the essential distinctiveness of God and his creation offers the solution that the saint's gracious acts are in fact God's gracious acts. But as noted above, this runs counter to Edwards's explicit denials that the saints are made partakers of the divine essence.

If neither the "created grace" nor "essential participation" accounts offer a satisfactory explanation of the nature of the Spirit's union with the saint, is there an alternative? The answer is that Edwards seems to express the relationship between the Holy Spirit's acts and the holy acts of the saint in "compatibilist" language.[46] At the moment when the Holy Spirit begins to indwell the saint, the Holy Spirit is communicated to the saint and is united to the soul in such a way that the Spirit's life and actions may truly be said to be those of the saint.[47] The saint's holiness is properly his own holiness, while also being the Spirit's. To return to Edwards's illustration of light shining through a glass, the saint becomes a luminous thing and shines with the light of the Sun of Righteousness, not because an abiding

---

[45]. "Treatise on Grace," *WJE* 21:195.

[46]. In this I follow Caldwell, *Communion*, 111ff. Danaher, *Trinitarian Ethics*, 46–47, explores the ethical implication of this notion of Edwards's compatibilism, noting that for Edwards participation occurs when our minds "repeat, rather than merely replicate or represent, the perfect idea of God." The saint shares "the divine idea and love that animates the divine mind."

[47]. Echoing his "Blank Bible" comments on flesh and Spirit in Galatians 5:17 (above), Edwards explicitly defines "the divine nature" in a footnote in *Original Sin*. He explains that "the divine nature" refers to those "superior principles" that comprise divine love, and in which the spiritual image of God consists and in which is man's righteousness and true holiness. These superior principles are "supernatural" in that they do not belong to or flow from man's nature "merely as a man." They stand in contrast to the "natural principles" in man, which are denominated "flesh" in Scripture. These "supernatural principles" "immediately depend on man's union and communion with God, or divine communications and influences of God's spirit" but they belong to the saint in such a way that they define an individual as "not only a man, but a truly virtuous, holy and spiritual man." *Original Sin, WJE* 3:381–82 (381, n. 5).

Case Study

Thomistic habit has been created within his soul as Morimoto contends, but because he is united to the Spirit in such a way that the Spirit's light becomes his also.[48] At the same time, however, Edwards maintains that the essential particularity of the saint and the Spirit are preserved. He does not know how the Spirit's union with the soul happens nor how the Spirit's nature may be communicated to the saint so that it may truly be said to be the saint's also.[49] Rejecting both the "created grace" account of the union

48. Edwards may have borrowed the illustration from Turretin, *Institutes*, 12.2.23: "As the sun sending its rays into a crystal or any other diaphanous body makes it lucent, so as to shine like the sun, thus the Father of lights irradiates us with his light ... and makes us shine like so many suns." However, Danaher, *Trinitarian Ethics*, 45, notes that there is in Turretin's thought a distinction between "formal and essential" communication by which one receives the "intrinsic being" of something, and a communication by "resemblance and analogy" by which one reflects the "effects and works" of another in one's own being. In this way participation in the divine nature, according to Turretin, *Institutes*, 3.6.5, is "not univocally (by a formal participation of the divine essence), but only analogically (by benefit of the regeneration which impresses upon them the marks of holiness and righteousness most properly belonging to God, since they are renewed after the image of their Creator ...)." Mastricht's position initially appears closer to that of Edwards when he affirms that in regeneration "a divine nature is communicated to the regenerate." Once again, however, the holiness communicated is only "similar in kind to the holiness of the Deity." Mastricht, *Treatise on Regeneration*, 16-17 (17). By contrast, while Edwards distinguishes between essence (which is not communicated) and nature (which is communicated), his divine communication is no mere communication by analogy, but a real, though mysterious, communication of God's own nature to the creature such that the saints "not only ... partake of [the] holiness that God gives, but partake of that holiness by which he himself is holy." "Treatise on Grace," *WJE* 21:195.

49. McClenahan, "Justification," 244, highlights the distinction Edwards makes between "relative," and "real" or "vital" union with Christ, in his funeral sermon for missionary, David Brainerd, "True Saints, when Absent from the Body, are Present with the Lord," *WJE* 25:225-56 (231). Relative union is perfected at the moment of the soul's closing with Christ, while real or vital union is the union of affections, begun in this world and perfected in the next. Real or vital union is begun with the first discovery of divine excellency at conversion, "whereby the saint becomes a living branch of the true vine, living by a communication of the sap and vital juice of the stock and root ... by a kind of participation of Christ's own life." But while the saints are in the body the vital union is imperfect, due to indwelling sin. Perfection of vital union occurs when the soul is "perfectly filled with [Christ's] Spirit and [is] living as it were only by Christ's life, without any remainder of spiritual death, or carnal life." See also Edwards's description of real union in, "True Grace Distinguished from the Experience of Devils," *WJE* 25:639. This concept of vital union seems to lie behind Edwards's definition of holiness in his sermon, "The Way of Holiness," *WJE* 10:468-80 (471-73), as being: "First ... a conformity of the heart and the life unto God. ... Second, it is a conformity to Jesus Christ. ... Third, holiness is a conformity to God's laws and commands. When all God's laws without exception are written in our hearts, then are we holy." Similarly,

and any notion of essential participation in God, Edwards seems content to establish the boundaries in such discussions and leave the precise details of the union a mystery.

CONSENT AND JUSTIFICATION

In the summer of 1733 Edwards preached a sermon to his Northampton congregation on Matthew 16:17 ["Blessed art thou, Simon Barjona: for flesh and blood hath not revealed it unto thee, but my Father which is in heaven."] The doctrine of the sermon reads: "There is such a thing as a spiritual and divine light, immediately imparted to the soul by God, of a different nature from any that is obtained by natural means."[50] In this sermon Edwards argued that there is a distinction between "notional" or "speculative knowledge," and "spiritual knowledge" or the "true sense" of things. Speculative knowledge is mere "rational judging" and its seat is in the head. Unregenerate man is incapable of anything more than this knowledge since he does not know the indwelling of the Holy Spirit.[51] On the other hand spiritual knowledge, arising from the divine and supernatural light, does not comprise the suggestion of new truths or doctrines to the mind, but is rather a true sense of the excellency of spiritual things. As the Holy Spirit is united to the human soul and indwells the saint as a vital principle, so he infuses a "new sense" by which the saint is enabled to see the excellency, beauty and fitness of the gospel. Since the will always follows what it perceives to be best, the regenerate cannot help but respond to the revelation with consent. Spiritual knowledge, therefore, differs from speculative knowledge in that its seat is in the "will, or inclination, or heart." Spiritual knowledge or the "true sense" of things is an exercise of the new disposition, being entirely and immediately dependent on the

---

it lies behind Edwards's contention that some saints "attain to much greater acquaintance and communion with God, and conformity to Him, than others." "God the Best Portion of the Christian," in Kistler, *Altogether Lovely*, 1–13 (5).

50. "A Divine and Supernatural Light," *WJE* 17:410.

51. See, for example, "A Spiritual Understanding of Things Denied to the Unregenerate," *WJE* 14:70–96. Nichols argues in his *Absolute Sort of Certainty*, 68 that the "new sense" doctrine refers to both the work of regeneration and illumination. However, McClenahan, "Justification," 288–300 demonstrates that the only reference to the "vital principle" in "Divine and Supernatural Light," *WJE* 17:405–26 is an explicit reference to the indwelling Holy Spirit, while the "new sense" refers to the new foundation of supernatural life in the soul and the renewed soul's exercise of the faculties.

indwelling Holy Spirit.[52] In an earlier sermon Edwards explores the Spirit's conviction in more detail:

> The Holy Ghost convinces of the suitableness and sufficiency of this way of salvation. The believing soul, when thus enlightened, sees a suitableness.... He sees now a fitness in this way of acceptance into God's favor; how it is adapted to the case of such sinners as he; how well the remedy is suited to the disease, and how sufficient it is for him.... When the soul is thus convinced of the reality, suitableness and glory of this way of acceptance by Christ, the heart and inclination entirely embraces it. The whole soul accords and consents to it . . . The heart that before opposed, now yields; it opposes no longer, but entirely closes with it and adheres to it with the inclination and affection.... There is a sweet harmony now between the soul and the gospel.[53]

The spiritual sense is not the suggestion of new truths. Nor is it merely an emotional response to the things of God. Rather, it is a new inclination towards those things.[54] Thus the Holy Spirit's role *ad intra* as divine love and consent between Father and Son is mirrored *ad extra* in the saint's consent to the things of God.

What is the place of justification in Edwards's soteriology? Morimoto claims that, aside from his 1734 lectures, Edwards rarely treated the doctrine of justification.[55] He argues that Edwards's "Controversies" note-

---

52. "Divine and Supernatural Light," *WJE* 17:414, 413.

53. "The Threefold Work of the Holy Ghost," *WJE* 14:407-9.

54. In his "Faith" notebook Edwards further explores the notion of consent. He observes that consent is threefold, respecting: 1. Christ, the author of salvation. 2. The benefit or the salvation itself. 3. The way or method of salvation. No. 121, "Faith," *WJE* 21:458.

55. Morimoto mentions in a brief footnote (*Catholic Vision*, 71, n. 2) Edwards's M.A. thesis on justification, "*Quæstio: Peccator Non Iustificatur Coram Deo Nisis Per Iustitiam Christi Fide Apprehensam*," ["*Quæstio*: A Sinner is not Justified in the Sight of God except through the Righteousness of Christ Obtained by Faith"] and comments, "[T]here are a few sermons that contain cursory references to the subject [justification] . . . But as far as a systematic treatment of justification is concerned, the celebrated series of lectures he delivered in 1734 is the only substantial piece of work devoted to the subject." Morimoto, *Catholic Vision*, 71-72. Edwards's two lectures in 1734 were expanded for publication in 1738 in a collection of other works: Edwards, *Discourses*. All are available in *WJE* 19. In his first published sermon (published in Boston in 1731), "God Glorified in Man's Dependence," *WJE* 17:196-216, Edwards offers a robust defense of justification by faith by tying it to the doctrine of the Trinity. All of man's goodness is of, through and in God, and it is faith alone that acknowledges this absolute dependence on God.

book, in which he sketched out a major treatise on justification, reveals a basic structure that is concerned with ontological transformation from a state of corruption to a state of salvation, "much like in Roman Catholic soteriology."[56] Thus in Morimoto's framework of dispositional ontology justification occupies a "middle step in the economy of salvation, between God's emanation and remanation."[57] Justification is the event in which God "crowns his own gift," the event in which he rewards the saint for the holiness and goodness which has previously been created in him by the infusion of the Holy Spirit. That is, to Morimoto, a person may be regenerate—there may be goodness and virtue present in them—even before their union with Christ. When the correct conditions are present to activate the disposition, the consequent act of faith, by which the individual is united with Christ is a "rewardable" act. Its integrity as a human act is safeguarded by the fact that it has arisen from the new disposition, a created grace.

As I have argued, Edwards does not conceive of the new disposition as a Thomistic habit, but as the active presence of the indwelling Holy Spirit. The new disposition is not the seat of some potential faith, but is consent itself. So in an entry entitled, "Faith, Justifying" Edwards comments: "'Tis the same agreeing or consenting disposition that according to the divers objects, different state or manner of exerting, is called by different names. When 'tis exerted towards a Savior, [it is called] faith or trust . . . when towards persons excellent, love; when towards commands, obedience . . ."[58]

Edwards articulates the relationship between faith and justification most clearly in his 1738 discourse, *Justification by Faith Alone*.[59] Throughout the discourse Edwards makes clear that justification is not a reward of the righteous, but is a divine declaration pronounced upon the unrigh-

---

56. Morimoto, *Catholic Vision*, 73.

57. Ibid., 101.

58. "Miscellanies," no. 218, *WJE* 13:344–45.

59. McClenahan argues that the discourse has frequently been misunderstood in the secondary literature because its Arminian target has been wrongly identified. He argues that the work was intended as a response to the English Arminianism propounded by, among others, Archbishop John Tillotson and propagated in New England through his printed sermons. See particularly his discussion of Edwards's deliberate choice of language to articulate the role of faith, given the polemical context of the work. McClenahan, "Justification," 148–202. For a selection of the secondary literature, see also, Cherry, *Theology of Jonathan Edwards*, 90–107; Gerstner, *Rational Biblical Theology*, 3.191–223; Holmes, *God of Grace*, 142–59; Lee, "Grace and Justification," 130–46; Logan, "Doctrine of Justification," 26–42; Morimoto, *Catholic Vision*, 71–130; Schafer, "Justification by Faith," 55–67; Waddington, "Doctrine of Justification," 357–72.

teous.⁶⁰ On what basis then does God pronounce the sinner righteous? According to Edwards, God justifies "purely from the relation faith has to the person in whom this benefit is to be had, or as it is united to that Mediator, in and by whom we are justified."⁶¹ Faith is the instrumental cause, not the formal cause, of a sinner's justification.⁶² Furthermore, Edwards is all too aware of the threat of neonomianism—the belief that an individual's repentance and faith represent obedience to a new law that God has established and therefore constitute their saving righteousness.⁶³ He is at pains to establish that faith does not merit justification but is the very receiving of it. There is in God's sight not a *"moral* fitness" in faith that renders it meritorious, but a *"natural* fitness" between faith, union with Christ and justification such that the three are co-ordinate.⁶⁴ "Faith is the soul's active uniting with Christ, or is itself the very act of unition."⁶⁵ And justification is the sinner's receiving of the title to eternal life through

---

60. The *Westminster Confession*, 11.1, of which Edwards expressed approval, is explicit: "Those whom God effectually calleth He also freely justifieth; not by infusing righteousness into them, but by pardoning their sins. . . . not by imputing faith itself . . . as their righteousness; but by imputing the obedience and satisfaction of Christ unto them, they receiving and resting on Him and His righteousness by faith . . ."

61. *Justification by Faith Alone*, WJE 19:152–55.

62. Edwards thus follows a tradition expressed in, among others, the *Westminster Confession*, 11.2; Owen, *Justification by Faith*, 147; Turretin, *Institutes*, 16.7.1–23; and in New England in Mather, *Everlasting Gospel*, 23.

63. Neonomianism is often associated with the English Nonconformist, Richard Baxter (1615–91), though it was adopted by later Presbyterians and Congregationalists in both England and America. Edwards argues that faith cannot be considered to be the condition of receiving the covenant blessings because "it is the receiving itself." Edwards concludes one of his earliest observations on faith's relationship to the covenant of grace: "This making faith a condition of life fills the mind with innumerable difficulties about faith and works and how to distinguish them, tends to make us apt to depend on our own righteousness, tends to lead men into neonomianism, and gives principal force to their arguments." "Miscellanies," no. 2 [May–June, 1723], *WJE* 13:197-99. See also Edwards's Master's *Quæstio* of 1723 in which he explicitly identifies his opponents as "neonomians," *WJE* 14:55–66 (63).

64. Man's faith cannot be morally fit, according to Edwards, because: (i) an individual's own disobedience to the moral law of God is infinitely evil; (ii) the "divine constitution or law" established by God means that mankind already stands under God's judgment owing to Adam's breaking of the covenant of works. *Justification by Faith Alone*, *WJE* 19:159–65. On the origins and development of this distinction in Edwards's thought, see McClenahan, "Justification," 197–201, 205–13.

65. *Justification by Faith Alone*, *WJE* 19:158. See also Edwards's discussion regarding faith as a condition of the covenant of grace, in "Miscellanies," nos. 2, 30, 35, *WJE* 13:197–99, 217 and 219 respectively.

sharing in Christ's justification by this union with him.⁶⁶ "[W]hat is real in the union between Christ and his people, is the foundation of what is legal; that is, it is something really in them, and between them, uniting them, that is the ground of the suitableness of their being accounted as one by the Judge. . . . And thus it is that faith justifies, or gives an interest in Christ's satisfaction and merits, and a right to the benefits procured thereby, viz. as it thus make Christ and the believer one in the acceptance of the Supreme Judge."⁶⁷

Bombaro argues that Morimoto neglects the role of the Holy Spirit in this act and whether Edwards's framework is a "temporal or eternal recognition of ontological unition."⁶⁸ Edwards's concern is with the *pactum salutis* according to Bombaro. The "ontological basis of forensic imputation . . . concerns the Spirit in an eternal arrangement."⁶⁹ This covenant of redemption is the eternal arrangement under which Christ's righteousness is imputed to the elect since they are looked on as one with him. Therefore, according to Bombaro, the mutual "consent" by which God the Father accounts anyone united to His Son, is none other than the Holy Spirit in the *pactum salutis*.⁷⁰ McClenahan notes that Edwards's concern in the 1738 discourse is more limited than Bombaro supposes. Rather than intending to frame a statement about the nature of the union, Edwards is simply asserting in his argument against the Arminian Archbishop Tillotson that

---

66. Edwards maintained the Reformed distinction between Christ's active and passive obedience in the *historia salutis* and his imputation to those in him of his negative and positive righteousness. Among many possible examples see Edwards note on Rom 8:1–4, "Blank Bible," *WJE* 24:1008–12. Waddington argues that Edwards shares Calvin's *duplex gratia*—the two graces of justification and sanctification received together from union with Christ—in contrast to the Reformed Orthodoxy of, for example, Peter van Mastricht who saw them as consecutive in the *ordo salutis*. Waddington, "Doctrine of Justification," 360–68; Calvin, *Institutes*, 3.1.1; Mastricht, *Treatise on Regeneration*, 16–17.

67. *Justification by Faith Alone*, *WJE* 19:158.

68. Bombaro, "Vision of Salvation," 62.

69. Ibid.

70. Ibid., 62ff. Kevin Woongsan Kang similarly argues that Edwards's commitment to the "union with Christ" paradigm is rooted in his desire to understand how the believer's justification is secured in the *pactum salutis* and the *historia salutis*; Edwards is less concerned to elucidate the logical, causal or temporal order of the application of the graces of Christ in the *ordo salutis*. Kang, "Justified by Faith in Christ," *passim*. Under the covenant of redemption the Holy Spirit assumes the role of the Gift purchased for the elect and in this sense, as Bombaro notes, the divine recognition of the soul's consent with Christ is eternal.

on man's part faith is necessary for the establishment of this union.[71] That may be the case, but Edwards asserts that "what is real . . . is the foundation of what is legal" in the context of a reference to the "mutual act of both" parties. "God sees it fit, that in order to an union's being established between two intelligent active beings or persons, so as that they should be looked upon as one, there should be the mutual act of both, that each should receive the other, as actively joining themselves one to another."[72] Thus, while Edwards's immediate concern in *Justification by Faith* is to establish the necessity of man's faith for the union, there is an indication, albeit undeveloped, that Edwards is setting this against the background of the eternal divine arrangement of the grounds of redemption.[73]

In the eternal covenant of redemption the Father made an agreement with the Son and with the church in him. The blessings promised were conditional solely on the work of the Son. This eternal covenant is consummated in the temporal sphere and actualized through the covenant of grace as the elect consent with Christ by an action of the Holy Spirit.[74]

71. McClenahan, "Justification," 189 n. 51, notes that preferable to Bombaro's assessment is Caldwell's conclusion that because "the believer's own act of faith is the product of the Spirit's union to the soul's faculties, the whole affair, from the widest possible angle, is ultimately and entirely of God." Caldwell, *Communion*, 137. However, this seems to set Bombaro falsely against Caldwell. Bombaro is careful throughout his wider argument to acknowledge the that the manifestations of the Spirit are the personal acts of the saints, but that these acts are only by the Spirit dwelling in them and do not spring from a *gratia creata*.

72. *Justification by Faith Alone*, WJE 19:158.

73. McClenahan highlights that Morimoto's immediate concern is with Edwards's *Justification by Faith Alone* and argues that consequently Bombaro's criticisms are unfair. Nevertheless in his wider systematization of Edwards's theology it is still true to say that Morimoto neglects its covenantal character.

74. Though Conrad Cherry does not mention the role of the Holy Spirit in the "consent" that actualizes the covenant, his analysis that Edwards collapses the two covenants (of redemption and grace) into one is helpful. He rightly identifies Edwards's eternal perspective in the issue of justifying faith. Cherry, "Puritan Notion," 335–40. Edwards is determined to root justification in the *pactum salutis* and *historia salutis*. His innovation, that Christ purchases the Holy Spirit and with Him faith, underlines his commitment to this goal by rooting the "actualization" of the individual's redemption in the eternal covenant of redemption. This initially appears to leave Edwards open to the charge of eternal justification, a doctrine explicitly rejected by the Westminster Divines who maintained that although "God did, from all eternity, decree to justify all the elect . . . nevertheless they are not justified, until the Holy Spirit doth in due time actually apply Christ unto them." *Westminster Confession*, 11.4. For this reason Edwards notes that although the covenants of redemption and grace are not entirely different they must not be confounded, a point I noted in chapter 3. While the covenant of redemption concerns the Persons of the Trinity (and the elect in God the

Conrad Cherry summarizes: "Faith is . . . the covenant's actualization in man's concrete life; it is the saint's reception into covenant with God through God's covenant with him in Christ. And in receiving salvation through the covenant, faith is active dependence in hope and trust upon the God who covenants."[75] Covenantal theology is the vital backdrop to Edwards's understanding of justification.

To sum up thus far: Edwards is committed to an account of salvation wherein his concept of a new disposition plays a central and defining role. By this it is meant that in the covenantal activity of God a new disposition is brought about in the saint by the eternal act of the Holy Spirit. At the moment when the consenting Holy Spirit is infused, the elect soul's union with Christ is actualized; he or she gains a title to Christ's benefits and is declared righteous. In the language of the *ordo salutis* regeneration and justification are distinct aspects of the one event, logically but not temporally separated.

A Concatenation of Graces

In Morimoto's thesis the new disposition is a tendency or habit, ontologically real, which will be triggered in an expression of faith given certain conditions. Nevertheless, it is the disposition itself, as the meeting place of God and man, which is sufficient for salvation, irrespective of its exercise. Morimoto claims that this enables Edwards to answer the question of how the Old Testament saints were saved, given that their place in redemption history denied them the opportunity of exercising faith in Christ. He cites "Miscellanies," no. 27b, in which Edwards notes: "It need not be doubted but that many of the ancient Jews before Christ were saved without the sensible exertions of those acts in that manner which is represented as necessary by some divines, because they had not those occasions nor were

---

Son), the covenant of grace is between Christ and the elect soul. One of the distinctive aspects of Edwards's approach to the character of the covenant is his analogy of the marriage covenant and its centrality to his scheme. Edwards notes: "The revelation and offer of the gospel is not properly called a covenant till it is consented to. As when a man courts a woman [and] offers himself to her, his offer is not called a covenant, though he be obliged by it on his part. Neither do I think that the gospel is called a covenant in Scripture, but only when the engagements are mutual." "Miscellanies," no. 617, *WJE* 18:148–51. The gospel remains only an offer and cannot be considered to be "a proper covenant" until the soul consents to it. On eternal justification in the Reformed tradition, see Trueman, *Claims of Truth*, 113–18.

75. Cherry, "Puritan Notion," 338.

under circumstances that would draw them out; though without doubt they had the disposition, which alone is absolutely necessary now, and at all time and in all circumstances is equally necessary."[76]

Morimoto highlights Edwards's comment that what arises from the disposition "cannot be proved to be absolutely necessary" for salvation.[77] Morimoto's error, however, is to ignore the context of both "Miscellanies," nos. 27b and 393, which he quotes. In both Edwards's concern is not with the objective reality of saving faith, but with subjective awareness of it.[78] Elsewhere Edwards notes that many Christians erroneously identify the moment of their conversion. Since God often gives "special discoveries of his glory and grace after brokenness of spirit, not only at first conversion but through the whole Christian course . . . many have been wont to call their first remarkable discovery of God's grace their conversion."[79] This is a mistake, according to Edwards. Humiliation cannot be a distinct act of the Holy Spirit *prior* to conversion, since to receive the experience as humiliation is itself evidence of the consenting new disposition. A "natural man" is unable in the one experience to recognize the justice of God in damning him, to despair of himself and to throw himself on God's mercy. It is the soul's consent in humiliation that marks it out as already saved. "Now it is impossible that that weight which was upon the mind, through its thought of God's obligation to punish him, should be removed any other way but by a discovery of a sufficiency of mercy, the secret revelation of a way that God may save if he pleases, consistent with his own honor and majesty: which is faith."[80]

It is worth nothing that the fact that Edwards's own experience did not match the conversion narratives he would have heard frequently recounted in his father's and grandfather's churches clearly caused him some soul-searching. In his diary of 18 December 1722 he wrote,

> The reason why I, in the least, question my interest in God's love and favor, is, 1. Because I cannot speak so fully to my experience of that preparatory work, of which divines speak; 2. I do not remember that I experienced regeneration, exactly in those

---

76. "Miscellanies," no. 27b, *WJE* 13:213–15 (214). See Morimoto's use of this in his *Catholic Vision*, 37–69.

77. "Miscellanies," no. 27b, *WJE* 13:213–15, quoted in Morimoto, *Catholic Vision*, 62.

78. Bombaro, "Vision of Salvation," 51.

79. "Miscellanies," no. 393, *WJE* 13:456. See also "Miscellanies," no. 847, *WJE* 20:72–73.

80. "Miscellanies," no. 393, *WJE* 13:457.

steps, in which divines say it is generally wrought; 3. I do not feel the Christian graces sensibly enough, particularly faith. I fear they are only such hypocritical outside affections, which wicked men may feel, as well as others. They do not seem to be sufficiently inward, full, sincere, entire and hearty. They do not seem so substantial, and so wrought into my very nature, as I could wish. 4. Because I am sometimes guilty of sins of omission and commission.[81]

However, by the time Edwards composed his "Personal Narrative" some eighteen years later he had been pastor in Northampton for more than a decade, had witnessed two awakenings there and the concern expressed in his "Diary" gives way to conviction that the steps of conversion are less important than the *nature* of the change wrought in the soul. Thus Edwards recalls that the first occasion of his own "inward sweet delight" in God came after reading 1 Timothy 1:17 ["Now unto the King eternal, immortal, invisible, the only wise God, be honour and glory for ever and ever. Amen."]. "As I read the words, there came into my soul, and was as it were diffused through it, a sense of the glory of the divine being; a new sense, quite different from anything I had experienced before."[82]

Edwards's belief that authenticating signs of the Spirit's work are to be sought not in the steps to conversion, but in the nature of the professing soul itself, is further expressed in the "negative signs" of *The Distinguishing Marks of a True Work of the Spirit of God* (Boston, 1741) and in *Religious Affections* (Boston, 1746). For example, "Many do greatly err in their notions of a clear work of conversion; calling that a clear work, where the successive steps of influence, and method of experience is clear: whereas that indeed is the clearest work (not where the order of doing is clearest, but), where the spiritual and divine nature of the work done, and effect wrought, is most clear."[83]

---

81. "Diary," *WJE* 16:759.

82. "Personal Narrative," *WJE* 16:792. Patricia Tracy argues that Edwards's experience as reported in the "Personal Narrative" is not borne out by examination of the relevant entries in his "Diary," letters or notebooks, and that as late as May 1725 Edwards was unsure of his own conversion. Though Tracy acknowledges the probable didactic purpose of the "Personal Narrative" (to encourage and instruct Edwards's future son-in-law, Aaron Burr) and its consequently stylized report, she arguably places too much weight on the fact that there is a difference between the event itself and mature reflection on that event. Tracy, *Jonathan Edwards, Pastor*, 58–64. The difference need not be surprising. The subject may be assailed by doubts which only mature reflection is able to identify as having been those of one truly regenerate.

83. *Religious Affections, WJE* 2:162–63.

Case Study

In this vein "Miscellanies," no. 393 (quoted above) reveals Edwards questioning the morphology of conversion that he had inherited from the previous occupant of the Northampton pulpit, his grandfather Solomon Stoddard.[84] Stoddard consciously followed such divines as William Perkins (1558–1602), Thomas Shephard (1604–49) and Thomas Hooker (1586–1647) in emphasizing the necessity for the sinner's conversion of a preparatory sense of humiliation or "terror" under God's Law, a period during which the afflicted might become conscious of the weight of his sin and despair at God's righteousness judgment against him.[85] Crucially, in this preparationist tradition humiliation, while a divine preparatory act, was not itself a gracious saving work of the Spirit.[86] Elect and reprobate

---

84. Edwards's relationship to the doctrine of preparation is much debated. Bogue, *Covenant of Grace*, 279, describes it as "one of the most difficult aspects of his thought to correctly grasp." Miller, "'Preparation,'" 253–86, argues that the doctrine of preparation essentially constituted a pastoral attempt to retain Calvinist teaching on predestination, whilst giving the seeker something to do, to "predispose himself for grace." This, Miller argues, was thinly veiled Arminianism, which Edwards consequently rejected. Goen, "Editor's Introduction," *WJE* 4:4–18, follows Miller in his assessment of New England's Arminianism as being a home-grown product of ambiguities in Puritan federal theology. Knight, *Orthodoxies in Massachusetts*, 287 n. 2, follows Miller in arguing that Edwards abandoned the doctrine of preparation altogether. In response Emerson, "Calvin and Covenant Theology," 136–44, argues *contra* Miller that preparation was no Puritan invention, but was present in Calvin and the early Reformers. McClenahan, "Justification," 49–107, argues that Miller overlooked the significance of non-meritorious causes in Puritan teaching on preparation; that is, the Puritan doctrine of preparation did not hold that man could prepare himself for conversion, but that he could be prepared by God. He further argues that New England Arminianism was not home-grown, but was imported from England in the sermons of Archbishop Tillotson. Edwards's conception of preparation is beyond the scope of the present enquiry, but see, in addition to the above, Cherry, *Jonathan Edwards*, 56–70; Gerstner and Gerstner, "Edwardsean Preparation for Salvation," 5–71.

85. Solomon Stoddard names Perkins, Shephard and Hooker as authorities in his *Guide to Christ*. See also Laurence, "Preparationist Model," 269. Thomas Hooker, for example, argued in *Soules Preparation*, 57: "This true sight of sin is the onely doore to life and salvation"; and in his *Soules Humiliation*, 145: "You must come to this truth [of the necessity of humiliation]: for there is no faith can be infused into the Soule, before the heart bee thus fitted and prepared: no preparation, no perfection. Never humbled, never exalted." (Both quoted in Laurence, "Preparationist Model," 269).

86. Muller, *Dictionary*, s.v *preparatio ad conversionem*, notes that the Reformed conceived of preparation as an *actus praeparatorius* or *actus praecedaneus* in an effort to preserve their doctrine from synergism. Discussion of the varieties of preparationism in England and New England is beyond the present enquiry. On the origins of the doctrine of preparation, see Heppe, *Reformed Dogmatics*, 523–24. The literature surrounding Puritan morphologies of conversion and conversion narratives is large. See for example: Caldwell, *Puritan Conversion Narrative*; Goen, "Editor's Introduction,"

alike might be brought to humiliation by the Holy Spirit, but while the elect's humiliation was termed "evangelical" in that it led to regeneration, the reprobate's humiliation was merely "legal" and his path to salvation terminated there.

Edwards does not throw out the distinction between legal and evangelical humiliation, but of significance to him is the manner of the Spirit's work in each case.[87] Consonant with his distinction between "speculative" (or "notional") and "spiritual knowledge," the issue of humiliation turns for Edwards on whether the Spirit merely acts externally (as in legal fear), or internally (as in evangelical conviction). According to Edwards, evangelical humiliation is not a work of the Spirit *prior* to conversion. Rather it is evidence of regenerating grace itself: "there is an exercise of faith in that humiliation."[88] And so it is with any prescribed confessions of Christ.

Edwards, the young pastor, confides that his grandfather erred in directly equating the objective reality of conversion with the saint's subjective experience of it. At the root of this lay Stoddard's misconstrual of the act of faith. (I quote Edwards's note at some length because of its importance to my argument).

> A principal thing that made Mr. Stoddard think that there was no grace in humiliation, was because he looked upon an explicit act of faith in Jesus Christ as evermore the first gracious act that ever was exerted. And what seems to have made him think that, seems to be his sense of faith's being the only condition of salvation, and for want of a sufficient explaining of what was meant by our being justified by faith alone, as being that grace which alone God has respect to, as being what he accounts renders it a suitable thing, that we should be justified for the sake of Christ. The graces of the Spirit, especially those that more directly respect God and another world, are so nearly allied that they include one another; and where there is the exercise of one, there is something of the other exercised with it: like strings in

---

WJE 4:25–32; Hindmarsh, *Evangelical Conversion Narrative*; Morgan, *Visible Saints*; Pettit, *Heart Prepared*.

87. See for example, *Religious Affections*, WJE 2:311–44; *Faithful Narrative*, WJE 4:170; "God Makes Men Sensible of their Misery Before He Reveals His Mercy and Love," WJE 17:142–72. In acting as an extrinsic agent on the unregenerate the Spirit merely assists natural principles of reason or conscience towards legal terror. However, the Spirit acts *within* the elect, communicating to them his nature, "his own natural, essential and eternal act": love. "Miscellanies," no. 471, WJE 13:512–14. See also my discussion above on *theosis*.

88. "Miscellanies," no. 393, WJE 13:457.

consort, if one is struck, others sound with it; or like links in a chain, if one is drawn, others follow. So that humiliation that there is in repentance implies a principle of faith, and not only so, but something of the exercise too; so that a person according to the gospel may be in a state of salvation, before a distinct and express act of faith in the sufficiency and suitableness of Christ as Savior. Persons are justified upon the first appearance of a principle of faith in the soul by any of the soul's acts: but a principle of faith appears and shows itself by the exercise of true repentance and evangelical humiliation; for the graces are all the same in principle, especially those that more immediately respect God and Christ and another world.[89]

Fundamental to Edwards's argument is his belief that there is a "consententation" or "concatenation" of the Holy Spirit's graces.[90] They are "all from the Spirit of Christ sent forth into the heart, and dwelling there as an holy principle and divine nature. And therefore all the graces are only the different ways of acting of the same divine nature."[91] Where one is exercised, so all are exercised. Not only does one grace help promote another, but "one is really implied in the other: the nature of one involves the nature of another."[92] And the reason for this is that all graces have "one common essence, the original principal of all. . . . a principle of divine love," namely, the Holy Spirit acting in the saint after the manner of a principle of life and action.[93] It is for this reason that Edwards argues that no particular prescribed steps can be considered a prior necessity to the Spirit's inward work, nor can consciousness of faith be an authenticating mark of its beginning. "Persons are justified upon the first appearance of

---

89. Ibid., 457–58. See also Edwards's sermon, "No Such Experiences as the Devils in Hell are the Subjects of are Any Sure Sign of Grace," [no. 852], Dec. 1746; repreached, 28 September 1752 and published as Edwards, *True Grace*, under which title it appears in *WJE* 25:608–40. The sermon anticipates Edwards's renunciation of Stoddard's practices regarding church membership and communion. For an introduction to the "communion controversy" that underlay Edwards's ejection from Northampton, see Hall, "Editor's Introduction," *WJE* 12:1–86.

90. "Treatise on Grace," *WJE* 21:166; "Christian Graces Concatenated Together," *Charity and Its Fruits*, *WJE* 8:327. The *Westminster Confession*, 11.2 similarly states that faith, "the alone instrument of justification . . . is not alone in the person justified, but is ever accompanied with all other saving graces, and is no dead faith, but worketh by love."

91. "Christian Graces Concatenated Together," *Charity and Its Fruits*, *WJE* 8:332.

92. "Treatise on Grace," *WJE* 21:166.

93. Ibid.

faith in the soul by *any* of the soul's acts."[94] Indeed a person may have been regenerated and justified by faith some time before they are able to make an explicit confession of Christ. Edwards holds open the possibility of a distinction between the objective reality of conversion and the subjective experience of it.[95]

Edwards expresses the distinction between "objective reality" and "sensible awareness" most clearly in his analogy of first and second births. For Edwards, an "infusion" of the soul into the fetus marks the beginning of a living being with a rational soul, though the development of the life is imperceptible. So it is with the new birth. It occurs at a definite moment, yet its growth may be insensible.[96] In other words, particular confessions of faith are not essential to the act of conversion, but are evidence of the presence of regenerating grace. A few months later Edwards developed the

---

94. "Miscellanies," no. 393, *WJE* 13:458. Emphasis added. In *Justification by Faith Alone*, *WJE* 19:201, Edwards notes that, "it having been shown . . . that 'tis only by faith, or the soul's receiving, and uniting to the Savior, that has wrought our righteousness, that we are justified; it therefore remains that the acts of a Christian life can't be concerned in this affair any otherwise, than as they imply, and are the expressions of faith, and may be looked upon as so many acts of reception of Christ the Savior." However, his concern at this point in his discourse is to distinguish the significance of the *first* act of faith which justifies, from *later* acts of faith which do not, despite their necessity to salvation. The significance of the first act of faith is its chronological position in a Reformed *ordo salutis* as the act of union with Christ in whom the sinner is declared righteous. Edwards clarifies his point, noting: "[T]he difference whereby this first act of faith has a concern in this affair that is peculiar, seems to be as it were only an accidental difference, arising from the circumstance of time, or its being first in order of time; and not from any peculiar respect that God has to it, or any influence it has of a particular nature, in the affair of our salvation." *Justification by Faith Alone*, *WJE* 19:207. On the necessity of maintaining the Reformed distinction between justification and salvation in discussions of the role of good works in Edwards's thought, see McClenahan, "Justification," 234–50.

95. The same response to Morimoto's interpretation of "Miscellanies," no. 393 should be made to his interpretation of "Miscellanies," no. 27b in which Edwards notes: "[T]he disposition is all that can be absolutely necessary. 'Tis the disposition and principle is the thing God looks at. . . . Supposing a man dies suddenly and not in the actual exercise of faith, 'tis his disposition that saves him; for if it were possible that the disposition was destroyed, the man would be damned and all the former acts of faith would signify nothing." "Miscellanies," no. 27b, *WJE* 13:214. Once again Edwards is responding to "our divines" who insist that particular expressions of faith are requisite for salvation. Edwards argues that the particular acts the divines insist upon may possibly be considered necessary but only in that given particular circumstances the new disposition would be expressed in those acts. It is the source and principle of the concatenating graces that God looks at—the indwelling Holy Spirit. See also his identical argument in "Miscellanies," no. 77, *WJE* 13:244–45.

96. "Miscellanies," no. 241, *WJE* 13:357–58.

Case Study

birth analogy in a further entry: "If there ever are any that are regenerated in their infancy that live till they are adult, then doubtless there are some whose first exercise of grace is not such a particular manner of closing with Christ[97] as some think necessary, and as perhaps is commonly the first gracious act in those that have for some time lived in an allowed way of sinning. For such infants without doubt exercise grace gradually as they exercise their reason."[98]

In short, to those who argue that a particular conversion morphology or expression of faith is necessary for salvation, Edwards responds that the new disposition implies the presence of all the graces of the Spirit. The new disposition, as the Spirit's active presence in the human heart, unites the soul to Christ in justifying faith. Other graces of the Spirit, including repentance, humility, good works, perseverance, gratitude, even sensible awareness of salvation and particular conscious expressions of faith in Christ, can be expected to appear either immediately or much later. These graces are not merely potential (as in Morimoto's thesis), but real, albeit embryonic.[99]

I now turn to the question of the salvation of the Old Testament saints. I will argue that Edwards's notion of the concatenation of the Holy Spirit's graces is central to his account of salvation in the Old Testament.

THE NEW DISPOSITION AND THE OLD DISPENSATION

During the summer of 1723 while Edwards prepared his M.A. *Quæstio*, the subject of conversion was clearly on his mind. In "Miscellanies," no. 39 he comments: "I am now convinced, that conversion under the old testament [*sic*] was not only the same in general with what it is commonly

---

97. Edwards has deleted at this point, "and coming unto him, as our old divines [. . . illegible word)]."

98. "Miscellanies," no. 302, *WJE* 13:389.

99. The ecclesial implications of Stoddard's relation to the "Halfway Covenant" of 1662 and of Edwards's departure from Stoddard have been rehearsed elsewhere and are beyond the scope of the present enquiry. Edwards publicly defended his departure from Stoddard's inclusive policy of admission to communion in *Humble Inquiry*. This is published with his later riposte to his critics, *Misrepresentations Corrected* and his own "Narrative of the Communion Controversy" in *WJE* 12. In addition to Morgan, *Visible Saints*, and Tracy, *Jonathan Edwards, Pastor*, David Hall's "Editor's Introduction," *WJE* 12:1–90, offers an excellent survey of the historical and theological context in England and New England.

under the new, but much more like it as to the particular way and manner, than I used to think..."[100]

I have noted Morimoto's argument that the disposition is ontologically real, the created grace of the indwelling Holy Spirit at the moment of regeneration. To him, conversion, a later though unnecessary event in terms of salvation, represents the activation of the regenerate's disposition. Since this conversion depends on an encounter with Jesus Christ, the Old Testament saints were regenerate, though unconverted; they were saved by possessing the new disposition, though it remained "un-activated."[101] However, I have argued that when Edwards speaks of the "new disposition" he is referring to the manner and activity of the Holy Spirit's indwelling. The graces of the Spirit are concatenated together so that any one expression of the Spirit in the human soul at the moment of infusion is an expression of justifying faith.

In chapter 3 I explored the notion of "covenant" as a fundamental feature of Edwards's theology. The following may be noted by way of a brief recapitulation. Before creation God's decision to glorify himself led the Persons of the Trinity to confederate themselves in a covenant of redemption. The Son was elected the Mediator of redemption, as was fitting to the immanent Trinitarian relations. At creation God entered into a covenant with Adam, the covenant of works, in which He promised Adam salvation on the condition of perfect righteousness. Upon Adam's sin God entered into another covenant with humanity, the covenant of grace. The covenants of works and grace were essentially different expressions of the one covenant, sharing the same condition: perfect righteousness. However, whereas the former covenant demanded that man made an offering to God of that righteousness through his own obedience, in the latter covenant the direction was reversed: humanity must trust God and receive the perfect righteousness of Christ's active and passive obedience. The Old Testament was characterized by God's offering the covenant of grace in the shell of a covenant of works. The covenant thus appeared to be a legal one, promising salvation on the condition of perfect obedience. But in the Old Testament God also revealed enough of his "merciful nature and his inclination to pity them and to accept of a propitiation for them," so that the elect would cast themselves on his undeserved mercy.[102] That is, in his covenants with Israel God proposed as a condition for salvation "the fruits

---

100. "Miscellanies," no. 39, *WJE* 13:221–22 (221).
101. Morimoto, *Catholic Vision*, 63–64.
102. "Miscellanies," no. 250, *WJE* 13:362.

of faith ... instead of faith itself." The result of this was that only those who had faith could hope for life. "[B]y God's contrivance of that dispensation they were led not to depend on these [acts of obedience] as works, but as a disposition to receive, as so many manifestations of repentance and submission; and they depended on them as such only, for life."[103]

Edwards is aware of the objection that the conditions of salvation revealed in the Old and New Testament appear to differ. In the New Testament salvation is presented as justification by faith alone; in the Old Testament the condition appears to be obedience. He answers in "Miscellanies," no. 1354, entitled "Justification. Objection against the doctrine of justification by faith alone from the conditions of God's favor chiefly insisted on in the Old Testament." First he summarizes the objection: "It appears that obedience is not only insisted on as the thing consequentially necessary, and so a kind of secondary condition of the covenant, but as the main thing required, the grand condition of the covenant that was established between him and his people, the grand condition of God's mercy and favor and blessing, of escaping death and obtaining life, of being accepted as God's people and having him as our God."[104] Much of Edwards's answer is by now familiar. Though God insisted on obedience as the condition of salvation, he also made it clear that Israel's sin made it impossible for her to fulfill her obligations of obedience. God's design was to drive the ancient church to faith in the Mediator for the fruit of obedience that was required. Obedience in both Old and New Testaments is an expression of the new disposition. It is "that sure, attendant fruit and distinguishing mark of [faith]."[105] As such it was under the Old Testament the manner of accepting God's covenant. The Old Testament saints did not seek to obey God thinking that their obedience had any value in itself that merited God's reward. Rather, their obedience was "the proper expression of receiving Jehovah as their God and Savior, or uniting themselves to him as his people, and receiving him as their spiritual husband, captain and Redeemer." That is, obedience to God's commands was indeed the condition of life, not as "the price of life and happiness," but "as an accepting it, a closing with it and embracing it."[106] Obedience properly understood under

---

103. Ibid., 363.
104. Ibid., 509.
105. Ibid., 527.
106. Ibid., 520–21.

the old dispensation was a grace of the Holy Spirit, a non-meritorious act of justifying faith.[107]

Expressions of the new disposition fitted the conditions of the dispensation and therefore differed through redemption history, the observance of the (temporary) ceremonial Law being the most notable example.[108] The saints offered the sacrifices that the Law required, not in order to obtain salvation, since they knew their sacrifices had no efficacy in themselves; rather to the faithful Israelites the sacrifices were expressions of their trust in the true Sacrifice. Though its outward expression may have changed as redemption history unfolded, the manner of salvation remained constant: the saints were saved in turning to God for mercy through the Mediator He had provided. Thus using language more familiar to the New Testament, Edwards describes the way of salvation in the Old Testament.

"The way of justification by faith was truly revealed. Sufficient instructions were given concerning it to lead convinced, penitent sinners to hope for justification no other way. Thus trusting in God and hoping in his mercy, seeking God, waiting for or upon the Lord, calling on the name of the Lord, looking to God, looking towards God's holy temple, laying hold on God's strength ... are abundantly insisted on as the terms of acceptance and salvation."[109]

Effectual Calling and the Means of Grace

Morimoto's dispositional soteriology renders justification God's rewarding of his own gift, and conversion an epistemological event. The Christian message provides the opportunity for the God-given disposition to "bloom into full faith." "It is an invitation for self-realization" but it is not vital to salvation.[110] Steven Studebaker follows Morimoto in contending that for

---

107. See also "Miscellanies," no. 218, *WJE* 13:344–45, which I have quoted above. Similarly, in *Justification by Faith Alone*, *WJE* 19:208–9, Edwards addresses the objection that the promise of salvation is often made to our virtue or obedience, as in Rom 2:7. He argues: "Promises may rationally be made to signs and evidence of faith, and yet the thing promised not be upon the account of the sign, but the thing signified." For example, human governments often promise privileges to people who can show evidence of their being freemen of a certain city. The privilege is not granted for the sake of the evidence itself, but for that of which it is evidence.

108. "Miscellanies," no. 1353, *WJE* 23:493–94; "Miscellanies," no. 439, *WJE* 13:488.

109. "Miscellanies," no. 1354, *WJE* 23:506–43 (541).

110. Morimoto, *Catholic Vision*, 162. Morimoto rightly identifies "realization" as an element of Edwards's theology, but his dispositional soteriology means he wrongly

Edwards, "the dispositional transformation can occur without Christological specificity [which] reinforces the possibility of the communication of the Spirit through means other than hearing/reading the gospel."[111] In what follows I will argue that Morimoto's temporal separation of regeneration and conversion is a fatal error and that *contra* both Morimoto and Studebaker, Edwards understands the effectual calling of God to come through the divinely-ordained means of grace, his word.[112] The preaching of the gospel awakened the sinner to regeneration, not merely to the consciousness of an already-possessed salvation.

Gerald McDermott advances Morimoto's thesis a stage further. Although he is careful to state that Edwards never argued such a line himself, McDermott claims Edwards laid the foundations for the possibility of the salvation of those who had not heard the word of Christ. McDermott argues that particularly during his years among the Indians of Stockbridge Edwards expended great effort in considering the eschatological future of those who had never heard the Christian gospel. Edwards had always been fascinated with accounts of other religions and the subject appears to have become increasingly important to him throughout his life, if the space he gave it in his "Miscellanies" is any measure.[113] It was not only Edwards's

---

locates it. By recovering Edwards's belief that the preaching of the Word is the means of regeneration and not merely the means of the "activation" of an abiding dormant disposition to faith, it is apparent that an individual's "realization" occurs at the moment of their regeneration. Edwards affirms that the end of creation was not reached in the first (natural) birth. "To have a being [from the first birth] is one step towards man's obtaining the end of his being." This goal is found in regeneration, according to Edwards in his sermon, "Born Again," *WJE* 17:186-95. But so radical is the new birth that in the same sermon Edwards comments that not only is regeneration the moment when man receives the goal of his being, but when a man is born again "he doth, as it were, receive his being again." "Born Again," *WJE* 17:189. As my earlier examination of Edwards's understanding of "flesh" and "Spirit" revealed, humanity is truly human when its disposition is directed towards God—when the image of God is restored in him. Gal 5:17, "Blank Bible," *WJE* 24:1086-87; "Born Again," *WJE* 17:191. And this image is normally brought into being, according to Edwards, by the means of grace: the preaching of the gospel.

111. Studebaker, "Pneumatological Concept of Grace," 339. Brown, *Edwards and the Bible*, 47-49, similarly asserts that, while Edwards's later writings granted a greater role to the Bible, in "A Divine and Supernatural Light" the Holy Spirit works "immediately," that is, without means.

112. It is not denied that theologians in the Reformed tradition differed among themselves as to their conception of *how* the means of grace were effective, though this question is beyond the scope of the present enquiry. On this, see for example, Heppe, *Reformed Dogmatics*, 510-42. My purpose here is merely to demonstrate that Edwards did consider the preaching of the gospel to be instrumental to regeneration.

113. See Sweeney, "Editor's Introduction," *WJE* 23:1-36.

greater exposure to pagan religions through his years at Stockbridge that fuelled his interest, however. The fate of the (non-Christian) majority of the world was a driving force in Deist objections to the church's orthodox teaching of salvation through faith in Christ. Matthew Tindal (1657–1733) argued that God must have at all times given the whole world sufficient means of knowing what he required of them, otherwise he would be unjust in His judgment. Christianity must be as old as creation: "[T]he Christian Religion has existed from the Beginning; and that God, both Then, and Ever since, has continued to give all Mankind sufficient Means to know it; and that 'tis their Duty to know, believe, profess, and practise it: so that Christianity, tho' the Name is of a later Date, must be as old, and as extensive, as human Nature; and, as the Law of our Creation, must have been Then implanted in us by God himself."[114] A God who wanted to instruct his creation would surely do so from the beginning. To show special favor to one part of the world while leaving the rest in darkness constituted a "scandal of particularity," both unreasonable and unworthy of God. As knowledge of the religions of Asia and the Americas increased, so too did objections to the claim that there was no saving revelation outside the Christian Scriptures. The vast majority of humanity could not be damned simply for not having the chance to hear the gospel. Edwards employs the *prisca theologia* in response, claiming that the sum of mankind had in fact heard the gospel.

According to the *prisca theologia*, outlined above in chapter 2, at least twice in the history of the world all of humanity possessed knowledge of the true God: before the Fall and immediately after the Flood. This knowledge was subsequently passed down the generations in a process McDermott calls "trickle-down revelation." Yet accompanying this process another was at work, "religious entropy."[115] The knowledge of God that reached the Greeks and other nations deteriorated over time; it was an imperfect knowledge. Nevertheless, vestiges of the truth were observable in the religious practices of the heathen nations. Numbers of Edwards's "Miscellanies" are occupied with subjects such as the notion of the Trinity in Chinese religion and Plato's reliance on Moses.[116] Edwards saw in the *prisca theologia* a useful weapon against Deist criticisms. McDermott claims that Edwards's reliance on natural revelation and the *prisca theologia* offers the possibility of salvation for those who have not heard the

---

114. Tindal, *Christianity*, 4.

115. McDermott, *Edwards Confronts the Gods*, 87–109.

116. "Miscellanies," no. 1181, *WJE* 23:96–104; "Miscellanies," no. 1355, *WJE* 23:543–75.

Christian gospel. But Morimoto and McDermott fall into the same error. Their dispositional soteriology depends on the arbitrary exercise of God's grace. By this is not meant that God saves whomever he wills, a notion Edwards frequently endorses, but that he saves whomever he wills without their having to receive the eternal covenant of redemption through faith in Christ the Mediator held out in the gospel.[117]

It is true that in his later "Miscellanies" Edwards does consider the possibility of the heathen's "reconciliation" with God, but McDermott emphasizes these occasional references in Edwards's semi-public notebooks, over against his more numerous, explicit and public declarations that God's free practice is usually to call effectually through means.[118] In "Miscellanies," no. 27b, the very entry that is the foundation for much of Morimoto's dispositional soteriology, the young Edwards emphasizes the role of the gospel in the appearance of the new disposition: "'Tis most certain, both from Scripture and reason, that there must be a reception of Christ with the faculties of the soul in order to salvation by him, and that in this reception there is a believing of what we are taught in the gospel concerning him and salvation by him, and that it must be a consent of the will or an agreeableness between the disposition of the soul and those doctrines."[119]

I have already noted the importance Edwards gives to consent in regeneration. Now he notes that this is consent to things heard in the gospel. Using the metaphor of birth Edwards comments that regeneration is "brought to pass by stated means . . . according to a fixed law of nature." God could convert man without any means at all, "but he doth not so. But there are stated means which are appointed and fixed by the law of grace that are constantly made use of in producing this effect. *Conversion*

---

117. I do not deny that "the bestowal of grace without means" is not unknown in the Reformed tradition, but Edwards did not subscribe to such a position. Jerom Zanchius, discussing the pagan nations who had never heard the gospel, concedes, "It is not indeed improbable, but some individuals in these unenlightened countries might belong to the secret election of grace, and the habit of faith might be wrought in these." Zanchius, *Absolute Predestination*, 104. And later, Shedd, *Dogmatic Theology*, 2.707–8, quotes the *Westminster Confession*, 10.3 ["elect infants dying in infancy are regenerated and saved by Christ through the Spirit, who worketh when and where and how he pleaseth. . . . so also are all other elect persons who are incapable of being outwardly called by the ministry of the word"] and comments, "This is commonly understood to refer not merely . . . to idiots and insane persons, but to such of the pagan world as God pleases to regenerate without the use of the written revelation."

118. See for example, "Miscellanies," no. 1338, *WJE* 23:345–55.

119. "Miscellanies," no. 27b, *WJE* 13:213–15 (213).

is wrought by the Word and ordinances."[120] Thus according to Edwards, although God is free to infuse grace without means, his usual method is to employ them. "Grace is from God as immediately and directly as light is from the sun; and that notwithstanding the means that are improved, such as word, ordinances, etc. For though these are made use of, yet they have no influence to produce grace, either as causes or instruments, or any other way; and yet they are concerned in the affair of the production of grace, and are necessary in order to it . . ."[121]

Similarly, in a sermon, Edwards notes that "God exercises his right [of sovereignty] . . . in calling one people or nation, and giving them the means of grace, and leaving others without them. According to the divine appointment, salvation is bestowed in connexion with the means of grace. God may sometime make use of very unlikely means, and bestow salvation on men who are under very great disadvantages; but he does not bestow grace wholly without means. But God exercises his sovereignty in bestowing those means."[122] Given Edwards's expansion of types and his interest in the *prisca theologia*, as in McDermott's account, it is not clear how God could still withhold means of grace from some unless the effectual means of grace Edwards has in mind are the Hebrew Scriptures and the types peculiar to Israel, such as her ceremonial laws. Granted Edward's emphasis on God's freedom, McDermott is right to highlight the salvific possibilities that Edwards's theology opens up; there seems no reason in principle why Edwards's expansion of types should not also expand the effectual means of grace beyond the borders of Israel in the Old Testament. However, McDermott's error is that he arguably pays insufficient attention to Edwards's clear affirmations that God's *normal* economy is that effectual calling is through special revelation.

120. "Born Again," *WJE* 17:189. Emphasis added.

121. "Miscellanies," no. 539, *WJE* 18:84–88. McClenahan, "Justification," 279–300, argues persuasively that Edwards's discussion of the immediacy of God's grace in "A Divine and Supernatural Light" is directed specifically against the Arminianism of Tillotson, who rejected the Reformed notion that supernatural habits or principles are infused by a sovereign work of God at the moment of conversion. But his observation that the spiritual and divine light immediately imparted to the soul by God is immediate as to its formal cause but not its instrumental cause, needs qualifying in the light of "Miscellanies," no. 539, above. The spiritual and divine light is immediate formally but not instrumentally, *from our perspective*. The instrumental use of means of grace is God's arbitrary but usual method of working. See also Edwards's warning to Northampton of the danger of "Living Unconverted Under an Eminent Means of Grace," *WJE* 14:359–70.

122. "God's Sovereignty in the Salvation of Men," *WJE BoT*, 2.851.

Case Study

If Edwards insists that the normal method of God regenerating the elect to is employ means of grace, what means were employed in the Old Testament? How did the elect then hear the word of Christ? According to Edwards, they heard the gospel through prophecies and types that God gave them. To Edwards these means of grace are explicitly Christological. First, in the face of Deist accusations that the New Testament writers had misappropriated the Hebrew Scriptures Edwards argues that the entire prophetic *corpus* of the Old Testament was one unified presentation of the person and work of the Messiah, as I demonstrated in chapter 1. Under the guidance of the Holy Spirit the Old Testament elect were "much enlightened by the plain prophecies which they had of Christ."[123] Indeed even if the prophecies of the Messiah had been less plain than they actually were, Edwards argues, "it would have been no wonder if the saints, who delighted in God's word and made it their meditation day and night, had understood that he was to suffer and in that way make atonement for sin." Furthermore, there were many in Israel who excelled in wisdom, "especially of the righteous, who had their minds enlightened by the Spirit of God, and who had prophets and priests and the wisest of their nation to instruct them and teach 'em the meaning of God's word."[124] Second, Edwards's expanded typology contends that in the smallest detail the Old Testament dispensation was typical of the things concerning the Messiah, as I noted in chapter 2. The sacrifices of the Mosaic dispensation were pedagogical, teaching the Old Testament church of God's authority and holy majesty. By them God also taught that he would not pardon without satisfaction and that sin must be suffered for. But not only did the sacrifices teach these general truths, they also *typified* the work of Christ and as a means of grace led the church to trust in a Mediator: "By these types and shadows they were led to true faith and a Mediator."[125] The sacrifices offered were not efficacious in themselves but were effective as a means to lead the soul to "trust in the mere mercy of God." They typified the sacrifice of Christ, so that "by this ceremonial law, the gospel was preached to them [the Israelites]... Those sacrifices were to point forth Christ and to lead them to trust in him, to prepare the church for the reception and

---

123. "Christ's Sacrifice," *WJE* 10:594–604 (595).

124. "Question: In What Sense Did the Saints Under the Old Testament Believe In Christ to Justification?" "Controversies" notebook, *WJE* 21:402.

125. "Christ's Sacrifice," *WJE* 10:594.

entertainment of him when he came."¹²⁶ Edwards's expanded conception of types thus offers innumerable means of grace to the Old Testament saints.

In God's sovereign design prophecies and types worked together as means of grace. They "agree and sweetly harmonize as to the aim and design of both": to preach a message of justification by faith alone in Christ to Old Testament Israel.¹²⁷ With Edwards's expanded understanding of both types and prophecies come not only innumerably more means of grace, but also a greater clarity of faith among the Old Testament saints than could be proposed by those exegetes who held a narrow understanding of types and prophecies. "The more fully we are supplied with these notions [of religion], the greater opportunity has grace to act, and to act more suitably to the nature of things when God infuses it, because it has more objects to act upon, and one object illustrates another; so that we han't only more notions, but all our notions are the more clear, and more according to truth."¹²⁸ This greater clarity and fuller content of faith is the subject of our next section.

The Object and Content of Faith

According to Morimoto's notion of dispositional soteriology, the Old Testament saints are saved on their possession of a new disposition created in them by the Holy Spirit; the fact that their place in redemption history means that their dispositions remained unrealized is consequently irrelevant to their salvation. However, as I have argued, Morimoto misrepresents Edwards at this point. He is not alone in his error. Robert Caldwell emphasizes the objective reality of the believer's union with Christ by the Holy Spirit to the neglect of the object of faith. While he rejects Morimoto's dispositional soteriology he nevertheless denies conscious faith in Christ to the Old Testament saints. Instead Caldwell claims their faith in Christ was "implicit," since they did not have opportunity to exercise it consciously.¹²⁹ In support of his argument Caldwell quotes part of "Miscellanies," no. 663 as representing Edwards's position. However, what he quotes as Edwards's own position is in fact part of an objection that Edwards outlines before answering. In "Miscellanies," no. 663, "Faith

---

126. "The Sacrifice of Christ Acceptable," *WJE* 14:448.
127. "Miscellanies," no. 1354, *WJE* 23:514.
128. "Miscellanies," no. 539, *WJE* 18:86.
129. Caldwell, *Communion*, 125.

Case Study

Justification," Edwards first outlines the objection; it is this that Caldwell supposes represents Edwards's own position:

> If faith justifies, or gives us a right to divine benefits, only as 'tis the act [of] uniting to Christ as a savior, then it may be inquired why we have so many instances of the old testament [sic] saints obtaining these and those benefits by their believing of God's promises and trusting in God ... when yet they had no distinct respect to Christ in those acts of faith that are mentioned. They believed in God, and trusted in him, without any distinct notion of, or respect to a distinction of persons and offices in the deity...[130]

Having outlined the objection Edwards then answers it, a fact which Caldwell unfortunately neglects:

> *I answer*, it was the Lord Jesus Christ, the second person in the Trinity, that was wont to appear and to reveal himself to the people of God of old, and that manifested himself as the husband of the church, and as the author of all that good and salvation to the saints ... And by those instances of faith before mentioned, they closed with and cleaved to this their God, husband and Savior, in a way agreeable to the dispensation they were under, and [in] the manner in which Christ revealed himself to them, and according to the manifestations Christ made of himself as their Savior and the author of their good and happiness, in those days.[131]

That the first part of the entry cannot represent Edwards's own position is further apparent when compared with the essay in his "Controversies" notebook, "Question: In What Sense Did the Saints Under the Old Testament Believe in Christ to Justification?"[132] In this essay, which I will consider further below, Edwards argues at length that the Old Testament saints were aware of a distinction of Persons of the Godhead and indeed trusted in the Second Person as their Mediator before the First Person. Again, in another note he writes of the Old Testament saints' faith in the divine Mediator, the Messiah: "God's people under the old testament [sic] were not only instructed in the way of faith in general, but... they were particularly led by the revelation they were under to faith in the second

---

130. "Miscellanies," no. 663, *WJE* 18:200–1.
131. Ibid. Emphasis added.
132. "Controversies" notebook, *WJE* 21:372–413.

person in the Godhead as their Mediator and advocate, and in the Messiah as their great high priest and sacrifice."[133]

It is true that Edwards speaks of the possibility of "implicit" faith in Christ. But *contra* Morimoto and Caldwell, such faith has nothing to do with a saint's place in redemption history denying them knowledge of Christ. Edwards's commitment to a deeply Christological and expanded understanding of types and prophecies as means of grace shows the error of this view, as does his interpretation of God's economic activity as I will show, below. To Edwards, "implicit" faith in Christ was not a characteristic peculiar to Old Testament religion, but was an occasional feature of every age. In 1735 Edwards the pastor recounts the same occasional phenomenon in his own day among the recently-awakened in Northampton, men and women who had heard the message of Christ preached clearly to them, but some of whom did not initially confess Christ by name.

> It must needs be confessed that Christ is not always distinctly and explicitly thought of in the first sensible act of grace (though most commonly he is); but sometimes he is the object of the mind only implicitly. Thus sometimes when persons have seemed evidently to be stripped of all their own righteousness, and to have stood self-condemned as guilty of death, they have been comforted with a joyful and satisfying view, that the mercy and grace of God is sufficient for them; that their sins, though never so great, shall be no hindrance to their being accepted; that there is mercy enough in God for the whole world, and the like, when they give no account of any particular or distinct thought of Christ; but yet when the account they give is duly weighed, and they are a little interrogated about it, it appears that the revelation of the mercy of God in the Gospel is the ground of this their encouragement and hope; and that it is indeed the mercy of God through Christ that is discovered to them, and that 'tis depended on in him, and not in any wise moved by anything in them.[134]

Thus this so-called "implicit faith" in Christ does not refer to the *objective* grounds of salvation, but is only a temporary stage in the *subjective* awareness of some saints and is an occasional feature of every era. Edwards does not assume that the saints of the Old Testament exerted implicit faith in Christ any more than saints in awakened Northampton. As attention to Edwards's wider *corpus* reveals, he is unequivocal that the normal state of

---

133. "Miscellanies," nos. 1354, *WJE* 23:506–43 (540).
134. *A Faithful Narrative, WJE* 4:172–73.

affairs was that the Old Testament saints consciously closed with Christ for their justification, just as they did in the Apostolic era and in his own day.

When both Morimoto and Caldwell cite "Miscellanies," no. 27b to deny conscious faith in Christ on the part of the Old Testament saints, they not only misread it as describing the objective reality of saving faith rather than the subjective experience of the saint as I have argued above, but they also do not read it in the light of Edwards's many other clear affirmations of the revelation of Christ to the Old Testament saints, and of their faith in him. For example, early in his 1739 history of redemption sermons Edwards notes:

> [W]hen . . . we read in the sacred history what God did from time to time towards his church and people, and what he said to them, and how he revealed himself to them, we are to understand it especially of the second person of the Trinity. When we read after this of God's appearing time after time in some visible form or outward symbol of his presence, we are ordinarily if not universally to understand it of the second person of the Trinity, which may be argued from John 1:18. . . . Colossians 1:15, intimating that though God the Father be invisible, yet Christ is his image or symbol by which he is seen . . .[135]

Similarly, in a late "Miscellanies" entry entitled, "The Two Dispensations Compared, That under Moses and That under Christ," Edwards declares that "The spirit or principle of faith in the heart was the same [in each dispensation]; *and the person who is the object of faith is the same, viz. the Son of God as Mediator. . .*"[136] Again, returning to his "Controversies" notebook, a collection of notes, compiled from the late 1740s to the late 1750s, and to its lengthy essay entitled, "Question: In What Sense Did the Saints Under the Old Testament Believe in Christ to Justification?" Edwards answers the question in typically precise fashion under thirteen points.[137] His argument begins with the claim that the ancient church of

---

135. "Work of Redemption," WJE 9:131.

136. "Miscellanies," no. 1353, WJE 23:502. Emphasis added. See also, "Miscellanies," no. 1354, WJE 23:506–43 and my discussion of Edwards's "Controversies" notebook below. Of many possible examples among Edwards's sermons, see "Christ's Sacrifice," WJE 10:594–604.

137. "Controversies" notebook, WJE 21:372–413. It is significant that Morimoto makes no reference to this important essay. The essay is the third of three essays on justification, the others being: "Of the Meaning of the Words 'Righteous,' 'Righteousness,' etc. in the Old Testament"; the other is in two parts: "Question: Wherein Do the Two

Israel knew there was a differentiation of divine Persons of the Godhead and concludes with the assertion that "dependence on the divine Mediator. . . was the revealed and known condition of peace and acceptance with God."[138] Edwards argues that the Person who led Israel through the wilderness, who dwelt in the Holy of Holies in the Tabernacle and who was revealed to them under the titles of "the Angel of the Lord," "the Angel of God's presence" and "the Messenger of the covenant" was none other than the eternal Son, a divine Person on earth distinct from another divine Person in heaven. "It was plainly and fully revealed to the church of Israel that his person was a different person from him in heaven that sustained the dignity and maintained the rights of the Godhead, and acted as first and head and chief in the affairs of God's kingdom; and that this person, that had espoused the church of Israel to himself and dwelt amongst them as their spiritual husband, acted under him as a messenger from him. And as this was sufficiently revealed to that people, so that church of Israel all along understood it."[139] To prevent the Jewish church from conceiving of two Gods, and to lead them to understand that the divine Person in heaven and the divine Person who dwelt among them were of "one nature and substance," the latter was called God's "Name." This Name is spoken of as an object of worship, fear, love, prayer and trust and Edwards notes that where in Scripture we read of God's intention regarding the Temple, "I will put my Name there," it is in the Hebrew, "I will cause my Name to inhabit there," "plainly speaking of God's name as a person."[140] Thus to Edwards, through the economic activity of God the Israelites were capable of possessing not only an understanding of the unity and distinction of the divine Persons, but also something of their manner of subsistence and relations.

In the previous chapter I described Edwards's notebook, "The Harmony of the Genius, Spirit, Doctrines and Rules of the Old Testament and the New" and noted the first two points of doctrinal harmony that he observes: "Faith In God The Grand Design Of God's Salvation, Protection,

---

Covenants Agree as to the Method of Justification, and Appointed Qualification for it?" and "The Things Wherein the Way of Justification by Mere Law and that by Grace through Christ Differ as to the Qualification of the Subject that Primarily Entitles him to Justification." In addition there are other entries and notes. Lee suggests that the notebook represents Edwards's preparation for a significant work on justification which he never wrote. See his introductory notes in *WJE* 21:328–31.

138. "Controversies" notebook, *WJE* 21:406.

139. Ibid., 372.

140. Ibid., 376–77.

Deliverance Etc."; and "Faith In A Mediator, In The Son Of God, In The Messiah." To Edwards these do not represent two independent objects of faith, nor two stages in the conversion of the saint, nor *normally* two stages of subjective awareness of the object of faith on the part of the saint. Rather, by the two headings Edwards wishes to expresses something of the economy of salvation by which the distinctions and relations of the divine Persons are revealed. The "great Turretine" makes a similar point.[141] The doctrine concerning Christ "proposes for its object God, not simply as Creator and Lord, but as a Redeemer and Father in Christ; as covenanted and ours, who wishes to be our God that he may bestow salvation upon us. And here God and Christ ought to be indissolubly joined together. God as the supreme good, in whom we are to be made happy; Christ as the only and infallible means by which we are to be led to God."[142]

English Puritan, Thomas Goodwin (1600-80), whose works Edwards makes use of in his own biblical notes, similarly remarks, "Christ is the object of faith, in joint commission with God the Father . . . [I]t is God that justifies, and Christ that died. They are both of them set forth as the foundation of a believer's confidence. . . . Now as both these meet to justify us, so faith in justification is to look at both these."[143]

In Edwards's thought the Old Testament saints were able to distinguish between Father and Son in their Persons and roles, while the nomenclature of the divine Persons was designed to express to Israel God's one nature and substance.[144] Edwards grounds the justifying faith of the

---

141. Edwards denominates him thus in *Religious Affections*, WJE 2:289 n. 4.

142. Turretin, *Institutes*, 15.11.15.

143. Goodwin, *Christ Set Forth*, 23-24. However, Goodwin makes the distinction between the Old Testament, under which faith "had a more usual recourse unto God, who had promised the Messiah, of whom they then had not so distinct, but only confused thoughts; though this they knew, that God accepted and saved them through the Messiah," and the New Testament under which Christ exists not only in promise but is come in the flesh. "Hence [under the New Testament] the more usual and immediate address of our faith is to be made unto Christ, who as he is distinctly set forth in the new testament [*sic*], so he is as distinctly to be apprehended by the faith of believers." Goodwin, *Christ Set Forth*, 25. The degree to which Edwards believes the Old Testament saints were aware of a distinction of divine Persons means that in practice he does not hold to the kind of Testamental difference that Goodwin advocates.

144. Turretin argues against a Socinian practice of distinguishing between the Father (as the primary object of faith in whom our faith terminates) and the Son (as the secondary object of faith through whom our faith is ultimately directed to God and rests in him). He claims that the distinction between the Father and Son in person and work does not destroy the "mutual equality of the persons (since they always remain mutually equal in essence [*homoousioi*])." Therefore the distinction precipitates

Israelites on their understanding the peculiar relations of the divine Mediator to them and to God: to them, as their "head, husband, captain and Redeemer," having taken them as his own people; and as his "most near" relation as God's Son, to the transcendent divine Person who took delight in him as his own "glory" and "beauty." Knowing these relations, it was natural for the Israelites to "trust in him as the Mediator . . . by whom they were recommended to [God's] acceptance and favor; and so when their minds were oppressed with a sense of guilt, and under all their straits and difficulties, to have the refuge of their souls in him. . . . The saints in Israel looked on this person as their Mediator, through whom they had acceptance with God in heaven and the forgiveness of their sins, and trusted in him as such."[145] Through God's economy towards Israel, Edwards ascribes to the faith of the saints remarkable theological depth.

In contrast to Morimoto's depiction of a Catholic Edwards, this "Controversies" essay, his 1739 sermon series, and his notes for the "Harmony" place Edwards squarely in a Reformed and Puritan tradition that saw Christ as the object of faith in both Old and New Testaments. English nonconformist divine, John Owen (1616–83), for example, entitles the eighth chapter of his *Christologia*, "The Faith of the Church Under the Old Testament in and Concerning the Person of Christ." He writes:

> [T]he faith of the saints under the Old Testament did principally respect the person of Christ—both what it was, and what it was to be in the fullness of time, when he was to become the seed of the woman. What his especial work was to be, and the mystery of the redemption of the church thereby, they referred unto his own wisdom and grace;—only, they believed that by him they should be saved from the hand of all their enemies, or all the evil that befell them on the account of the first sin and apostasy from God.[146]

For Owen, the faith of the Old Testament saints was in the person of Christ, though their understanding of the manner of his redemption was slight due to the shadowy nature of their dispensation. Turretin holds

---

no disparity "whether of object [of faith] or of religious worship." Turretin, *Institutes*, 15.11.16–21.

145. "Controversies" notebook, *WJE* 21:386–87.

146. Owen, *Christologia*, 1.101. See also Edwards's reliance on Owen's commentary on the book of Hebrews in "Miscellanies," no. 1283, *WJE* 23:229–30 (229): "It is manifest that all that ever obtained the pardon of their sins, from the foundation of the world till Christ came (if any at all were pardoned), obtained forgiveness through the sacrifice of Christ, by Heb 9:26 . . . (see Owen on the place . . .)."

a similar position. In arguing for the substantial unity of the covenant of grace in Old and New Testament, he notes that he wages "this most important controversy" against those who hold that "the fathers of the Old Testament were not saved by the gratuitous mercy of God in Christ, the Mediator . . . *through faith in him about to come*."[147] Turretin argues that since faith and the word are related, in the dispensation of shadows and types faith was similarly obscure. Nevertheless, "The same thing . . . was always known and proposed as the object of faith, but the mode was less clearly discovered before the advent of Christ than after it . . ."[148] Christ was ever the object of justifying faith, though the revelation of him was veiled in the Old Testament. Though Edwards asserts this mainstream Reformed position, nevertheless in practice he goes beyond it. His expanded conception of prophecies and types as the means of grace means he is prepared to grant to the Old Testament saints a greater understanding of the work of Christ than were, for example, Owen or Turretin. Since I have already discussed the role of prophecies and types as means of grace in Edwards's theology, I offer only a brief recapitulation at this point. In a remarkable passage on the Holy of Holies in the "Controversies" essay Edwards argues that the "mercy seat" of the ark is better translated the "propitiatory" and points out that in Scripture heaven, not earth, is represented as the place of God's throne where He sits to hear and accept the offerings made. Earth is the place where those sacrifices are made—at the propitiatory, God's footstool. Those who offered sacrifices looked on the Angel of the Covenant "who abode there as their most eminent high priest, through whom their sacrifices came up for a sweet savor to God in heaven, and on whom they [were] entirely dependent for a real atonement and peace with God . . ."[149] Old Testament sacrifices did not provide "real atonement" *ex opere operato*, but were called "sacrifices of atonement" because of their typical character grasped by faith, the shadow being called by the name of the substance. The sacrifices were appointed to "stand instead of, or to represent, the real atonement," and the saints of Israel knew this because their Scriptures spoke of the true expiation of sin coming only through the Messiah.[150] Types and prophecies bore witness together to that "real

147. Turretin, *Institutes*, 12.5.1. Emphasis added. Turretin names among his opponents, "the Socinians, Remonstrants, [and] Anabaptists."

148. Ibid., 12.5.38.

149. "Controversies" notebook, *WJE* 21:394.

150. "Miscellanies," no. 1069, *WJE* 11:308-15 (312). Edwards does not explicitly respond to the question that Turretin expounds in his *Institutes*, 12.10.1-32, namely whether the Old Testament saints enjoyed *aphesin* (a full remission of sins under the

atonement" which came through the work of the Messiah. Similarly, in his "Controversies" essay Edwards follows his discussion of the didactic nature of Tabernacle/Temple types by arguing that the saints knew from the prophets (among others he cites Zech 6:12–13, Mal 3:1, and Hag 2:7) that "that divine person who was to come as the Messiah was that Angel whom they knew . . . who used to appear in the tabernacle and temple in the cloud of glory."[151] From there it was a short step to Edwards's further point that the Old Testament saints understood that the Messiah would make atonement for sin by his own sufferings and by offering himself up to God. It is "not credible," Edwards argues, that Israel should have so many prophecies of the Messiah's coming "yet . . . all along be totally ignorant of the main errand of the Messiah . . . and of the main thing that he should do for their benefit."[152]

Edwards multiplies the means of grace in the Old Testament through his expanded typology and through his conception of the prophetic *corpus* as one vast unified presentation of the person and work of the Messiah. As a result he pushes the boundaries of the Reformed tradition regarding the

---

Law in virtue of the future death of Christ—the position to which Turretin subscribes) or whether they only enjoyed a *paresin* (a passing-by of their sins until Christ's death). However, he may be said to address the question at a number of points in his theology, among them: (1) his theology of history demands that the saints in every age are affectively involved in God's self-glorification, which is inconsistent with them being under guilt and fear; (2) the gracious nature of the covenant that the Old Testament saints entered implies the communication of all spiritual happiness, or else reconciliation can co-exist with wrath; (3) for Edwards types are no longer simply temporal prefigurations of a later event, but are shadows of spiritual substance that convey the reality they portray. Consequently, the effect of Christ's atoning death is "common to all ages from the fall of man <to the end of the world>." *WJE* 9:120–21. In this Edwards follows Mastricht, *Theoretico-practica Theologia*, 5.1.34. Mastricht ties *aphesin* to the eternal covenant, rather than to the testamentary character of the Mediator's death: "Those brethren who follow . . . Cocceius . . . in order more conveniently to hold that in spite of the eternal promise the faithful of the O.T. were liable right up to the actual satisfaction, insist that the *sponsio* was a *fideiussio* by which the chief debtor remains under liability right up to the actual payment. The rest of the Reformed hold the view that by his eternal promise the Son had absolutely promised a payment or satisfaction without reservation of the benefits of order and quittance . . . had taken upon himself once for all the complete case of the elect sinner and his liability therewith and had undertaken them once for all and had thereby delivered those to be redeemed from all liability." See Heppe, *Reformed Dogmatics*, 378–81. On Edwards's response to the question of the relationship between Christ as the bond in the eternal covenant of redemption and the temporal application of his satisfaction, see above n. 74.

151. "Controversies" notebook, *WJE* 21:396.

152. Ibid., 400–01.

content of the faith possessed by the saints of the Old Testament. Though Edwards maintains that the revelation of the gospel in the Old Testament was shadowy and dark, in principle his multiplied means of grace seem capable of delivering to the Old Testament saints an understanding of the gospel more commonly associated in his tradition with its New Testament administration.

Conclusion

In the first of his sermons in the Redemption discourse, Edwards comments that the work of redemption can be considered in two respects. First, it may be conceived as the grand scheme that unites history (the *historia salutis*), which Edwards expounds in the following twenty-nine sermons. Second, however, it may be understood

> with respect to the effect wrought on the souls of the redeemed, which is common to all ages from the fall of man <to the end of the world>. [This is] the application of redemption with respect to the souls of particular persons in converting, justifying, sanctifying and glorifying of them. . . . The way that the Work of Redemption with respect to these effects of it respecting the souls of the redeemed is carried on from the fall <of man to the end of the world> is by repeating after continually working the same work over again, though in different persons from age to age.[153]

It is with this second sense (of the work of redemption) that this chapter has been concerned. I have argued that Edwards sees a close harmony in soteriology between Old and New Testaments. His commitment to the coherence of prophecy in things concerning the Messiah, coupled with his expansion of types in the Old Testament bears fruit in this soteriological harmony. This harmony is ultimately expressed in a common object of faith. *Contra* Morimoto's account of dispositional soteriology, Edwards maintains that the Old Testament saints closed with Christ, though in a manner fitting to their dispensation. And as with the saints of his own day, Edwards argues that the Old Testament saints may have grown in their subjective awareness of their salvation. Though at points he affirms the revelatory superiority of the new dispensation, in practice Edwards seems to grant to the Old Testament saints a content of faith normally associated in his tradition only with the New Testament church.

153. "Work of Redemption," *WJE* 9:120–21.

General Conclusion

THAT MORE WORK REMAINS to be done on Jonathan Edwards's understanding and interpretation of Scripture scarcely needs stating, nor that such work needs to be done in order for our understanding of Edwards to sharpened. The present study has sought to offer an account of Edwards's conception of the relationship between Old and New Testaments through examination of his wider *corpus* but principally of his largely neglected notes for, "The Harmony of the Old and New Testament." What may be learned from Edwards on this subject? Does this eighteenth-century colonial theologian have anything of value to say on the question this side of Hans Frei's "eclipse"?[1] I noted in my introduction that before Edwards can be retrieved he must be understood. And he must be understood as an eighteenth-century pastor, theologian and biblical scholar. The present study has sought to do that.

In chapter 1 I set Edwards's understanding of prophecy against the backdrop of the debate initiated by the Deist, Anthony Collins concerning the Apostolic use of Old Testament prophecy. I argued that, like Collins, Edwards follows Locke in believing the language of prophecy must be ruled and rational, but in keeping with his tradition Edwards demands that attention to authorial intention must include taking notice of the divine author, the Holy Spirit, whose words are capable of polyvalence. Only one enjoying the Spirit-given "new sense," who pays attention to the wider analogy of Scripture may correctly understand Scripture's idiom. I argued that whereas previous accounts have painted Edwards as an unprincipled and unrestrained exegete, there is significant continuity with his Puritan and Reformed exegetical heritage, principally his reliance on the analogy of Scripture. Turning to his notes for the "Harmony," I argued that "Miscellanies," no. 1347 is a crucial but hitherto unrecognized part of

---

1. Frei, *Eclipse*.

Edwards's preparation for the work, displaying clearly the method he employs in it elsewhere. In the section of the "Harmony" concerning prophecy Edwards confines himself to the text of the Old Testament, arguing that figural language and predictive prophecy are features of its literal sense and that its prophecies are only coherent when read as prophecies of the coming Messiah. By this method he seeks to establish key phenomena in the defense of the coherence of the Bible as a whole. The scale of Edwards's account of prophecy is vast and provides context to the relatively few prophecies whose Apostolic interpretation Collins had objected to.

In chapter 2 I examined Edwards's typology and argued that previous accounts have failed to pay sufficient attention to the priority and constraining role of Scripture in his identification and interpretation of types. I argued, in contrast to previous accounts, that Edwards's typologizing of Scripture, history and nature are all of one piece, explicable by reference to his philosophical commitments, in particular his idealism and his notion of being as relational and communicative within a teleology of divine self-glorification. As with Edwards's approach to prophecy, it is Scripture that helps the saint identify and interpret the divine language of types. To Edwards the existence of types within the Bible is evidence of a universal nexus of types and antitypes that runs throughout creation and history. When he reads the Bible through the lens of this universal imaging system, Edwards sees in Scripture a degree of typological harmony that surpasses that acknowledged by his tradition. To Edwards, Old and New Testaments are not linked at finite explicit points, but at every moment. Turning to his "Harmony" notes, Edwards follows the approach he has pursued with prophecy. He defends the phenomenon of types from within the Old Testament, and argues that the Old Testament is itself only coherent when understood as "one great and vastly complicated and variegated prediction of this event [the coming of the Messiah, his redemption and kingdom]."[2]

Chapter 3 was concerned with the third aspect of Testamental harmony Edwards perceives: that of doctrine and precept. Redemption history and a covenantal system, apparent in Edwards's wider *corpus*, provide the unseen framework to this part of his "Harmony." I argued that Edwards follows Calvin and a continental Reformed tradition in holding to the substantial similarity but administrative difference of the covenant of grace in Old and New Testaments. The response of the saints to the gospel is similarly temporally conditioned. Yet as Edwards develops the

---

2. "Miscellanies," no. 1347, *WJE* 23:384.

complexity of the Old Testament "veil," expanding the category of types and the Messianic nature and interconnectedness of prophecy whose meaning is made available to those in possession of the "new sense," so he inevitably emphasizes the substantial similarity between Old and New Testament expressions of the covenant of grace. As with prophecies and types, so Edwards is willing to find parallels in doctrine and precept that go beyond the familiar categories employed by his tradition.

Chapter 4 attempted to draw together the three forms of harmony that Edwards observes, in a case study of Edwards's doctrine of salvation. Engaging with the thesis of dispositional soteriology, it sought to answer the question of how, on Edwards's account, the Old Testaments saints were saved. In contrast to the (anachronistic) accounts offered by Morimoto, McDermott and Studebaker I argued that the soteriological harmony Edwards observes between Old and New Testaments is ultimately expressed in a common object of saving faith, namely Christ, as was common to Edwards's tradition. He maintains that the Old Testament saints "closed with Christ" in a manner fitting to their dispensation, though they may have grown in their subjective awareness of their salvation, just as the saints of his own day did.

In seeking some estimation of the value of Edwards's approach it must be admitted that there are difficulties inherent in it. Granted that it is the Holy Spirit who alone engenders in the believer a "new sense" of things, yet for Edwards, another factor plays a central role in his epistemology: spiritual maturity, both personal and ecclesial. The importance of spiritual maturity in the life of the individual saint is highlighted by the scope of the coherence between the Testaments that Edwards proposes. Edwards is optimistic in the ability of his framework to account for the smallest detail of reality presented in Old and New Testaments. This is because Edwards understands the world of the Old Testament to be one part of the typical world, as his notes for the "Harmony" indicate. The saint has both the ability and the responsibility to mine the Scriptures and the world around him for spiritual truth with the tools learned through the Bible's own exegesis. But Edwards's scheme leaves him with few controls in his exegetical practice. It is true that Edwards presupposes some basic rules for the interpretation of types, rules I outlined in my discussion in chapter 2. Nevertheless, his conception of types as "a certain sort of language" leaves them relatively open to error, being ultimately dependent on the competence of the interpreter to understand the language. Operating on a "pre-critical" notion of the perspicuity of Scripture, Edwards assumes that

General Conclusion

as a language typology's idiom may be learnt by acquaintance. But as with all languages typology is capable of being mis-heard, misinterpreted and misunderstood. Therefore, although in principle God has done enough to teach us the language of types Edwards concedes that great care must be taken to have a right notion of the language's idiom lest we use "barbarous expressions that fail entirely of the proper beauty of the language."[3] Only as the believer grows in his understanding of the Scriptures and in familiarity with typology's idiom may he interpret the types around him accurately. In the final analysis, the correct understanding of types is dependent on the believer's spiritual maturity.

Personal spiritual maturity is crucial to a correct understanding of the language of types, but so too is the spiritual maturity of the church. Edwards argues that the church's place in redemption history affects her ability to understand the types and prophecies presented to her. "The types of the Old Testament were given, not without an aim at their instruction to whom they were given, but yet they were given much more for our instruction under the New Testament; for they understood but little, but we are under vastly greater advantage to understand them than they. That they were given chiefly for us seem to be evident by those texts, I Corinthians 9:910, I Corinthians 10:11."[4] Edwards argues that the New Testament church is able to understand the types and prophecies of the Old Testament far better than could the Old Testament church to whom they were first given. Referring to the Apostle Paul, Edwards comments that by his writings "a child may come to know more of the doctrines of the gospel in many respects than the greatest prophets knew under the darkness of the Old Testament."[5] And yet Edwards himself, well practiced in typological interpretation, at times offers several discrete interpretations of the one type. An example of this is Edwards's observations on the significance of stars. In his "Blank Bible" he comments on Genesis 15:5, "The stars were designed by the creator to be a type of the saints, the spiritual seed of Abraham. And the seeming multitude of them, which is much greater than the real multitude of visible stars, was designed as a type of the multitude of the saints."[6] In his notebook, "Images or Shadows of Divine Things" Edwards repeats this observation on two occasions.[7] However, elsewhere in

---

3. "Types," *WJE* 11:151.
4. "Types," *WJE* 11:148-49.
5. "Work of Redemption," *WJE* 9:367.
6. "Blank Bible," *WJE* 24:157.
7. "Images," nos. 53 and 86, *WJE* 11:65-66 and 85-86 respectively.

the notebook he suggests that the stars might signify other spiritual truths altogether. In "Images," no. 40 Edwards notes that the gradual vanishing of the stars when the sun begins to appear is "a type of the gradual vanishing of Jewish ordinances as the Gospel dispensation was introduced."[8] Again, towards the end of the notebook the stars take on yet another significance when Edwards notes that in Job 38 "the dominion of the stars in the earth" is spoken of as "an image of the dominion of angels in the earth."[9] The one type is thus capable of at least three distinct interpretations: as the (glorified) saints; as the Jewish ordinances; and as angels. Since Scripture is for Edwards a grammar book for the language of types, it is reasonable to expect that types might be more accurately understood once that grammar book was complete. Consequently, if a type is capable of numerous interpretations by an eighteenth-century observer in possession of the complete Christian canon, it is questionable whether the saint living much earlier in redemption history, and more dependent on "un-interpreted" types due to the incompleteness of the canon, really has the ability to understand the spiritual truth communicated by the type to the degree that Edwards's system requires. That is, are natural types in the Old Testament really able to bear the theological weight Edwards asks of them, or to play the didactic role Edwards demands of them for the redemption of the Old Testament elect? This objection may be answered by the claim that Edwards's conception of types is analogous to his understanding of prophecy. Both type and prophecy are polyvalent. Thus the Old Testament saint, looking up at the stars, might understand the types he saw in terms of just one of the several interpretations available to a saint, such as Edwards, who lived much later in redemption history. Both prophecy and types are capable of a manifold instruction which is increasingly known as redemption history unfolds. However, in practice Edwards's treatment of types and prophecy differs. While he argues that the full import of a Messianic prophecy only becomes apparent as redemption history unfolds, Edwards is adamant that the Messianic *nature* of the prophecy was always known. But the fact that Edwards's own interpretations of the one type are so very different from each other suggests a degree of latitude in interpreting types that casts doubt on Edwards's ability to identify and rely upon the type's

8. "Images," no. 40, *WJE* 11:60.

9. "Images," no. 184, *WJE* 11:120. See also Edwards's series of observations under the heading "SCRIPTURES," that follows the main body of "Images." Edwards again refers to stars in "Images," no. 38, *WJE* 11:134, cross-referencing to his "Blank Bible" entry on Joshua 10:13 in which he notes that "the angels are called stars," "Blank Bible," *WJE* 24:326–27.

General Conclusion

meaning at an earlier stage in redemption history.[10] That is, at issue is not necessarily the polyvalence of types, nor the ability of a particular type to hold a fixed meaning at a particular stage in redemption history, nor even the possibility of that meaning being known by an Old Testament saint. Rather, the difficulty lies with Edwards's confidence in being able to isolate and identify a type's meaning at any stage in redemption history and to rely on it in his account of the faith of the saints in Old and New Testament.

A similar difficulty is found in Edwards's treatment of polyvalent prophecy. It is clear that Edwards was aware of this problem and wrestled throughout his life to answer to his own satisfaction the question of what the prophets or their first audiences understood of their messages. I noted this in chapter 2. Edwards did not consider it necessary that the prophets themselves understood the full import of what the Holy Spirit intended by their words; redemption history would reveal the depth of their messages. Yet Edwards assumed that the Messianic referent of the prophets' messages did not only become apparent retrospectively, but was available from the start. After all, did not the prophets themselves search out the time and circumstances of the sufferings and glory of Christ that the Spirit of Christ in them had testified to beforehand (1 Pet 1:10-11)?[11] As the means of grace were multiplied through redemption history, with the gifts of the covenants, sacrificial system, Law, Temple, prophecy etc., so were multiplied the presentations of the Messiah, his redemption and kingdom. In principle a saint living after the return from the Exile could be expected to understand far more of the coming Messiah than a saint living before the Flood. However, Edwards's typological system that takes in the natural world has the effect of blunting the gains made by his commitment to "progressive revelation." Though prophecies and types might yield greater truth through redemption history, yet at every stage in her history the church always had held before her eyes innumerable images and shadows of spiritual reality. Those enlightened by the Holy Spirit and in possession

---

10. In chapter 2 I drew attention to a note in Edwards's "Blank Bible" on Daniel 5:25ff. in which he argued that a single prophecy might have two distinct meanings at the same time—meanings not related as type-antitype—providing that both are linguistically permitted, are instructive and are agreeable to the analogy of faith. This suggests that in Edwards's thought type and prophecy were both in principle capable of multiple unrelated senses. However, Edwards rarely employs this thesis in his treatment of prophecies, preferring instead to relate the multiple senses of a prophecy typologically.

11. "Work of Redemption," *WJE* 9:339.

of the "new sense" could in principle understand a great deal of spiritual reality, on Edwards's system.

In Edwards's account the degree of spiritual understanding enjoyed by those in the Old Testament in possession of the "new sense" is remarkable. I noted above that in "Miscellanies," no. 1353 Edwards makes what could have been a useful distinction between the content of faith of the post-Apostolic Christian church and that of the Old Testament church under Moses. Such a distinction, if exploited, might have safeguarded Edwards from charges of eisegesis in his handling of the Old Testament and offer for retrieval a more moderate Edwards. But, as soon as Edwards makes this distinction he goes on to invalidate it in practice by noting, "Not only were these things, mentioned under the last head, in some sort exhibited and represented under both dispensations, but also were in some degree made known and revealed under both."[12] The same conviction is apparent elsewhere. In "Types of the Messiah" it is clear that the difference between "exhibition" and "revelation" is, to all intents, irrelevant to Edwards: "We find by the Old Testament that it has ever been God's manner from the beginning of the world to exhibit and reveal future things by symbolical representations, which were no other than types of the future things revealed."[13] His insistence that the Old Testament saints could "understand such like things [types] as representations of divine things, and receive the particular instruction exhibited in them, even before they are particularly explained to 'em by God by a new revelation" suggests that in practice a distinction between "exhibition" and "revelation" is invalid. Thus despite Edwards's assertions to the contrary, there appears to be little discernible difference in his account between the degree of understanding enjoyed by the church living in each Testamental era. In short, though Edwards affirms the greater revelatory clarity of the new dispensation, his multiplication of (Messianic) types and the interconnectedness of (Messianic) prophecy whose content is revealed to the regenerate, means that in practice he often seems to grant to the Old Testament saints a content of faith normally associated with the New Testament.

In the course of this work I have noted that Edwards operates according to a number of "pre-critical" assumptions, chief among them the analogies of Scripture and faith. Though these assumptions may not be readily shared by all today, nevertheless a number of benefits emerge from Edwards's approach. First, the scale of Edwards's "Harmony," which

12. "Miscellanies," no. 1353, *WJE* 23:493.
13. "Miscellanies," no. 1069, *WJE* 11:192.

was intended to take in "a very great part of the holy Scripture," is vast. Edwards's account of the relationship of the Old and New Testaments is able to account for temporally-disparate and seemingly-marginal texts, as well as more familiar ones. In short, the scale of Edwards's "Harmony" means that future studies of the unity of the Christian Bible cannot afford to ignore it. Furthermore, in a contemporary academic atmosphere of disciplinary specialization that often exist in isolation from each other, Edwards offers an example of a "grand unified theory" of the Bible, a comprehensive interpretation capable of embracing the *minutiae* of Old and New Testaments. Second, Edwards's approach takes seriously the nature of the Bible as the Scriptures of the Christian church, Scriptures whose scope and meaning are made available to those who profess faith in Jesus the Messiah and are indwelt and illumined by his Holy Spirit. Third and related, in principle Edwards's conception of the Old and New Testaments as God's grammar book of a typological language offers a way of connecting the world that the Christian experiences to the world he or she professes to inhabit. Fourth, by grounding the unity of the Christian Bible on a discrete witness of the Hebrew Scriptures that is Messianic, Edwards in principle offers to resource a conversation between the church and the synagogue regarding the identity of the Messiah and the object of faith.

Edwards's Bible presents modern sensibilities with "a strange new world" indeed. Yet arguably there is value in its very strangeness. John Webster's comment that theologies of retrieval are valuable precisely because they "de-centre" the accepted norms of critical judgment by trying to stand with the Christian past, may be applied to Edwards's theology of the Bible. Precisely because it is foreign to contemporary conventions it can "function as an instrument for the enlargement of vision."[14]

---

14. Webster, "Theologies of Retrieval," 583-99.

Bibliography

Jonathan Edwards

"Miscellanies," nos. 891, 922, 1067, 1068, *Works of Jonathan Edwards*. Vol. 30. Online: http://www.edwards.yale.edu.
"Scripture Prophecies of the Old Testament," *Works of Jonathan Edwards*. Vol. 30. Online: http://www.edwards.yale.edu.
"A History of the Work of Redemption," *Works of Jonathan Edwards*. Vol. 31. Online: http://www.edwards.yale.edu.
Discourses on Various Important Subjects. Boston, 1738.
An Humble Inquiry into the Rules of the Word of God, Concerning the Qualifications Requisite to a Complete Standing and Full Communion in the Visible Christian Church. Boston, 1749.
Misrepresentations corrected and truth vindicated. In reply to the Rev. Mr. Solomon Williams's book intitled, The true state of the question concerning the qualifications necessary to lawful communion in the Christian sacraments. Boston, 1752.
Remarks on important theological controversies. Edinburgh, 1796.
True grace, distinguished from the experience of devils; in a sermon, preached before the Synod of New-York, convened at New-Ark, in New-Jersey, on September 28. N.S. 1752. New York, 1753.

Collected Works

Works of Jonathan Edwards. 26 vols. New Haven: Yale University Press, 1957–2008:

Vol. 1. *Freedom of the Will*, edited by Paul Ramsey, 1957.
Vol. 2. *Religious Affections*, edited by John E. Smith, 1959.
Vol. 3. *Original Sin*, edited by Clyde A. Holbrook, 1970.
Vol. 4. *The Great Awakening*, edited by C. C. Goen, 1972.
Vol. 5. *Apocalyptic Writings*, edited by Stephen J. Stein, 1977.
Vol. 6. *Scientific and Philosophical Writings*, edited by Wallace E. Anderson, 1980.
Vol. 7. *The Life of David Brainerd*, edited by Norman Pettit, 1985.
Vol. 8. *Ethical Writings*, edited by Paul Ramsey, 1989.
Vol. 9. *A History of the Work of Redemption*, edited by John F. Wilson, 1989.

Bibliography

Vol. 10. *Sermons and Discourses, 1720-23*, edited by Wilson H. Kimnach, 1992.
Vol. 11. *Typological Writings*, edited by Wallace E. Anderson and Mason I. Lowance Jr. with David Watters, 1993.
Vol. 12. *Ecclesiastical Writings*, edited by David D. Hall, 1994.
Vol. 13. *The "Miscellanies" a-z, aa-zz, 1-500*, edited by Thomas A. Schafer, 1994.
Vol. 14. *Sermons and Discourses, 1723-29*, edited by Kenneth P. Minkema, 1997.
Vol. 15. *Notes on Scripture*, edited by Stephen J. Stein, 1998.
Vol. 16. *Letters and Personal Writings*, edited by George S. Claghorn, 1998.
Vol. 17. *Sermons and Discourses, 1730-33*, edited by Mark Valeri, 1999.
Vol. 18. *The "Miscellanies" 501-832*, edited by Ava Chamberlain, 2000.
Vol. 19. *Sermons and Discourses, 1734-38*, edited by M.X. Lesser, 2001.
Vol. 20. *The "Miscellanies" 833-1152*, edited by Amy Plantinga Pauw, 2002.
Vol. 21. *Writings on the Trinity, Grace and Faith*, edited by Sang Hyun Lee, 2003.
Vol. 22. *Sermons and Discourses, 1739-42*, edited by Harry S. Stout and Nathan O. Hatch with Kyle P. Farley, 2003.
Vol. 23. *The "Miscellanies" 1153-1360*, edited by Douglas A. Sweeney, 2004.
Vol. 24. *The Blank Bible*, edited by Stephen J. Stein, 2006.
Vol. 25. *Sermons and Discourses, 1743-58*, edited by Wilson H. Kimnach, 2006.
Vol. 26. *Catalogues of Books*, edited by Peter J. Thuesen, 2008.
Dwight, Sereno, editor. *The Works of President Edwards*. 10 vols. New York: Converse, 1830.
Hickman, Edward, editor. *The Works of Jonathan Edwards*. 2 vols. London: Westley and Davis, 1834. Reprinted, Edinburgh: Banner of Truth, 1974.

Separately Published Works

Bailey, Richard A. and Gregory Wills, editors. *The Salvation of Souls: Nine Previously Unpublished Sermons on the Call of Ministry and the Gospel by Jonathan Edwards*. Wheaton, IL: Crossway, 2002.
Helm, Paul, editor. *Treatise on Grace and Other Posthumously Published Writings*. Cambridge: James Clark, 1971.
Kimnach, Wilson H., et al. editors. *The Sermons of Jonathan Edwards: A Reader*. New Haven: Yale University Press, 1999.
Kistler, Don, editor. *Altogether Lovely: Jonathan Edwards on the Glory and Excellency of Jesus Christ*. Morgan, PA: Soli Deo Gloria Publications, 1997.
Miller, Perry, editor. *Images or Shadows of Divine Things*. New Haven: Yale University Press, 1948.
Sermons of Jonathan Edwards. Peabody, MA: Hendrickson, 2005.

OTHER WORKS

Aaron, Richard I. *John Locke*. Oxford: Clarendon, 1955.
Althaus, Paul. *The Theology of Martin Luther*. Philadelphia: Fortress, 1966.
Ames, William. *The Marrow of Theology*. Translated from the third Latin edition, 1629, and edited by John D. Eusden. Boston: Pilgrim, 1968.

Bibliography

Anderson, Wallace E. "Editor's Introduction to 'Images of Divine Things' and 'Types.'" In *Typological Writings*. Vol. 11 of *The Works of Jonathan Edwards*, 3–48. New Haven: Yale University Press, 1993.

———. "Editor's Introduction." In *Scientific and Philosophical Writings*. Vol. 6 of *The Works of Jonathan Edwards*, 1–143. New Haven: Yale University Press, 1980.

———. "Note on 'The Mind.'" In *Scientific and Philosophical Writings*. Vol. 6 of *The Works of Jonathan Edwards*, 313–29. New Haven: Yale University Press, 1980.

Aquinas, Thomas. *Summa Theologica*. Translated by the Fathers of the English Dominican Province. Christian Classics Ethereal Library. Benziger, 1947. Online, http://www.ccel.org/aquinas/summa

Asselt, Willem J. van. *The Federal Theology of Johannes Cocceius 1603–1669*. Translated by Raymond A. Blacketer. Leiden: Brill, 2001.

Auerbach, Erich. *Mimesis: The Representation of Reality in Western Literature*. Translated by Willard R. Trask. Princeton: Princeton University Press, 1968.

———. *Scenes from the Drama of European Literature*. Theory and History of Literature 9. New York: Meridian, 1959.

Augustine. "On Faith and the Creed." In *On Faith and the Creed: Dogmatic Teaching of the Church of the Fourth and Fifth Centuries*, translated by Charles A. Heurtley Oxford: Parker, 1886.

———. *The Trinity*. Introduced, translated and notes by Edmund Hill. Edited by John E. Rotelle. New York: New City, 1991.

Baker, David L. *Two Testaments, One Bible: A study of the theological relationship between the Old and New Testaments*. Leicester: Apollos, 1991.

Balserak, Jon. *Divinity Compromised: A Study of Divine Accommodation in the Thought of John Calvin*. Dordrecht: Springer, 2006.

———. "The God of Love and Weakness: Calvin's Understanding of God's Accommodating Relationship with His People." *Westminster Theological Journal* 62 (2000) 177–95.

Barr, James. *The Concept of Biblical Theology: An Old Testament Perspective*. London: SCM, 1999.

———. *Holy Scripture: Canon, Authority, Criticism*. Oxford: Clarendon, 1983.

Barrera, Julio Trebolle. *The Jewish Bible and the Christian Bible: An Introduction to the History of the Bible*. Translated by Wilfred G. E. Watson. Cambridge: Eerdmans, 1998.

Barth, Karl. *Church Dogmatics* II.1. Edinburgh: Clark, 2004.

———. *Credo*. London: Hodder & Stoughton, 1964.

Bartholomew, Craig, et al., editors. *Canon and Biblical Interpretation*. Scripture and Hermeneutics 7. Milton Keynes: Paternoster, 2006.

Basnage, Jacques. *The History of the Jews from Jesus Christ to the Present Time: Containing their Antiquities, their Religion, their Rites, the Dispersion of the Ten Tribes in the East, and the Persecutions this Nation has Suffered in the West. Being a Supplement and Continuation of The History of Josephus*. Translated by Thomas Taylor. London, 1708.

Bauckham, Richard. *Bible and Mission: Christian Witness in a Postmodern World*. Milton Keynes: Authentic, 2003.

Baumgartner, Paul R. "Jonathan Edwards: the theory behind his use of figurative language," *Proceedings of the Modern Language Association* 78.4 (1963) 321–25.

Bibliography

Beale, Gregory K. *The Temple and the Church's Mission: A Biblical Theology of the Dwelling Place of God.* New Studies in Biblical Theology 17. Downers Grove, IL: Apollos, 2004.

Beale, Gregory K., and D. A. Carson, editors. *Commentary on the New Testament Use of the Old Testament.* Grand Rapids: Baker, 2007.

Bentley, Richard. *Remarks upon a Late Discourse of Free-Thinking, Occasion'd by the Rise and Growth of a Sect Call'd Free-Thinkers.* London, 1713.

Bercovitch, Sacvan. *The American Jeremiad.* Madison: University of Wisconsin, 1978.

———. *The Puritan Origins of the American Self.* New Haven: Yale University Press, 1975.

———, editor. "Special Typology Issue." *Early American Literature*, 2 parts, 5.1 (1970).

———, editor. *Typology and Early American Literature.* Amherst: University of Massachusetts Press, 1972.

Berkeley, George. *An Essay Towards a New Theory of Vision.* Dublin, 1709.

———. *The Principles of Human Knowledge and Three Dialogues.* Dublin, 1710. Edited by Howard Robinson. Oxford World Classics Series. Oxford: Oxford University Press, 1999.

Berman, David. *A History of Atheism in Britain from Hobbes to Russell.* London: Routledge, 1990.

Biehl, Craig. *The Infinite Merit of Christ: The Glory of Christ's Obedience in the Theology of Jonathan Edwards.* Jackson, MS: Reformed Academic, 2009.

Bogue, Carl W. *Jonathan Edwards and the Covenant of Grace.* Cherry Hill, NJ: Mack, 1975.

Bombaro, John J. "Jonathan Edward's [sic] Vision of Salvation." *Westminster Theological Journal* 65 (2003) 45–67.

Boston, Thomas. *A View of the Covenant of Grace from the sacred records: wherein the parties in that covenant, the making of it, its parts conditionary and promissory, and the administration thereof, are distinctly considered: together with the trial of a personal inbeing in it... To which is subjoin'd, a memorial concerning personal and family fasting....* Edinburgh, 1742. Reprinted, Philadelphia, 1827.

Bray, Gerald *Biblical Interpretation: Past and Present.* Leicester: Apollos, 1996.

———. "The Church Fathers and Biblical Theology." In *Canon and Biblical Interpretation*, edited by Craig Bartholomew et al., 23–40. Scripture and Hermeneutics 7. Milton Keynes: Paternoster, 2006.

Brown, Robert E. "The Bible." In *The Princeton Companion to Jonathan Edwards*, edited by Sang Hyun Lee, 87–102. Princeton: Princeton University Press, 2005.

———. "Edwards, Locke and the Bible." *Journal of Religion* 79.3 (1999) 361–84.

———. *Jonathan Edwards and the Bible.* Bloomington: Indiana University Press, 2002.

———. "The Sacred and the Profane Connected: Edwards, the Bible, and Intellectual Culture." In *Jonathan Edwards at 300: Essays on the Tercentenary of His Birth*, edited by H. Stout et al., 38–53. Lanham, MD: University Press of America, 2005.

Brumm, Ursula. *American Thought and Religious Typology.* New Brunswick, NJ: Rutgers University Press, 1970.

Bryant, Louise May and Mary Patterson. "The List of Books Sent by Jeremiah Dummer." In *Papers in Honor of Andrew Keogh*, edited by Mary C. Withington, 423–92. New Haven: Yale University Press, 1938.

Buren, Paul M. van. "On Reading Someone Else's Mail: The Church and Israel's [sic] Scriptures." In *Die Hebräische Bibel und ihre zweifache Nachgeschichte: Festschrift*

für Rolf Rendtorff zum 65. Gebertstag, herausgegeben Erhard von Blum, Christian Macholz und Ekkehard W. Stegemann Neukirchen-Vluyn: Neukirchener, (1990), 595–606.
Buxtorf, Johannes. *Lexica Hebriacum et Chaldacicum*. London, 1646.
Caldwell, Patricia. *The Puritan Conversion Narrative: The Beginnings of American Expression*. Cambridge: Cambridge University Press, 1983.
Caldwell, Robert W. *Communion in the Spirit: The Holy Spirit as the Bond of Union in the Theology of Jonathan Edwards*. Milton Keynes: Paternoster, 2006.
Calvin, John. *Commentaries on the First Book of Moses Called Genesis*. Vol. 1 of Calvin's Commentaries. Translated by John King. Grand Rapids: Baker 2005.
———. *Commentaries on the Second Epistle of Peter*. Vol. 22 of *Calvin's Commentaries*. Translated by John King. Grand Rapids: Baker, 2005.
———. *Institutes of the Christian Religion*. The Library of Christian Classics 20–21. Edited by John T. McNeill. Translated by Ford Lewis Battles. London: SCM, 1960.
Chai, Leon. *Jonathan Edwards and the Limits of Enlightenment Philosophy*. New York: Oxford University Press, 1998.
Chamberlain, Ava. "Editor's Introduction." In *The "Miscellanies" 501–832*. Vol. 18 of *The Works of Jonathan Edwards*, 1–48. New Haven: Yale University Press, 2000.
Chandler, Edward. *A Defence of Christianity from the Prophecies of the Old Testament*. London, 1725.
Chandler, Samuel. *A Vindication of the Christian Religion*. 2nd ed. 2 vols. London. 1727–28.
Chappell, Vere, editor. *The Cambridge Companion to Locke*. Cambridge: Cambridge University Press, 1994.
Charity, A. C. *Events and Their Afterlife: The Dialectics of Christian Typology in the Bible and Dante*. Cambridge: Cambridge University Press, 1966.
Cherry, Conrad. *Nature and Religious Imagination: From Edwards to Bushnell*. Philadelphia: Fortress, 1980.
———. "The Puritan Notion of the Covenant in Jonathan Edwards' [sic] Doctrine of Faith." *Church History* 34 (1965) 328–41.
———. "Symbols of Spiritual Truth." *Interpretation* 39.3 (1985) 263–71.
———. *The Theology of Jonathan Edwards: A Reappraisal*. Bloomington, IN: Indiana University Press, 1990.
Chubb, Thomas. *A collection of tracts, on various subjects*. London, 1730.
Clarke, Samuel. *A Discourse concerning the connexion of the Prophecies in the Old Testament and the Application of them to Christ*. London, 1725.
———. *A Discourse concerning the unchangeable Obligations of Natural Religion and the Truth . . . of the Christian Revelation*. 4th ed. London, 1716.
Cohen, Charles H. "The Post-Puritan Paradigm of Early American Religious History." *William and Mary Quarterly* 3rd series, 54.4 (1997) 695–722.
Collins, Anthony. *A Discourse on the Grounds and Reasons of the Christian Religion*. London, 1724.
———. *The Scheme of Literal Prophecy Considered; in view of the controversy occasion'd by a late book, intitled, A discourse of the grounds and reasons of the Christian religion*. London, 1726.
Cooey, Paula M. *Jonathan Edwards on Nature and Destiny: A Systematic Analysis* Studies in American Religion 16. New York: Edwin Mellen, 1985.

Bibliography

Coombe, Thomas. *The Harmony Between the Old and New Testaments Respecting the Messiah; being the substance of two sermons* . . . Philadelphia, 1774.

Cooper, John W. *Panentheism: The Other God of the Philosophers*. Nottingham: Apollos, 2007.

Crisp, Oliver D. "How 'Occasional' was Edwards's Occasionalism?" In *Jonathan Edwards: Philosophical Theologian*, edited by Paul Helm and Oliver D. Crisp, 61–77. Aldershot: Ashgate, 2003.

———. "Jonathan Edwards on Divine Simplicity." *Religious Studies* 39 (2003) 23–41.

———. "Jonathan Edwards's God: Trinity, Individuation and Divine Simplicity." In *Engaging the Doctrine of God: Contemporary Protestant Perspectives*, edited by Bruce L. McCormack, 83–103. Grand Rapids: Baker, 2008.

———. *Jonathan Edwards and the Metaphysics of Sin*. Aldershot: Ashgate, 2005.

———. "Jonathan Edwards's Ontology: A Critique of Sang Hyun Lee's Dispositional Account of Edwardsean Metaphysics." *Religious Studies* 46 (2010) 1–20.

Cudworth, Ralph. *True Intellectual System of the Universe*. London, 1678.

Danaher, William J., Jr. *The Trinitarian Ethics of Jonathan Edwards*. Louisville: Westminster John Knox, 2004.

Daniel, Stephen H. "Edwards as Philosopher." In *The Cambridge Companion to Jonathan Edwards* edited by Stephen J. Stein, 162–80. Cambridge: Cambridge University Press, 2007.

———. *The Philosophy of Jonathan Edwards: A Study in Divine Semiotics*. Bloomington: Indiana University Press, 1994.

Danielou, Jean. *From Shadows to Reality: Studies in the Biblical Typology of the Fathers*. Translated by Wulstan Hibberd. London: Burns & Oates, 1960.

Davidson, Edward H. *Jonathan Edwards: The Narrative of a Puritan Mind*. Cambridge: Harvard University Press, 1968.

Davis, Thomas M. "The Traditions of Puritan Typology" In *Typology and Early American Literature*, edited by Sacvan Bercovitch, 11–45. Amherst: University of Massachusetts Press, 1972.

De Jong, Peter Y. *The Covenant Idea in New England Theology, 1620–1847*. Grand Rapids: Eerdmans, 1945. Online: http://www.monergism.com/thethreshold/books/The_Covenant_Idea.pdf

Dictionary of National Biography. Oxford: Oxford University Press, 1885–1901.

Doddridge, Philip. *The Family Expositor: Or, A Paraphrase and Version of the New Testament: with Critical Notes; and a Practical Improvement of each Section*. 6 vols. London, 1739–56.

Drury, John, editor. *Critics of the Bible, 1724–1873*. Cambridge: Cambridge University Press: 1989.

Edwards, John. *The Preacher. A discourse, shewing, what are the particular offices and employments of those of that character in the church*. . . , 3 pts. in 1 vol. London, 1705–07. Reprinted, Memphis: General, 2009.

Emerson, Everett H. "Calvin and Covenant Theology." *Church History* 25 (1956) 136–44.

Endy, Melvin B., Jr. *William Penn and Early Quakerism*. Princeton: Princeton University Press, 1973.

English, Thomas. *The Harmony of the Old and New Testaments; or, The truths of the gospel irrefutably proved and fully established, from the Scriptures of the Old and New Testament, by the infallible comments of the Holy Spirit*. London, 1790.

Erskine, John. *Miscellaneous observations on important theological subjects, original and collected. By the late Reverend Mr Jonathan Edwards.* Edinburgh, 1793.

Eusden, John D. "Editor's Introduction." *The Marrow of Sacred Theology* by William Ames. Trans. from the third Latin edition, 1629 and edited by John D. Eusden. Boston: Pilgrim, 1968.

Eversley, Walter V. L. "The Pastor as Revivalist." In *Edwards in our Time: Jonathan Edwards and the Shaping of American Religion*, edited by Sang Hyun Lee and Allen C. Guelzo, 113–30. Grand Rapids: Eerdmans, 1999.

Fabiny, Tibor. "Edwards and Biblical Typology." In *Understanding Jonathan Edwards: An Introduction to America's Theologian*, edited by Gerald R. McDermott, 91–108. New York: Oxford University Press, 2009.

Fairbairn, Patrick. *The Interpretation of Prophecy.* Edinburgh, 1865. Reprinted, London: Banner of Truth, 1964.

———. *The Typology of Scripture Viewed in Connection with the Whole Series of Divine Dispensations.* Edinburgh: T. & T. Clark, 1870.

Feldmeth, Nathan P. "William Tyndale." In *Dictionary of Major Biblical Interpreters*, edited by Donald McKim, 996–100. 2nd ed. Downers Grove, IL: InterVarsity Press, 2006.

Fiering, Norman. *Jonathan Edwards's Moral Thought and Its British Context.* Chapel Hill: University of North Carolina Press, 1981.

———. *Moral Philosophy at Seventeenth Century Harvard.* Chapel Hill: University of North Carolina Press, 1981.

John Flavel. *Husbandry Spiritualized: Or, the Heavenly Use of Earthly Things.* 3rd ed. London, 1674.

———. *The Works of John Flavel.* 6 vols. London: Banner of Truth, 1968.

Fowl, Stephen E., editor. *The Theological Interpretation of Scripture.* Oxford: Blackwell, 1997.

Frei, Hans W. *The Eclipse of Biblical Narrative: A Study in Eighteenth and Nineteenth Century Hermeneutics.* New Haven: Yale University Press, 1974.

Froehlich, Karlfried. *Biblical Interpretation in the Early Church.* Philadelphia: Fortress, 1984.

Gale, Theophilus. *The Court of the Gentiles; or, A discourse touching the original of human literature, both philology and philosophie, from the Scriptures & Jewish church . . .* 4 vols. Oxford, 1672.

Gay, Peter. *A Loss of Mastery: Puritan Historians in Colonial America.* Berkeley: University of California Press, 1966.

Gerstner, John H. "Jonathan Edwards and the Bible." In *Inerrancy and the Church*, edited by John D. Hannah, 257–78 Chicago: Moody, 1984.

———. "Jonathan Edwards and the Bible." *Tenth: An Evangelical Quarterly* 9.4 (1979) 1–71.

———. *Jonathan Edwards on Heaven and Hell.* Grand Rapids: Baker, 1980.

———. *The Rational Biblical Theology of Jonathan Edwards, In Three Volumes.* Vols. 1–3. Powhatan, VA: Berea, 1991–93.

———. "The View of the Bible held by the Church: Calvin and the Westminster Divines." In *Inerrancy*, edited by Norman L. Geisler, 383–410. Grand Rapids: Zondervan, 1979.

Gerstner, John H., and Jonathan Neil Gerstner, "Edwardsean Preparation for Salvation." *Westminster Theological Journal* 42.1 (1979) 5–71.

Bibliography

Gill, John. *Prophecies of the Old Testament Respecting the Messiah*. London, 1728.
Goen, C. C. "Editor's Introduction." In *The Great Awakening*. Vol. 4 of *The Works of Jonathan Edwards*, 1–95. New Haven: Yale University Press, 1972.
Goldman, Shalom. *God's Sacred Language: Hebrew & the American Imagination*. Chapel Hill: University of North Carolina Press, 2004.
———. editor. *Hebrew and the Bible in America: The First Two Centuries*. Hanover, NH: University Press of New England, 1993.
Goodwin, Thomas. *Christ Set Forth in His Death, Resurrection, Ascension, Sitting at God's Right Hand, and Intercession*. London, 1642. Reprinted, Ligonier, PA: Soli Deo Gloria, 1992.
Goppelt, Leonhard. *Typos: The Typological Interpretation of the Old Testament in the New*. Translated by Donald H. Madvig. Grand Rapids: Eerdmans, 1982.
Goudriaan, Aza. *Reformed Orthodoxy and Philosophy, 1625–1750: Gisbertus Voetius, Petrus van Mastricht, and Anthonius Driessen*. Brill's Series in Church History 26. Leiden: Brill, 2006.
Greenslade, S. L., editor. *The West from the Reformation to the Present Day*. Vol. 3 of *The Cambridge History of the Bible*. Cambridge: Cambridge University Press, 1963.
Grotius, Hugo. *Opera omnia theologica*. Amsterdam, 1679.
———. *The Truth of the Christian Religion in Six Books... Corrected and Illustrated by Mr. Le Clerc. To Which is Added a Seventh Book Concerning This Question, What Christian Church Ought We To Join Ourselves To; By the said Mr. Le Clerc. The Second Edition with Additions. Done into English by John Clarke, D. D. and Chaplain in Ordinary to His Majesty*. London, 1719.
Guild, William. *Moses Unveiled: or, Those figures which served unto the pattern and shadow of heavenly things, pointing out the messiah Christ Iesus, briefly explained. Whereunto is added the harmony of all the prophets, breathing with one mouth, the mystery of his coming, and of that redemption which by his death he was to accomplish*. London, 1620.
Hagen, Kenneth. "Martin Luther." In *Dictionary of Major Biblical Interpreters*, edited by Donald McKim, 687–94. 2nd ed. Downers Grove, IL: InterVarsity Press, 2006.
Hall, David D. "Editor's Introduction." In *Ecclesiastical Writings*. Vol. 12 of *The Works of Jonathan Edwards*, 1–90. New Haven: Yale University Press, 1994.
———. *The Faithful Shepherd: A History of the New England Ministry in the Seventeenth Century*. Harvard Theological Studies 54. Cambridge: Harvard University Press, 2006.
———. *World of Wonder, Days of Judgment: Popular Religious Belief in Early New England*. Cambridge: Harvard University Press, 1989.
Hannah, John D., editor. *Inerrancy and the Church*. Chicago: Moody Press, 1984.
Harris, William. *Practical Discourses on the Principal Representation of the Messiah Throughout the Old Testament*. London, 1724.
Harrisville, Roy A. and Walter Sundberg, *The Bible in Modern Culture: Baruch Spinoza to Brevard Childs*. Cambridge: Eerdmans, 2002.
Hauser, Alan J. and Duane F. Watson, editors. *The Ancient Period*. Vol. 1 of *A History of Biblical Interpretation*. Grand Rapids: Eerdmans, 2003.
Hays, Richard B. *Echoes of Scripture in the Letters of Paul*. New Haven: Yale University Press, 1989.

Bibliography

Heering, Jan Paul. *Hugo Grotius as Apologist for the Christian Religion: A Study of His Work De veritate religionis christianae 1640.* Translated by J. C. Grayson. Leiden: Brill, 2004.

———. "Hugo Grotius' *De Veritate Religionis Christianae*," in *Hugo Grotius, Theologian: Essays in Honour of G. H. M. Posthumus Meyjes*, edited by Henk J. M. Nellen and Edwin Rabbie, 41–52. Leiden: Brill, 1994.

Heimert, Alan. *Religion and the American Mind from the Great Awakening to the Revolution.* Cambridge: Harvard University Press, 1966.

Helm, Paul. *Calvin and the Calvinists.* Edinburgh: Banner of Truth, 1982.

———. "The Great Christian Doctrine *Original Sin*." In *A God-Entranced Vision of All Things: The Legacy of Jonathan Edwards*, edited by John Piper and Justin Taylor, 175–200. Wheaton, IL: Crossway Books, 2004.

———. *John Calvin's Ideas.* Oxford: Oxford University Press, 2006.

Helm, Paul, and Oliver D. Crisp, editors. *Jonathan Edwards: Philosophical Theologian.* Aldershot: Ashgate, 2003.

Hengel, Martin. *The Septuagint as Christian Scripture: Its Prehistory and the Problem of Its Canon.* Translated by Mark E. Biddle. Edinburgh: T. & T. Clark, 2002.

Henry, Matthew. *An Exposition of the Old and New Testaments* 6 vols. 3rd ed. London, 1725.

Heppe, Heinrich. *Reformed Dogmatics.* Revised and edited by Ernst Bizer. Translated by G. T. Thomson. London: Wakeman Trust, 2002.

Hindmarsh, D. Bruce. *The Evangelical Conversion Narrative: Spiritual Autobiography in Early Modern England.* Oxford: Oxford University Press, 2005.

Hirsch, E. D. Jr. *The Aims of Interpretation.* Chicago: University of Chicago Press, 1976.

Hobbes, Thomas. *Leviathan.* Edited by. J. C. A. Gaskin. Oxford World Classics Oxford: Oxford University Press, 1998.

Holbrook, Clyde A. "Editor's Introduction." In *Original Sin*. Vol. 3 of *The Works of Jonathan Edwards*, 1–101. New Haven: Yale University Press, 1970.

Holifield, E. Brooks. *The Covenant Sealed: The Development of Puritan Sacramental Theology in Old and New England, 1570-1720.* New Haven: Yale University Press, 1974.

———. *Theology in America: Christian Thought from the Age of the Puritans to the Civil War.* New Haven: Yale University Press, 2003.

Holmes, Stephen R. "The Attributes of God." In *The Oxford Handbook of Systematic Theology*, edited by John Webster, Kathryn Tanner and Iain Torrance, 54–71. Oxford: Oxford University Press, 2007.

———. "Does Jonathan Edwards Use a Dispositional Ontology? A Response to Sang Hyun Lee." In *Jonathan Edwards: Philosophical Theologian*, edited by Paul Helm and Oliver D. Crisp, 99–114. Aldershot: Ashgate, 2003.

———. *God of Grace and God of Glory: An Account of the Theology of Jonathan Edwards.* Edinburgh: T. & T. Clark, 2000.

———. *Listening to the Past: The Place of Tradition in Theology.* Carlisle: Paternoster, 2002.

———. "*Religious Affections* by Jonathan Edwards (1703–58)." In *The Devoted Life: An Invitation to the Puritan Classics*, edited by Kelly M. Kapic and Randall C. Gleason, 285–97. Downers Grove, IL: InterVarsity, 2004.

Bibliography

———. "'Something Much Too Plain to Say': Towards a Defence of the Doctrine of Divine Simplicity." In *Neue Zeitschrift für Systematische Theologie und Religionsphilosophie* 43 (2001) 137–54.

Hooker, Thomas. *The soules humiliation*. London, 1638.

———. *The soules preparation for Christ, or, A treatise of contrition*. London, 1632.

Hopkins, Samuel. *The Life and Character of the Late Reverend Mr. Jonathan Edwards*. Boston, 1765.

Hunsinger, George. "Dispositional Soteriology: Jonathan Edwards on Justification by Faith." *Westminster Theological Journal* 66 (2004) 107–20.

Irenaeus. *Against Heresies*. In *Irenaeus, I*. Vol. 5 of *Ante-Nicene Christian Library: translations of the writings of the Fathers down to A. D. 325*, edited by Alexander Roberts and James Donaldson. Edinburgh: T. & T. Clark, 1868.

Jenson, Robert W. *America's Theologian: A Recommendation of Jonathan Edwards*. New York: Oxford University Press, 1988.

———. "Christology." In *The Princeton Companion to Jonathan Edwards*, edited by Sang Hyun Lee, 72–86. Princeton: Princeton University Press, 2005.

———. "The End is Music." In *Edwards in Our Time: Jonathan Edwards and the Shaping of American Religion*, edited by Sang Hyun Lee and Allen C. Guelzo, 161–71. Cambridge: Eerdmans, 1999.

Jonge, Henk Jan de. "Grotius as an Interpreter of the Bible, Particularly the New Testament." In *Hugo Grotius a Great European, 1583–1645: Contributions Concerning his Activities as a Humanist Scholar*, 59–65 [Complete Translation of the Dutch Articles abridged for the Exhibition Catalogue Het Delfts orakel, Hugo de Groot 1583–1645]. Delft: Meinema, 1983.

———. "Grotius' View of the Gospels and the Evangelists." In *Hugo Grotius, Theologian: Essays in Honour of G. H. M. Posthumus Meyjes*, edited by Henk J. M. Nellen and Edwin Rabbie, 65–74 Leiden: Brill, 1994.

Justin. *First Apology; Second Apology; Dialogue with Trypho the Jew*. In *Justin Martyr and Athenagoras*. Vol. 2 of *Ante-Nicene Christian Library: translations of the writings of the Fathers down to A. D. 325*, edited by Alexander Roberts and James Donaldson. Edinburgh: T. & T. Clark, 1870.

Kang, Kevin Woongsan. "Justified by Faith in Christ: Jonathan Edwards' Doctrine of Justification in Light of Union with Christ." PhD diss., Westminster Theological Seminary, PA., 2003.

Kapic, Kelly M. *Communion with God: The Divine and the Human in the Theology of John Owen*. Grand Rapids: Baker Academic, 2007.

Keach, Benjamin. *Tropologia: A Key to Open Scripture Metaphors... Together with Types of the Old Testament*. London, 1681.

Kelly, J. N. D. *Early Christian Doctrines*. 5th ed. London: Continuum, 2004.

Kendall, R. T. *Calvin and English Calvinism to 1649*. Oxford: Oxford University Press, 1979.

Kevan, E. F. *The Puritan Doctrine of Conversion*. The Annual Lecture at the Evangelical Library. London: The Evangelical Library, 1952.

Kidder, Richard, *A Demonstration of the Messias in which the Truth of the Christian Religion is Proved, against all the Enemies thereof; But especially against the Jews*. 2nd ed. corrected. London, 1726.

Bibliography

Kimnach, Wilson H. "Editor's Introduction." In *Sermons and Discourses, 1720–23*. Vol. 10 of *The Works of Jonathan Edwards*, 3–258. New Haven: Yale University Press, 1992.

———. "Edwards as Preacher." In *The Cambridge Companion to Jonathan Edwards*, edited by Stephen J. Stein, 103–24. Cambridge: Cambridge University Press, 2007.

Kling, David W., and Douglas A. Sweeney, editors. *Jonathan Edwards at Home and Abroad: Historical Memories, Cultural Movements, Global Horizons*. Columbia: University of South Carolina, 2003.

Knight, Janice. "Learning the Language of God: Jonathan Edwards and the Typology of Nature." *William and Mary Quarterly* 3rd series, 48 (1991) 531–51.

———. *Orthodoxies in Massachusetts: Rereading American Puritanism*. Cambridge: Harvard University Press, 1994.

———. "Typology." In *The Princeton Companion to Jonathan Edwards*, edited by Sang Hyun Lee, 190–209. Princeton: Princeton University Press, 2005.

Kugel, James L., and Rowan A. Greer. *Early Biblical Interpretation*. Philadelphia: Westminster, 1986.

Kuklick, Bruce. "Review Essay: An Edwards for the Millennium." *Religion and American Culture: A Journal of Interpretation* 11 (2001) 109–17.

Lampe, G. W. H., and K. Woollcombe. *Essays on Typology*. London: SCM, 1957.

LaSor, William Sanford. "The *Sensus Plenior* and Biblical Interpretation." In *A Guide to Contemporary Hermeneutics: Major Trends in Biblical Interpretation*, edited by Donald K. McKim, 47–64. Grand Rapids: Eerdmans, 1986.

Laurence, David. "Jonathan Edwards, Solomon Stoddard, and the Preparationist Model of Conversion." *Harvard Theological Review* 72 (1979) 267–83.

Le Clerc, Jean. *Bibliothèque choisie*. Amsterdam, 1713.

Lee, Sang Hyun. "Editor's Introduction." In *Writings on the Trinity, Grace and Faith*. Vol. 21 of *The Works of Jonathan Edwards*, 1–108. New Haven: Yale University Press, 2003.

———. "Grace and Justification by Faith Alone." In *The Princeton Companion to Jonathan Edwards*, edited by Sang Hyun Lee, 130–46. Princeton, NJ: Princeton University Press, 2005.

———. *The Philosophical Theology of Jonathan Edwards*. Princeton, NJ: Princeton University Press, 2000.

———, editor. *The Princeton Companion to Jonathan Edwards*. Princeton, NJ: Princeton University Press, 2005.

Lee, Sang Hyun, and Allen C. Guelzo, editors. *Edwards in Our Time: Jonathan Edwards and the Shaping of American Religion*. Grand Rapids: Eerdmans, 1999.

Leigh, Edward. *A Treatise of Divinity*. London, 1646.

Leithart, Peter J. *Deep Exegesis: The Mystery of Reading Scripture*. Waco, TX: Baylor University Press, 2009.

Leland, John. *A view of the principal deistical writers*. 2 vols. with a one-volume supplement. London, 1754–56.

Lesser, M. X. *Reading Jonathan Edwards: An Annotated Bibliography in Three Parts, 1729–2005*. Grand Rapids: Eerdmans, 2008.

Letham, Robert. *The Westminster Assembly: Reading its Theology in Historical Context*. Philipsburg, NJ: Presbyterian & Reformed, 2009.

Levin, David. editor. *Jonathan Edwards: A Profile*. New York: Hill & Wang, 1969.

Bibliography

Lightfoot, John. *The harmony, chronicle, and order of the New Testament, the text of the four evangelists methodized, story of the Acts of the apostles analyzed, order of the Epistles manifested, times of the revelation observed*... London, 1655.

Locke, John. *An Essay Concerning Human Understanding*. London, 1690. Edited by Peter H. Nidditch. Oxford: Clarendon, 1979.

———. *The Reasonableness of Christianity as Delivered in the Scriptures*. London, 1695. Edited by John C. Higgins-Biddle. Oxford: Clarendon, 1999.

Logan, Samuel T., Jr. "The Doctrine of Justification in the Theology of Jonathan Edwards." *Westminster Theological Journal* 46 (1984) 26–52.

———. "The Hermeneutics of Jonathan Edwards." *Westminster Theological Journal* 43 (1980) 79–96.

Lombard, Peter. *The Sentences, Book 1, The Mystery of the Trinity*. Translated by Giulio Silano. Toronto: Pontifical Institute of Medieval Studies, 2007.

Lowance, Mason I. Jr. "'Images or Shadows of Divine Things' in the Thought of Jonathan Edwards." In *Typology and Early American Literature*, edited by Sacvan Bercovitch, 209–44. Amherst: University of Massachusetts Press, 1972.

———. *The Language of Canaan: Metaphor and Symbol in New England from the Puritans to the Transcendentalists*. Cambridge: Harvard University Press, 1980.

Lowance, Mason I., Jr., and David H. Watters. "Editor's Introduction to 'Types of the Messiah.'" In *Typological Writings*. Vol. 11 of *The Works of Jonathan Edwards*, 157–82. New Haven: Yale University Press, 1993.

———. "Note on the Manuscript of 'Types of the Messiah.'" In *Typological Writings*. Vol. 11 of *The Works of Jonathan Edwards*, 183–86. New Haven: Yale University Press, 1993.

Lubac, Henri de. *Medieval Exegesis*. Vol. 2, *The Four Senses of Scripture*. Translated by E. M. Macierowski. Grand Rapids: Eerdmans, 2000.

Mastricht, Peter van. *Theoretico-practica theologia: qua, per singula capita theologica, pars exegetica, dogmatica, elenchtica & practica, perpetua successione conjugantur*. Amsterdam, 1699.

———. *A Treatise on Regeneration, By Peter Van Mastricht, D.D. Professor of Divinity in the Universities of Francfort, Duisburgh, and Utrecht. Extracted from his system of divinity, called Theologia theoretico-practica; and faithfully translated into English; with an appendix, containing extracts from many celebrated divines of the Reformed Church, upon the same subject*. New Haven: Thomas & Samuel Green, 1770.

Marsden, George M. *Jonathan Edwards: A Life*. New Haven: Yale University Press, 2003.

———. "Perry Miller's Rehabilitation of the Puritans: A Critique." *Church History* 39 (1970) 91–105.

———. *A Shorter Life of Jonathan Edwards*. Grand Rapids: Eerdmans, 2008.

Malebranche, Nicolas. *Treatise Concerning the Search After Truth*. 2nd ed. London, 1700.

Mather, Cotton. *Agricola*. Boston, 1727.

———. *Blessed Union*. Boston, 1692.

———. *The Everlasting Gospel*. Boston, 1699.

———. *Magnalia Christi Americana, or the Ecclesiastical History of New-England*. London, 1702. Reprinted, Edinburgh, Banner of Truth, 1979.

Mather, Samuel. *The Figures or Types of the Old Testament*. 2nd ed. London, 1705.

McClenahan, Michael. "Jonathan Edwards' Doctrine of Justification in the Period up to the First Great Awakening." DPhil diss., University of Oxford, 2006.

Bibliography

McClymond, Michael J. *Encounters with God: An Approach to the Theology of Jonathan Edwards.* New York: Oxford University Press, 1998.

———. "Salvation as Divinization: Jonathan Edwards, Gregory Palamas and the Theological Uses of Neoplatonism." In *Jonathan Edwards: Philosophical Theologian,* edited by Paul Helm and Oliver D. Crisp, 139–55. Aldershot: Ashgate, 2003.

———. "A Different Legacy? The Cultural Turn in Edwards's Later Notebooks and the Unwritten *History of the Work of Redemption.*" In *Jonathan Edwards at Home and Abroad: Historical Memories, Cultural Movements, Global Horizons,* edited by David W. Kling and Douglas A. Sweeney, 16–39. Columbia, SC: University of South Carolina, 2003.

McDermott, Gerald R. "Alternative Viewpoint: Edwards and Biblical Typology." In *Understanding Jonathan Edwards: An Introduction to America's Theologian* edited by Gerald R. McDermott, 109–12. New York: Oxford University Press, 2009.

———. *Can Evangelicals Learn from World Religions? Jesus, Revelation & Religious Traditions.* Downer's Grove, IL: InterVarsity Press, 2000.

———. *Jonathan Edwards Confronts the Gods: Christian Theology, Enlightenment Religion and Non-Christian Faiths.* New York: Oxford University Press, 2000.

———. "Jonathan Edwards, John Henry Newman and non-Christian Religions." In *Jonathan Edwards: Philosophical Theologian,* edited by Paul Helm and Oliver D. Crisp, 127–37. Aldershot: Ashgate, 2003.

———. "Jonathan Edwards on Justification by Faith—More Protestant or Catholic?" *Pro Ecclesia* 17.1 (2008) 92–111.

———. *One Holy and Happy Society: The Public Theology of Jonathan Edwards.* University Park: Pennsylvania State University Press, 1992.

———. "A Possibility of Reconciliation: Jonathan Edwards and the Salvation of Non-Christians." In *Edwards in our Time: Jonathan Edwards and the Shaping of American Religion,* edited by Sang Hyun Lee and Allen C. Guelzo, 173–202. Grand Rapids: Eerdmans, 1999.

———, editor. *Understanding Jonathan Edwards: An Introduction to America's Theologian.* New York: Oxford University Press, 2009.

McGrath, Alister E., *Iustitia Dei: A History of the Christian Doctrine of Justification.* 2nd ed. Cambridge: Cambridge University Press, 2003.

McKim, Donald, editor. *Dictionary of Major Biblical Interpreters.* 2nd ed. Downers Grove, IL: InterVarsity, 2006.

———. editor. *A Guide to Contemporary Hermeneutics: Major Trends in Biblical Interpretation.* Grand Rapids: Eerdmans, 1986.

McNeill, J. T. "The Significance of the Word of God for Calvin." *Church History* 28 (1959) 131–46.

Meyjes, G. H. M. Posthumus, "Grotius as a Theologian." In *Hugo Grotius a Great European, 1583–1645: Contributions Concerning his Activities as a Humanist Scholar,* 51–58. Delft: Meinema, 1983.

Miller, Perry. "From Edwards to Emerson." *New England Quarterly* 13 (1940) 589–617.

———. "Edwards, Locke and the Rhetoric of Sensation." In *Perspectives in Criticism,* edited by Harry Levin Cambridge, 103–23. MA: Harvard University Press, 1950.

———. *Errand into the Wilderness.* Cambridge: Harvard University Press, 1956.

———. "Introduction." *Images or Shadows of Divine Things,* 1–41. New Haven: Yale University Press, 1948.

———. *Jonathan Edwards.* Toronto: Sloane Associates, 1949.

Bibliography

———. *The New England Mind: From Colony to Province.* Cambridge: Harvard University Press, 1953.

———. *The New England Mind: The Seventeenth Century.* Cambridge: MA: Harvard University Press, 1954.

———. "'Preparation for Salvation' in Seventeenth-Century New England." *Journal of the History of Ideas* 4 (1943) 253–86.

Minkema, Kenneth P. "Preface to the Period." In *Sermons and Discourses, 1723–29.* Vol. 14 of *The Works of Jonathan Edwards,* 3–46. New Haven: Yale University Press, 1997.

———. "Jonathan Edwards: A Theological Life." In *The Princeton Companion to Jonathan Edwards,* edited by Sang Hyun Lee, 1–15. Princeton: Princeton University Press, 2005.

———. "The Other Unfinished 'Great Work': Jonathan Edwards, Messianic Prophecy, and 'The Harmony of the Old and New Testaments [sic]'." In *Jonathan Edwards' Writings: Text, Context, Interpretation,* edited by Stephen J. Stein, 52–65. Bloomington: Indiana University Press, 1996.

Møller, Jens, G. "The Beginnings of Puritan Covenant Theology." *Journal of Ecclesiastical History* 14 (1963) 46–67.

Moody, Josh. *Jonathan Edwards and the Enlightenment: Knowing the Presence of God.* Lanham, MD: University Press of America, 2005.

More, Henry. *An Antidote Against Atheisme.* London, 1653.

———. *Enchiridion Ethicum.* London, 1668.

———. *The Immortality of the Soul.* London, 1659.

Morgan, Edmund S. *Visible Saints: The History of a Puritan Idea.* New York: New York University Press, 1963.

Morimoto, Anri. *Jonathan Edwards and the Catholic Vision of Salvation.* University Park: Pennsylvania State University Press, 1995.

———. "Salvation as the Fulfillment of Being: The Soteriology of Jonathan Edwards and its Implications for Christian Mission." *The Princeton Seminary Bulletin* 20 (1999) 13–23.

Morris, William S. *The Young Jonathan Edwards: A Reconstruction.* Eugene, OR: Wipf & Stock, 2005.

Muller, Richard A. "Biblical Interpretation in the Sixteenth and Seventeenth Centuries." In *Dictionary of Major Biblical Interpreters,* edited by Donald McKim, 22–44. 2nd ed. Downers Grove, IL: InterVarsity, 2006.

———. *Christ and the Decree: Christology and Predestination in Reformed Theology from Calvin to Perkins.* Grand Rapids: Baker, 1988.

———. *Dictionary of Latin and Greek Theological Terms Drawn Principally from Protestant Scholastic Theology.* Grand Rapids: Baker, 1985.

———. *Post-Reformation Reformed Dogmatics: The Rise and Development of Reformed Orthodoxy, ca. 1520 to ca. 1725.* 4 vols. Grand Rapids: Baker, 2003–06.

Muller, Richard A., and John L. Thompson, editors. *Biblical Interpretation in the Era of the Reformation: essays presented to David C. Steinmetz in honor of his sixtieth birthday.* Grand Rapids: Eerdmans, 1996.

Mulsow, Martin, and Jan Rohls, editors. *Socinianism and Arminianism: Antitrinitarians, Calvinists and Cultural Exchange in Seventeenth-Century Europe.* Leiden: Brill, 2005.

Murray, Ian H. *Jonathan Edwards: A New Biography.* Edinburgh: Banner of Truth, 1987.

Bibliography

Nassif, Bradley. "Antiochene θεωρία in John Chrysostom's Exegesis." In *Ancient & Postmodern Christianity: Paleo-Orthodoxy in the 21st Century: Essays in Honor of Thomas C. Oden*, edited by Kenneth Tanner and Christopher A. Hall, 49–67. Downers Grove, IL: InterVarsity, 2002.

Neele, Adriaan C. *The Art of Living to God. A Study of Method and Piety in the Theoretico-practica theologia of Petrus van Mastricht (1630-1706)*. Pretoria: University of Pretoria Press, 2005.

———. *Petrus van Mastricht 1630-1706: Reformed Orthodoxy – Method and Piety*. Brill's Series in Church History 35. Leiden: Brill, 2009.

Neil, W. "The Criticism and Theological Use of the Bible, 1700-1950." In *The West from the Reformation to the Present Day*. Vol. 3 of The Cambridge History of the Bible, edited by S. L. Greenslade, 238–93. Cambridge: Cambridge University Press, 1963.

Nellen, H. J. M. "Tension between Church Doctrines and Critical Exegesis of the Old Testament." In *From the Renaissance to the Enlightenment*. Vol. 2 of *Hebrew Bible/Old Testament: The History of Its Interpretation*, edited by Magne Sæbø, 802–26. Göttingen: Vandenhoeck & Ruprecht, 1996–2008.

Nichols, Stephen J. *An Absolute Sort of Certainty: The Holy Spirit and the Apologetics of Jonathan Edwards*. Phillipsburg, NJ: Presbyterian & Reformed Publishing, 2003.

Niebuhr, H. Richard *The Kingdom of God in America*. London: Harper, 1959.

Niebuhr, Richard R. "Being and Consent." In *The Princeton Companion to Jonathan Edwards*, edited by Sang Hyun Lee, 34–43. Princeton: Princeton University Press, 2005.

Nineham, Dennis. *The Use and Abuse of the Bible: A Study of the Bible in an Age of Rapid Cultural Change*. London: Macmillan, 1976.

Noble, Paul R. *The Canonical Approach: A Critical Reconstruction of the Hermeneutics of Brevard S. Childs*. Leiden: E. J. Brill, 1995.

Ocker, Christopher. "Biblical Interpretation in the Middle Ages." *Dictionary of Major Biblical Interpreters*, edited by Donald McKim, 14–21. 2nd ed. Downers Grove, IL: InterVarsity, 2006.

O'Higgins, James S. J. *Anthony Collins: The Man and His Works*. The Hague: Martinus Nijhoff, 1970.

Old, Hughes Oliphant. *The Reading and Preaching of the Scriptures in the Worship of the Christian Church*. 6 vols. Grand Rapids: Eerdmans, 1998–2007.

Ortlund, Dane. *A New Inner Relish: Christian Motivation in the Thought of Jonathan Edwards*. Fearn: Christian Focus, 2008.

Owen, John. *Christologia: Or, A Declaration of the Glorious Mystery of the Person of Christ*. In *The Glory of Christ*. Vol. 1 of *The Works of John Owen*, 2–272. London, 1679. Reprinted, Edinburgh: Banner of Truth, 1981.

———. *The Doctrine of Justification by Faith through the Imputation of the Righteousness of Christ*. London, 1677.

———. *A Review of the Annotations of Hugo Grotius in Reference unto the Doctrine of the Deity etc. with a Defence of the Charge formerly laid against them*. Oxford, 1656.

Patrides, C. A. *The Cambridge Platonists*. Cambridge: Cambridge University Press, 1980.

Pauw, Amy Plantinga. "Editor's Introduction." In *The "Miscellanies" 833–1152*. Vol. 20 of *The Works of Jonathan Edwards*, 1–39. New Haven: Yale University Press, 2002.

Bibliography

———. "'One Alone Cannot be Excellent': Edwards on Divine Simplicity." In *Jonathan Edwards: Philosophical Theologian*, edited by Paul Helm and Oliver D. Crisp, 115–25. Aldershot: Ashgate, 2003.

———. *The Supreme Harmony of All: The Trinitarian Theology of Jonathan Edwards*. Grand Rapids: Eerdmans, 2002.

———. "The Trinity." In *The Princeton Companion to Jonathan Edwards*, edited by Sang Hyun Lee, 44–58. Princeton: Princeton University Press, 2005.

Perkins, William. *The Arte of Prophecying: or A Treatise Concerning the sacred and onely true manner and methode of Preaching*. Translated by Thomas Tuke. London, 1607.

Pettit, Norman. *The Heart Prepared: Grace and Conversion in Puritan Spiritual Life*. New Haven: Yale University Press, 1966.

Pfisterer, Karl Dietrich. *The Prism of Scripture: Studies on History and Historicity in the Work of Jonathan Edwards*. Frankfurt: Herbert Lang Bern, 1975.

Pilkington, Matthew. *The Evangelical History and Harmony*. London, 1747.

Piper, John and Justin Taylor, editors. *A God-Entranced Vision of All Things: The Legacy of Jonathan Edwards*. Wheaton, IL: Crossway Books, 2004.

Plantinga, Alvin, editor. *The Ontological Argument: From St. Anselm to Contemporary Philosophers*. London: Macmillan, 1968.

Poole, Matthew. *Synopsis Criticorum Aliorumque Sacrae Scripturae Interpretum* 5 vols. London, 1669–76.

Pope, Alexander. *An Essay on Man*. Edited by Maynard Mack. London: Methuen, 1950.

Popkin, Richard H. "Spinoza and Bible Scholarship." In *The Books of Nature and Scripture: Recent Essays on Natural Philosophy, Theology, and Biblical Criticism In the Netherlands of Spinoza's Time and the British Isles of Newton's Time*. International Archives of the History of Ideas 139, edited by James E. Force and Richard H. Popkin, 1–20. Dordrecht: Kluwer, 1994.

Porter, Roy. *Enlightenment: Britain and the Creation of the Modern World*. London: Penguin, 2000.

Poythress, Vern S. "Analyzing a Biblical Text: Some Important Linguistic Distinctions." *Scottish Journal of Theology* 32.2 (1979) 113–31.

Pratt, Anne Stokely. "The Books Sent from England by Jeremiah Dummer to Yale College." In *Papers in Honor of Andrew Keogh*, edited by Mary C. Withington, 7–44. New Haven: Yale University Press, 1938.

Proudfoot, Wayne. "*Perception and Love* in Religious Affections' [sic]." In *Jonathan Edwards's Writings: Text, Context, Interpretation*, edited by Stephen J. Stein, 122–38. Bloomington: Indiana University Press, 1996.

Rabbie, Edwin. "Grotius and Judaism." In *Hugo Grotius, Theologian: Essays in Honour of G. H. M. Posthumus Meyjes*, edited by Henk J. M. Nellen and Edwin Rabbie, 99–120. Leiden: Brill, 1994.

Ramsay, Chevalier [Andrew Michael]. *Philosophical Principles of Natural and Revealed Religion*. Glasgow, 1748–49.

———. *Travels of Cyrus. To Which is Annexed, a Discourse upon the Theology and Mythology of the Pagans*. 8th ed. London, 1752.

Ramsey, Paul. "Editor's Introduction." In *Ethical Writings*. Vol. 8 of *The Works of Jonathan Edwards*, 1–121. New Haven: Yale University Press, 1989.

Reventlow, Henning Graf. *The Authority of the Bible and the Rise of the Modern World*. London: SCM, 1984.

Rohr, John von. "Covenant and Assurance in Early English Puritanism." *Church History* 34 (1965) 195–203.

———. *The Covenant of Grace in Puritan Thought.* Atlanta, GA: Scholars Press, 1986.

Rolston III, Holmes. "Responsible Man in Reformed Theology: Calvin versus the Westminster Confession." *Scottish Journal of Theology* 23 (1970), 129–56.

Rowley, H. H. *The Re-Discovery of the Old Testament.* London: T. & T. Clark, 1946.

Ryle, Herbert Edward. *The Canon of the Old Testament: An Essay on the Gradual Growth and Formation of the Hebrew Canon of Scripture.* London: Macmillan, 1892.

Sæbø, Magne, editor. *Hebrew Bible/Old Testament: The History of Its Interpretation* 2 vols. Göttingen: Vandenhoeck & Ruprecht, 1996–2008.

Schafer, Thomas. "Editor's Introduction." In *The "Miscellanies" a-z, aa-zz, 1–500.* Vol. 13 of *The Works of Jonathan Edwards,* 1–160. New Haven: Yale University Press, 1994.

———. "Jonathan Edwards and Justification by Faith." *Church History* 20 (1951) 55–67.

Scholder, Klaus. *The Birth of Modern Critical Theology.* Translated by John Bowden. London: SCM Press, 1990.

Schweitzer, William M. "Interpreting the Harmony of Reality: Jonathan Edwards' Theology of Revelation." PhD diss., University of Edinburgh, 2008.

Seitz, Christopher. *Word Without End: The Old Testament as Abiding Theological Witness.* Grand Rapids: Eerdmans, 1998.

Shedd, William G. T. *Dogmatic Theology.* 3 vols. New York: Scribner, 1888–94. Reprinted, Nashville, TN: Thomas Nelson, 1980.

Sheehan, Jonathan. *The Enlightenment Bible: Translation, Scholarship, Culture.* Princeton: Princeton University Press, 2005.

Sheppard, G. T. "Brevard Childs." In *Handbook of Major Biblical Interpreters,* edited by Donald K. McKim, 575–84. 2nd ed. Downers Grove, IL: InterVarsity Press, 2006.

Sherlock, Thomas. *The Use and Intent of Prophecy in the Several Ages of the World: in Six Discourses Delivered at the Temple Church in April and May, 1724. . . to which are Added Three Dissertations.* London, 1725.

Sherlock, William. *Concerning the Knowledge of Jesus Christ.* London, 1674.

Simon, Irène. *Three Restoration Divines: Barrow, South, Tillotson: Selected Sermons.* 2 vols. Paris: L'Université de Liège, 1967–76.

Simon, Richard. *A Critical History of the Old Testament translated by 'a Person of Quality'.* London, 1682.

Simonetti, Manilo. *Biblical Interpretation in the Early Church: An Historical Introduction to Patristic Exegesis.* Translated by John A. Hughes. Edinburgh: T. & T. Clark, 1994.

Simonson, Harold P. *Jonathan Edwards: Theologian of the Heart.* Macon, GA: Mercer University Press, 1982.

Skelton, Philip. *Deism revealed; or, The attack on Christianity candidly reviewed in its real merits, as they stand in the celebrated writings of Lord Herbert, Lord Shaftesbury, Hobbes, Toland, Tindal, Collins, Mandeville, Dodwell, Woolston, Morgan, Chubb, and others.* 2 vols. London, 1751.

Smith, John E. "Editor's Introduction." In *Religious Affections.* Vol. 2 of *The Works of Jonathan Edwards,* 1–83. New Haven: Yale University Press, 1959.

———. *Jonathan Edwards: Puritan, Preacher, Philosopher.* London: Chapman, 1992.

———. "Religious Affections and the "Sense of the Heart." In *The Princeton Companion to Jonathan Edwards,* edited by Sang Hyun Lee, 103–14. Princeton, Princeton University Press, 2005.

Bibliography

Smolinksi, Reiner. "*Israel Redivivus*: The Eschatological Limits of Puritan Typology in New England." *The New England Quarterly* 63.3 (1990) 357–95.

Sparks, Adam. "Salvation History, Chronology and Crisis: A Problem with Inclusivist Theology of Religions [Part 1]." *Themelios* 33.2 (2008) 7–18.

———. "Salvation History, Chronology and Crisis: A Problem with Inclusivist Theology of Religions [Part 2]." *Themelios* 33.3 (2008) 48–62.

Spinoza, Baruch. *Ethics & "De Intellectus Emendatione."* Translated by A. Boyle. Introduction by George Santayana. Everyman's Library 481. London: Dent, 1948.

[———.] *Tractatus Theologico-Politicus cui adjunctus est Philosophia s. Scripturæ interpres. Ab authore longe emendatior.* Amsterdam, 1674.

Sprunger, Keith L. *The Learned Doctor William Ames.* Chicago: University of Illinois Press, 1972.

Stanford, Donald E., editor. *The Poems of Edward Taylor.* New Haven: Yale University Press, 1960. Reprinted 1989.

Stapfer, Johann Friedrich. *Institutiones Theologiae Polemicae Universae.* 5 vols. Zurich, 1743–47.

Steiger, Johann Anselm. "The Development of the Reformation Legacy: Hermeneutics and Interpretation of the Sacred Scriptures in the Age of Orthodoxy." In *Hebrew Bible/Old Testament: The History of Its Interpretation*, 2 vols, edited by Magne Sæbø, 2.725–32. Göttingen: Vandenhoeck & Ruprecht, 1996–2008.

Stein, Stephen J., editor. *The Cambridge Companion to Jonathan Edwards.* Cambridge: Cambridge University Press, 2007.

———. "Cotton Mather and Jonathan Edwards on the Number of the Beast: Eighteenth-Century Speculation about Antichrist." *Proceedings of the American Antiquarian Society* 84 (1974) 293–315.

———. "Editor's Introduction" In *Apocalyptic Writings.* Vol. 5 of *The Works of Jonathan Edwards*, 1–93. New Haven: Yale University Press, 1977.

———. "Editor's Introduction." In "The Blank Bible." Vol. 24 of *The Works of Jonathan Edwards*, 1–117. New Haven: Yale University Press, 2006.

———. "Editor's Introduction." In *Notes on Scripture.* Vol. 15 of *The Works of Jonathan Edwards*, 1–46. New Haven: Yale University Press, 1998.

———. "Edwards as Biblical Exegete." In *The Cambridge Companion to Jonathan Edwards*, edited by Stephen J. Stein, 181–95. Cambridge: Cambridge University Press, 2007.

———. "Eschatology." In *The Princeton Companion to Jonathan Edwards*, edited by Sang Hyun Lee, 226–42. Princeton: Princeton University Press, 2005.

———. "Jonathan Edwards and the Cultures of Biblical Violence." In *Jonathan Edwards at 300: Essays on the Tercentenary of His Birth*, edited by H. Stout et al., 54–64. Lanham, MD: University Press of America, 2005.

———. "Jonathan Edwards and the Rainbow: Biblical Exegesis and Poetic Imagination." *New England Quarterly* 47.3 (1974) 440–56.

———. "'Like Apples of Gold in Pictures of Silver': The Portrait of Wisdom in Jonathan Edwards' Commentary on the Book of Proverbs." *Church History* 54 (1985) 324–37.

———. "A Notebook on the Apocalypse by Jonathan Edwards." *The William and Mary Quarterly* 3rd series, 29 (1972) 623–34.

———. "Providence and Apocalypse in the Early Writings of Jonathan Edwards." *Early American Literature* 13 (1978–79) 250–67.

Bibliography

———. "The Quest for the Spiritual Sense: The Biblical Hermeneutics of Jonathan Edwards." *Harvard Theological Review* 70.1–2 (1977) 99–113.
———. "The Spirit and the Word: Jonathan Edwards and Scriptural Exegesis." In *Jonathan Edwards and the American Experience*, edited by Nathan O. Hatch and Harry S. Stout, 118–30. New York: Oxford University Press, 1988.
Steinmetz, David C. "The Superiority of Precritical Exegesis." In *A Guide to Contemporary Hermeneutics: Major Trends in Biblical Interpretation*, edited by Donald K. McKim, 65–77. Grand Rapids: Eerdmans, 1986.
Stendahl, Krister. "Biblical Theology, Contemporary." In *Interpreter's Dictionary of the Bible* 1.418–31. New York: Abingdon Press, 1962.
Stephen, Leslie. *English Thought in the Eighteenth Century*. 2 vols. London: Smith and Elder, 1902. Reprinted, Bristol: Thoemmes, 1991.
Stephens, Bruce M. *God's Last Metaphor: The Doctrine of the Trinity in New England Theology*. Chico, CA: Scholars Press, 1981.
Stoddard, Solomon. *A guide to Christ. Or, The way of directing souls that are under the work of conversion. Compiled for the help of young ministers: and may be serviceable to private Christians, who are enquiring the way to Zion. By Solomon Stoddard, A.M. and Pastor of the church in Northampton. With an epistle prefixed, by the Reverend Dr. Increase Mather*. Boston, 1714.
Stoever, William K. B. *"A Faire and Easie Way to Heaven": Covenant Theology and Antinomianism in Early Massachusetts*. Middletown, CT: Wesleyan University Press, 1978.
Stout, Harr, S. "The Puritans and Edwards." In *Jonathan Edwards and the American Experience*, edited by Nathan O. Hatch and Harry S. Stout, 142–59. New York, Oxford University Press, 1988.
Stout, Harry S. et al., editors. *Jonathan Edwards at 300: Essays on the Tercentenary of His Birth* Lanham. MD: University Press of America, 2005.
Strange, Daniel. *The Possibility of Salvation Among the Unevangelised: An Analysis of Inclusivism in Recent Evangelical Theology*. Carlisle: Paternoster, 2002.
Studebaker, Steven M. "Jonathan Edwards' Pneumatological Concept of Grace and Dispositional Soteriology: Resources for an Evangelical Inclusivism." *Pro Ecclesia* 14.3 (2005) 324–39.
Sumpter, Philip. "Brevard Childs as Critical and Faithful Exegete." *Princeton Theological Review* 14.1, No. 38 (2008) 95–116. Online: http://www.princetontheologicalreview.org/issues_pdf/38.pdf
Sundberg, Albert C. Jr. *The Old Testament of the Early Church*. Harvard Theological Studies 20. London: Oxford University Press, 1964.
Surenhusius, William. Βίβλος Καταλλαγῆς *in quo secundum veterum Theologorum Hebraeorum Formulas allegandi, et Modos interpretandi conciliantur Loca Ex V. in N.T. Allegata*. Amsterdam, 1713.
Sweeney, Douglas A. "Editor's Introduction." In *The "Miscellanies" 1153–1360*. Vol. 23 of *The Works of Jonathan Edwards*, 1–36. New Haven: Yale University Press, 2004.
———. "'Longing for More of It'? [sic] The Strange Exegetical Career of Jonathan Edwards's Exegetical Exertions." in *Jonathan Edwards at 300: Essays on the Tercentenary of His Birth*, edited by Harry S. Stout et al., 25–37. Lanham, MD: University Press of America, 2005.
Sykes, Arthur Ashley. *An Essay upon the Truth of the Christian Religion* (London, 1725).

Bibliography

Sykes, Norman. "The Religion of Protestants." In *The West from the Reformation to the Present Day*. Vol. 3 of *The Cambridge History of the Bible*, edited by S. L. Greenslade, 175–98. Cambridge: Cambridge University Press, 1963.
Tanner, Kenneth and Christopher A. Hall, editors. *Ancient & Postmodern Christianity: Paleo-Orthodoxy in the 21st Century: Essays in Honor of Thomas C. Oden*. Downers Grove, IL: Inter Varsity Press, 2002.
Terry, Milton S. *Biblical Hermeneutics: A Treatise on the Interpretation of the Old and New Testaments*. New York, 1883. Reprinted, Grand Rapids: Zondervan, 1974.
Thuesen, Peter J. "Editor's Introduction." In *Catalogues of Books*. Vol. 26 of *The Works of Jonathan Edwards*, 1–113. New Haven: Yale University Press, 2008.
―――. "Edwards' Intellectual Background." In *The Princeton Companion to Jonathan Edwards*, edited by Sang Hyun Lee, 16–33. Princeton: Princeton University Press, 2005.
Tindal, Matthew. *Christianity as Old as Creation* (With a New Introduction by John Vladimir Price). London: Routledge/Thoemmes, 1995.
Tomkins, John. *The Harmony of the Old and New Testament. And the Fulfilling of the Prophets Concerning Our Blessed Lord and Saviour Jesus Christ, and His Kingdom. And the Grace and Glory that Shall be Reveal'd in the Latter Days. Published for the benefit of Christians and Jews by J. T. one of the people in scorn call'd Quakers. With an appendix to the Jews by W.P.* London, 1694.
Toulouse, Teresa. *The Art of Prophesying: New England Sermons and the Shaping of Belief*. Athens: University of Georgia Press, 1987.
Tracy, Patricia J. *Jonathan Edwards, Pastor: Religion and Society in Eighteenth-Century Northampton*. New York: Hill & Wang, 1980.
Trembath, Kern Robert. *Evangelical Theories of Biblical Inspiration: A Review and Proposal*. Oxford: Oxford University Press, 1987.
Trueman, Carl R. *The Claims of Truth: John Owen's Trinitarian Theolog.y* Carlisle: Paternoster, 1998.
―――. *John Owen: Reformed Catholic, Renaissance Man*. Aldershot: Ashgate, 2007.
Turnbull, Ralph G. "Jonathan Edwards – Bible Interpreter." *Interpretation: A Journal of Bible and Theology* 6 (1952) 422–35.
Turretin, Francis. *The Institutes of Elenctic Theology*. 3 vols. Translated by George Musgrave Giger. Edited by James T. Dennison Jr. Philipsburg, NJ: Presbyterian & Reformed, 1992–97.
Waddington, Jeffrey C. "Jonathan Edwards's 'Ambiguous and Somewhat Precarious' Doctrine of Justification?" *Westminster Theological Journal* 66 (2004) 357–72.
Wainwright, William J. "Jonathan Edwards." *The Stanford Encyclopaedia of Philosophy*. Online: http://www.plato.stanford.edu/entries/edwards/
―――. "Jonathan Edwards and the Language of God." *Journal of the American Academy of Religion* 48.4 (1980) 519–30.
―――. "Jonathan Edwards, William Rowe, and the Necessity of Creation." In *Faith, Freedom, And Rationality: Philosophy of Religion Today*, edited by Jeff Jordan and Daniel Howard-Snyder, 119–33. London: Rowman & Littlefield, 1996.
Walker, D. P. *The Ancient Theology: Studies in Christian Platonism from the Fifteenth to the Eighteenth Century*. London: Duckworth, 1972.
Wall, Ernestine van der. "Between Grotius and Cocceius: the 'Theologia Prophetica' of Campegius Vitringa 1659–1722." In *Hugo Grotius, Theologian: Essays in Honour*

of G. H. M. Posthumus Meyjes, edited by Henk J. M. Nellen and Edwin Rabbie, 195-215. Leiden: Brill, 1994.

Warburton, William. *The Divine Legation of Moses Demonstrated, on the Principles of a Religious Deist, from the Omission of the Doctrine of a Future State of Reward and Punishment in the Jewish Dispensation. In Six Books*... 2 vols. London, 1738-41.

Warch, Richard. *School of the Prophets: Yale College, 1701-1740*. New Haven: Yale University Press, 1973.

Warfield, Benjamin B. *The Works of Benjamin B. Warfield*. Vol. 2, *Biblical Doctrines*. Oxford: Oxford University Press, 1929.

Watson, Francis. *Text, Church and World: Biblical Interpretation in Theological Perspective*. Edinburgh: T. & T. Clark, 1994.

———. *Text and Truth: Redefining Biblical Theology*. Edinburgh: T. & T. Clark, 1997.

Webster, John. "Theologies of Retrieval." In *The Oxford Handbook of Systematic Theology*, edited by John Webster, Kathryn Tanner and Iain Torrance, 583-99. Oxford: Oxford University Press, 2007.

Weinsheimer, Joel C. *Eighteenth-Century Hermeneutics: Philosophy of Interpretation in England from Locke to Burke*. New Haven: Yale University Press, 1993.

Weir, David A. *Early New England: A Covenanted Society*. Cambridge: Eerdmans, 2005.

Westminster Confession of Faith. Glasgow: Free Presbyterian Publications, 2006.

Westra, Helen P. "Divinity's Design: Edwards and the History of the Work of Revival." In *Edwards in Our Time: Jonathan Edwards and the Shaping of American Religion*, edited by Sang Hyun Lee and Allen C. Guelzo, 131-57. Cambridge: Eerdmans, 1999.

Whiston, William. *The Accomplishment of Scripture Prophecies*. Cambridge, 1708.

———. *An Essay Towards Restoring the True Text of the Old Testament, and for vindicating the Citations thence made in the New Testament*. London, 1722.

———. *The Eternity of Hell's Torments Considered*. London, 1740.

———. *A short view of the chronology of the Old Testament: and of the harmony of the four evangelists*. Cambridge, 1702.

Whitaker, William. *Disputation on Holy Scripture Against the Papists*. Cambridge, 1588. Translated and edited by William Fitzgerald. Cambridge: Cambridge University Press, 1849.

Williams, Rowan. *Why Study the Past? The Quest for the Historical Church*. London: Darton, Longman & Todd, 2005.

Wilson, Andrew. *The creation the ground-work of revelation, and revelation the language of nature; or, a brief attempt to demonstrate, that the Hebrew language is founded upon natural ideas, and that the Hebrew writings transfer them to spiritual objects*. Edinburgh, 1750.

Wilson, John F. "Editor's Introduction." In *A History of the Work of Redemption*. Vol. 9 of *The Works of Jonathan Edwards*, 1-109. New Haven: Yale University Press, 1989.

———. "History." In *The Princeton Companion to Jonathan Edwards*, edited by Sang Hyun Lee, 210-25. Princeton: Princeton University Press, 2005.

———. "History, Redemption and the Millenium." In *Jonathan Edwards and the American Experience*, edited by Nathan O. Hatch and Harry S. Stout, 131-41. New York: Oxford University Press, 1988.

Winslow, Ola E. *Jonathan Edwards, 1703-1758: A Biography*. New York: Macmillan, 1940.

Bibliography

Withington, Mary C., editor. *Papers in Honor of Andrew Keogh*. New Haven: Yale University Press, 1938.

Withrow, Brandon G. "'Full of Wondrous and Glorious Things': The Exegetical Mind of Jonathan Edwards in his Anglo-American Cultural Context." PhD diss., Westminster Theological Seminary, PA., 2007.

Wollebius, John. *The Abridgment of Christian Divinitie*. 3rd ed. Translated by Alexander Ross. London, 1660.

Wolterstorff, Nicholas. "Locke's Philosophy of Religion." In *The Cambridge Companion to Locke*, edited by Vere Chappell, 172–98. Cambridge: Cambridge University Press, 1994.

Yarchin, William. *History of Biblical Interpretation: A Reader*. Peabody, MA: Hendrickson, 2004.

Yolton, John W. et al., editors. *The Dictionary of Eighteenth-Century British Philosophers*. 2 vols. Bristol: Thoemmes, 1999.

Young, Frances. "Alexandrian and Antiochene Exegesis." In *The Ancient Period*. Vol. 1 of *A History of Biblical Interpretation*, edited by Alan J. Hauser and Duane F. Watson, 334–54. Grand Rapids: Eerdmans, 2003.

Zakai, Avihu. "The Conversion of Jonathan Edwards." *Journal of Presbyterian History* 76.2 (1998) 127–38.

———. *Jonathan Edwards's Philosophy of History: The Reenchantment of the World in the Age of Enlightenment*. Princeton: Princeton University Press, 2003.

———. "The Theological Origins of Jonathan Edwards's Philosophy of Nature." *Journal of Ecclesiastical History* 60.4 (2009) 708–24.

Zanchius, Jerom. *The Doctrine of Absolute Predestination Stated and Asserted*. Translated by Augustus M. Toplady. London: Sovereign Grace, 1930.

Index

Abridgment (Wollebius), 135
accommodatio, 38n84
actus purus, 145, 146, 148
Adam, covenant of works and, 127
adoption, 129
affective knowledge, 23
Agricola (C. Mather), 63, 67
Alexandrian exegesis, 60
allegories
    scriptural, 62
    allusive, 41
    simple, 41
    vertical nature of, 60
Ambrose, 61
Ames, William, 118–19, 123, 129, 135
Anderson, Wallace, 72
antitypes, 22, 31, 32, 33–34, 58n1, 59, 75
aphesin, 186n
Apostles, interpretation of prophecies, 18–19
Aquinas, Thomas, 148–49
Arminianism, 121–22, 123, 165n84, 176n121
Arte of Prophesying, The (Perkins), 22
atonement, 104n172, 185
Auerbach, Erich, 58, 59
Augustine, 61
awareness, sensible, 168

baptism, 93

Basnage, Jacques, 46–47
Baxter, Richard, 159n63
beauty, 7, 75
Bedford, Arthur, 2
being, 71–76
Bellamy, Joseph, 5n21
Berkeley, George, 1, 2, 72–73
Bible. *See* New Testament; Old Testament; Scripture
biblical typology, resurgence of, 64
births, first and second, 168
"Blank Bible" (Edwards), 2n5, 6, 37, 49n, 78n90, 90–91, 136–37, 149–50
bodies, existence of, dependent on God's action, 69–71
Bogue, Carl, 118, 122–23
Bombaro, John J., 160, 161n71
Boston, Thomas, 128n68
Brainerd, David, x
Brown, Robert E., 2, 3, 132–33, 134

Cabbalism, 78n92
Caldwell, Robert, 153, 178–79, 181
calling, 129
Calvin, John, 10n41, 14, 21, 62, 87, 118, 121, 123
Cambridge Platonists, 1, 73n
central dogma theory, 122
Chamberlain, Ava, 27–28
Chandler, Samuel, 32, 33
Cherry, Conrad, 120, 123, 124, 161n74, 162

219

Index

Christ
  centrality of, in redemption history, 114–15
  common to Old and New Testaments, 13, 14
  covenant of, with his bride, 128
  implicit faith in, 180–81
  kingdom of, 113
  perfect righteousness of, 128
  performing the condition of the new covenant, 124
  revelation of, to Old Testament saints, 181–85
  union with, 155n49, 159–60, 178
Christianity
  rationality of, 27–28
  truth of, judging, 18
Christianity as Old as Creation (Tindal), 86
Christologia (Owen), 184
Christian Scriptures. *See* New Testament
Chrysostom, John, 60–61
church, spiritual maturity of, 191
Clarke, Samuel, 20–21n15, 32
Clement of Alexandria, 60, 79
Collegiate School (Weathersfield, CT), 118–19
Collins, Anthony, xiii, 12, 18–19, 20, 21, 26–27, 30, 37, 42
  committed to literal sense of text, 43
  on New Testament interpretations of Old Testament prophecies, 27
  rationalist criticisms of, 52
communication, divine, 38n84
Compendium Theologiae Christiannae (*The Abridgment of Christian Divinity*; Wollebius), 119

Concerning the End for Which God Created the World (Edwards), 5n21
condescensio, 38n84
consciousness, imagistic, 63
consistency, 7
conversion
  as activation of disposition, 170
  means of, 175–76
  moment of, 163
  morphology of, 165, 169
  preparation for, 165
  reality and experience of, 166, 168
  steps of, 164
Court of the Gentiles, The (Gale), 79–80
covenant, 118–31
covenantal system, 14, 108
covenant theology, 119–23, 124–25, 128n68, 162
created grace, 151, 154
creation
  divine glory of, 146
  harmony and, 8
  purpose of, 76, 108–10
  representing spiritual things, 65–66
  shadowing spiritual truths, 76
  as system of signs, x
  typological significance of, 76
Crisp, Oliver, 70n, 72n
Cudworth, Ralph, 73n, 80

Danielou, Jean, 59
Davis, Thomas, 63
Deists, 20, 21, 27–28, 55, 86, 109, 174
De Jong, Peter, 123
Descartes, Rene, 69
Diodore of Tarsus, 60
Discourse of the Grounds and Reasons of the Christian Religion (Collins), 18–19, 56

Index

dispensations, stages in, 129, 130
disposition, activation of, 158
dispositional ontology, 70n, 71–72n62, 144, 158
dispositional soteriology, 11, 14, 87n122, 142–44, 172–73, 175, 178
Dissertation Concerning the End for Which God Created the World (Edwards), 146
Distinguishing Marks of a True Work of the Spirit of God, The (Edwards), 164
Divine Legation of Moses, The (Warburton), 36–37
divine nature, 145–46, 152, 154n47, 155n48, 167
doctrine
  practice and, 135
  precept and, 14, 135, 138–39, 141
Doddridge, Philip, 49n
Dummer Collection, 70n

Edwards, John, 25–26
Edwards, Jonathan
  attempting to harmonize four gospel accounts, 6
  on being, 71–76
  biblical theology of, 14
  citing New Testament in third part of "Harmony," 140–41
  conversion of, 163–64
  as defender of Reformed orthodoxy, 1
  defending rationality of Christian religion, 27–28
  on the Deists, 20
  on excellency, 7–8, 9
  exegesis of, 2–3
  fast sermons of, 125
  harmony's significance to, 7
  Hebrew language an interest for, 78–79
  on historical character of types, 84–85
  hostility of, toward Arminianism, 121–22
  idealism of, 68, 73, 80, 90
  influences on, 1, 25, 70n
  as interpreter of Scripture, 1–2
  interests of, ix–x
  on language and Scripture interpretation, 28–29
  metaphysics of, 69–74
  misunderstood, 11, 13
  on natural revelation and natural theology, 85–86
  notebooks of, 4, 11, 19–20, 69, 89, 114 133–34
  obsessed with Scripture, xi
  pagan religions an interest for, 174
  as pastor-theologian, 1, 15
  on the Psalter, 138–39
  reading interests of, ix, 19–20
  on the relationship between the Old and New Testaments, 4
  relevance of, 3
  scholarship about, x
  on Scripture interpreting nature, 87
  soteriology of, 11, 142–44, 157–58
  study of, 1
  on substance, 69–71
  on texts having more than one referent, 27
  theme of prophecy in work of, 17
  theological solipsism of, 106–7
  theology of, 3–4, 15, 140, 143
  thought of, Bible's importance to, 1–2
  typological unity of, 68–69, 98–104
  typology of, 13, 76, 89–95
  understanding, in his context, 4

221

Index

Edwards, Jonathan (*cont.*)
    unrestricted by Bible's literal sense, 24
Edwards, Jonathan, Jnr., 5n21
election, 129
Emerson, Ralph Waldo, 67
End of Creation (Edwards), 110, 146, 151, 153
epistemic progress, 83n107
equality, 7
Erskine, John, 5n21
eschatology, prophetic, 17
essence, nature and, 152–53
essentialism, 70n
eternal justification, 161
events, typological significance of, 104n172
excellency, 7–8, 9
exegesis
    Alexandrian, 60, 61
    allegorical, 60
    figural, 58n1

faith, 124, 130
    as acceptance of grace, 127–28
    analogy of, 25, 30, 31, 55
    awareness of, 163
    expressions of, and salvation, 168–69
    grace and, 159n63
    justification and, 158–60
    as means for interpreting Scripture, 25
    obscurity of, 185
    reception of, 123
    salvation and, 170–72
    unity of, 132
figural (figurative) exegesis, 58n1
figural hermeneutics, 58
figures, 22
Figures or Types of the Old Testament (S. Mather), 64, 96
Flavel, John, 63
Frei, Hans, 3, 19, 188

"The Fulfillment of the Prophecies of the Messiah" (Edwards), 54–55

Gale, Theophilus, 79–80
Gay, Peter, 3
"Genius, Spirit, Doctrine and Rules" notebook. *See* "Harmony of the Genius, Spirit, Doctrines and Rules of the Old Testament and the New, The" (Edwards)
Gerstner, John, 17
glorification, 129
God
    as act, 145
    action of, 69–71
    activity *ad extra* of, 148
    attributes of, 150n30
    communicating his nature, 153
    consciousness of, 74
    distinct from creature, 152
    glorification of, 75
    grace of, 121
    harmony of, 8
    holiness of, 146
    knowledge of, 151
    naming of, 182
    nature of, participating in, 151–52
    plurality in, 8
    self-glorification of, 98, 106, 109–10, 111, 125, 126–27, 170
    self-love of, 146–47, 151
    self-reflection of, 144–45
    space and, 72, 74
Goldman, Shalom, 78, 81
Goodwin, Thomas, 183
Goppelt, Leonard, 59
gospel
    preaching and hearing of, 173–75
    response to, 132
    spirit of, 131–32

Index

grace
  application of, 129
  arbitrary exercise of, 175
  concatenation of, 167, 169, 170
  covenant of, 14, 120–24, 127–31, 136, 139, 161–62n74, 170, 185
  created, 149, 151, 154
  essence of, 167
  evidence of, 138
  expression of the Spirit's activity, 151
  faith and, 127–28, 159n63
  humiliation and, 166
  means of, 124, 176–79, 186–87, 193
  spiritual sense and, 23
gratia creata, 149
gratia increata, 149
Grotius, Hugo, 42–43, 47n114
Grounds and Reasons. See *Discourse of the Grounds and Reasons of the Christian Religion* (Collins)
Guild, William, 62

Halfway Covenant, 169n99
harmony
  creation and, 8
  in Edwards's work, 10–11
  genre of, 6
  spiritual, 7
  theological significance of, 7, 8
  Trinity and, 8
"Harmony of the Old and New Testament, The" (Edwards), xi, xiii, 30
  compilation of, 132–33, 134
  cross-references in, 46, 49–50
  development of, 140
  Edwards's description of, 6
  Edwards's intention in, 12, 21, 43
  purpose of, 10, 54
  scale of, 15, 195
  scope of, 10
  structure of, threefold, 46–47
  title of, 131
  writing of, 4–5
"Harmony of the Genius, Spirit, Doctrines and Rules of the Old Testament and the New, The" (Edwards), 132, 133–35, 182–83
heathens, religious practices of, 174–75
Hebrew language
  Edwards's interest in, 78–79
  importance of, 77–80
Hebrew Scriptures. *See* Old Testament
Henry, Matthew, 49n
hieroglyphs, 80
historia salutis, 187
historical biblical criticism, x
history
  prophecy explicating, 53
  typical nature of, 42
  typological interpretation of, 94
History of the Jews, The (Basnage), 46–47
History of the Work of Redemption (Edwards), 5, 47, 89–90, 92, 93–94, 110
Hobbes, Thomas, ix, 69
holiness, 152, 154
Holmes, Stephen, 70n
Holy Spirit
  grace of, 167, 169
  in the human heart, 148–50
  indwelling of, 9–10, 154, 156–58, 170
  infusion of, 151
  instruction from, 29
  light of, 9
  name of, 145–46
  needed for reading Scripture properly, 28–32

223

Index

Holy Spirit (*cont.*)
   new disposition and, 148–50
   redemption history and, 112
   representing mutual love of Father and Son, 145, 153
   Scripture and, 12
Hooker, Thomas, 165
Hopkins, Samuel, 5n21
Hume, David, ix
humiliation, 163, 165–66
Husbandry Spiritualized (Flavel), 63

Images or Shadows of Divine Things (Miller), 66–67
immaterialism, 72
immediate revelation, 34
individual redemption, 115–18
Institutes (Calvin), 10n41, 122
Institutio Theologiae Elencticae (*The Institutes of Elenctic Theology*; Turretin), 119
instruction, methods of, 38

Jerome, 61
Jesus, Messiahship of, 12
John of Cassian, 61
justification, 2, 124, 129, 157–58, 167–68
   eternal, 161
   faith and, 158–60
Justification by Faith Alone (Edwards), 158–59, 161

Keach, Benjamin, 41
Kidder, Richard, 102n167
Kimnach, Wilson, 83n107
knowledge
   experiential, 8–9
   types of, 23, 156
Kuklick, Bruce, 3
language
   common, for spiritual things, 28
   figural, literal nature of, 42

   figurative, 13
   limiting, to expressions in Scripture, 68–69, 82–83
   meaningful use of, 26–27
   metaphorical, 37–43
   rules for, 27
Law, Christological character of, 62
Lee, Sang Hyun, 70n, 71–72n62, 109n2, 143, 144, 146
Leland, John, 20
life, spiritual substance of, 136
Lightfoot, John, 6
Locke, John, 1, 2, 17–18, 26–27, 28, 30, 37, 38
Lombard, Peter, 148–49
Lord's Supper, 87–88
Lowance, Mason I., Jr., 64, 67–68, 69, 85, 88, 89, 92, 96–97, 99, 102n167, 106
Luther, Martin, 61–62

Magnalia Christi Americana (C. Mather), 63
man, happiness of, 108–9, 110
Marrow, The (Ames), 129, 135
Marsden, George M., 110
Mastricht, Peter van, 22–23n25, 119, 135, 155n48, 186n
materialism, ix, 69
material world, reflecting the spiritual world, 77–78, 80
Mather, Cotton, 63, 67
Mather, Samuel, 64–65, 68, 69, 76, 81–84, 89, 90, 96, 100
maturity, spiritual, 190–91
McClenahan, Michael, 122, 160
McDermott, Gerald, 65n33, 87n122, 125n60, 142n1, 173, 174–75, 176
Medulla Theologiae (*The Marrow of Theology*; Ames), 118–19
Messiah, typified in the Old Testament, 99–106
Messianic prophecy, 12

metaphorical language, 37–43
metaphors, 40–41
millennialism, 17
Miller, Perry, 1, 3, 66–67, 68, 85, 87, 121, 122
Minkema, Kenneth P., 4, 17, 44, 45, 51, 140
miracles, proof of, 20–21
More, Henry, 73n
Morimoto, Anri, 14, 142–44, 148, 149, 150, 154, 155, 157–58, 161n73, 162–63, 172–73, 175, 178, 181
mystical union, 41n97

naming, 80, 104n172, 105, 182
naturalism, 67
natural revelation, 85–87
natural theology, 85–86
nature
 communicating spiritual truths, 86
 definition of, 152
 essence and, 152–53
 as network of types, 86
 principle of, 151
 typologizing of, 66–67
Nature of True Virtue, The (Edwards), 5n21
negative signs, 164
neonomianism, 159
new disposition, 143, 144, 148–57, 162, 169, 170
 expressions of, 172
 gospel's role in, 175
 obedience and, 171
New England, 94n146
 covenant theology in, 121, 123, 124–25
 Israel and, 63
 relationship of, with God, 125
new sense, 9, 15, 28, 31, 43
New Testament
 as antitype, 77

authority of, 79–80
types in, 100
Newton, Isaac, 1, 2, 69
notional knowledge, 23, 156

obedience, salvation and, 170–71
Old Testament
 antitypes in, 100–101
 Apostles' use of, 55, 56
 coherence of, 13, 42, 48–50, 55, 141
 grace in, means of, 186–87
 interpretation of, transformed, 58–59
 literal meaning of, 42
 literal sense of, reimagined, 56
 messianic witness of, 15, 20, 195
 prophecies in, unity of, 44–45, 48–50, 99–106
 redemption history and, 103
 saints in, grace for, 9, 11, 14–15, 177–80
 scope and sense of, 13
 Sermon on the Mount and, 138
 spiritual interpretation of, 61–62
 as type, 77
ontology, dispositional, 70n, 71–72n62, 144, 158
ordo salutis, 160nn66, 70
Origen, 61, 61
original revelation, 26
Owen, John, 41n97, 184, 185

pactum salutis, 160
paresin, 186n
participation, essential, 154
Pauw, Amy Plantinga, 132–33
Perkins, William, 22, 25, 165
perseverance, 124
Philo, 60
places
 conference of, 25
 typological significance of, 104n172

225

Index

Poole, Matthew, 2, 48–49n119
Pope, Alexander, 108–9n1
practice, doctrine and, 135
Preacher, The (John Edwards), 25
precept, doctrine and, 14, 135, 138–39, 141
predestination, 165n84
predictive prophecy, 52–53, 99, 100
preparation, doctrine of, 121–22, 165nn84, 86
Prideaux, Humphrey, 2
principle of nature, 151
prisca theologia (ancient theology), 79, 174–75
prophecies, 14, 15
   bearing witness to real atonement, 185–86
   conference of, 46–47
   double-referents of, 32, 33–34
   explicating history, 53
   fulfillment of, 33–35, 52–53
   historical function of, 27n
   interpreting, 82–83
   literal reading of, 39
   as means of grace, 178, 180
   Messianic nature of, 40–41, 43, 192
   metaphorical nature of, 42
   polyvalent, 193
   predictive, 13, 52–53, 99, 100
   proof of, 20–21
   rabbinical interpretation of, 47n114
   reference point for, 47–48
   sense of, 22
   theme of, overlooked in Edwards's work, 17
   types and, 32–37, 101–3, 118
   understanding of, 193
"Prophecies of the Messiah" (Edwards), 45–50, 138–39
propitiatory, 185
proportion, 7
protevangelion, 46, 76
Psalter, the, 138–39

quadriga, 61

Ramsay, Andrew Michael, 80
rationality, 27–28
reality
   objective, 168
   spiritual, 75
real union, 155n49
Reasonableness of Christianity, The (Locke), 17–18
redemption, 129, 130
   outside the Bible, 112–13
   covenant of, 120, 123–24, 125–30, 160, 161–62
   design of, 111–15
   grand scheme of, 187
   individual, 115–18
   Spirit-led nature of, 112
   understanding of, 110–11
   work of, 116
redemption history, 14, 34, 48, 94–95, 103, 108, 110, 192–93
   church's place in, 191
   complexity of, 113
regeneration, 43, 124, 173n
   consent and, 175
   through means of grace, 176–77
relationship, necessity of, for being, 74–75
relative union, 155n49
religion
   authenticating marks of, 137
   as end of creation, 86
   history of, typology in, 65n33
   as purpose of creation, 76
   revealed, 86
Religious Affections (Edwards), 24, 137–38, 164
religious entropy, 174
retrieval, theologies of, 195
revealed religion, 86
revelation, 26–27, 34, 87
   ancient universal, 79, 80–81

Index

revelation (*cont.*)
  clarity of, for New Testament saints, 84
  exhibition and, 194
  natural, 85–87
  plainness of, 131
  progressive, 193
  trickle-down, 174
revival, 53n135, 111, 137, 180
righteousness, 170

sacrifices, 105, 172, 185
salvation, 130
  causes of, 122
  before Christ, 162–63
  disposition sufficient for, 162–63
  faith and, 168–72
  ground for, 143
  and hearing the gospel, 173–75
  for individual souls, 115–18
  involving *theosis*, 148
  manner of, 172
  obedience and, 170–71
  as part of God's emanation, 143
  reception of, 124
  subjective awareness of, 180
salvation history, 60
sanctification, 129
Schafer, Thomas, 133
Scriptura Scripturae interpres, 56
Scripture
  allegories in, 41, 62
  constraining role of, on Edwards's typological exegesis, 84–95
  divine authorship of, 12, 30–31
  divine origin of, 8
  Edwards's trust in, x
  encompassing all history, 95
  four-fold sense of, 61
  as grammar book of typological language, 82, 85, 192, 195
  grasping, failure to, 29
  guiding Edwards's typological interpretation, 88–95
  harmony of, 6, 8
  interpretation of, 25, 62–63
  interpreting nature, 87
  intertestamental relationship in, three categories of, 11
  invitational role of, in Edwards's typological exegesis, 77–84
  meaning and message harmonized in, 29–30
  meanings of, multiple levels of, 24, 30–31
  Messianic reading of, 44–50
  metaphors in, 39–40
  as parable and interpretation, 81
  prophecies in, applicable to many things, 27
  self-authentication of, 21
  self-interpreting, 25–26, 29
  silence of, 82–83
  similarities and differences in, accounting for, 136
  soteriological harmony of Testaments, 144ff.
  spiritual sense of, 12, 23, 24, 63, 136–37
  testaments distinguished by manner, 62
  testaments related typologically in, 13
  theme of, 131
  types and antitypes in, 84, 93, 100–101, 103
  typology and, 13, 84, 98–104
  understanding of, 35
  unity of, xiii, 52–53, 61, 77, 139, 185, 195
Scripture Prophecies (Whiston), 18n6
"Scripture Prophecies of the Messiah" (Edwards), 50–54
sensation
  epistemology of, 26

227

Index

sensation (*cont.*)
  rhetoric of, 38
sense
  literal, 22–23
  mystical, 23
  spiritual, 23, 24
sense of the heart, 9, 23, 9. *See also* new sense
sensus allegoricus, 61
sensus anagogicus, 61
sensus historicus, 61
sensus literalis, 61
sensus tropologicus, 61
Sermon on the Mount, 136–38
Shephard, Thomas, 165
Sherlock, Thomas, 41n97, 44
Sherlock, William, 41n97
sin, effects of, 21
Skelton, Philip, 20
skepticism, ix
Socinianism, 183n144
soteriology, 14
  covenantal categories and, 124
  dispositional, 11, 87n122, 142–44, 172–73, 175, 178
space, 72, 74
speculative knowledge, 23, 156
Spinoza, Benedict (Baruch), 27n
Spirit-baptism, 93
Spirit of God, nature of, 153
spiritual knowledge, 23, 156–57
spiritual maturity, 190–91
spiritual sense, 9, 63. *See also* new sense
stars, signifying spiritual truths, 191–92
Stein, Stephen, 1–2, 17, 23, 24, 26, 32, 50, 56, 67, 84, 85, 138
Stoddard, Solomon, 165, 166–67, 169n99
Stout, Harry, 124–25
Studebaker, Steven, 172–73
substance, 69–71
sui interpres principle, 25–26

Surenhusius, William, 18n6
Sweeney, Douglas, 2, 52
Sykes, Arthur Ashley, 32–33

Taylor, Edward, 63
Temple, messianic significance of, 112
testaments, relationship between, x
texts
  conference of, 26, 29–30
  literal sense of, 22–23, 61
  mystical (spiritual) sense of, 23
  referents for, 27, 30–31
Theodore of Mopsuestia, 60
Theodoret, 60
theological scholarship, changes in, 3
theology
  covenant, 119–23, 124–25, 128n68, 162
  natural, 85–86
  of retrieval, 195
Theoretico-practica theologia (Mastricht), 119, 135
theosis, 110n5, 143, 148, 151, 153, 154
Tillotson, John, 39n89, 160–61
Tindal, Matthew, 20, 86, 174
Tracy, Patricia, 164n82
traditional revelation, 26
trickle-down revelation, 174
Trinity, 8, 145
  a priori account of, 144
  activity of, 125
  confederation of, 125–27
  equality of, 125–27, 150n30
  love of, participating in, 110
Tropologia (Keach), 41
True Intellectual System of the Universe (Cudworth), 80
true sense, 156–57
Turretin, Francis, 22, 119, 120, 155n48, 183, 184–85
Tyndale, William, 62

Index

types, 14, 15, 22, 31, 32, 58n1, 64
  bearing witness to real atonement, 185–86
  educational value of, 98
  figurative language as, 37
  historical character of, 84–85
  as images of spiritual substance, 92–93, 137
  as language, 81–82, 90, 190–91
  material, 75
  meaning of, in redemption history, 192–93
  as means of grace, 178, 180
  for Old Testament saints, 83
  prophecies and, 32–37, 101–3, 118
  in Scripture, 59, 87–88
  as spiritual truths, 93, 100–101
"Types of the Messiah" (Edwards), 96–106, 139–40
typology, 58n1
  allegory distinct from, 60
  competing versions of, 67–68
  conservative, 13, 64, 66–69, 84, 89, 90, 96
  as language, 81–82
  liberal, 13, 67–68, 85, 89, 90, 96
  linear nature of, 59–60
  misunderstanding of, 191
  Pauline, 59
  prophecy and fulfillment as, 59

unevangelized, salvation of, 87n122
Use and Intent of Prophecy in the Several Ages of the World, The (T. Sherlock), 44
use lines, 51, 52

vital union, 155n49

Warburton, William, 36–37
Watters, David, 96–97, 99
Webster, John, 195
Westminster Confession, 121
Westminster Shorter Catechism, 118
wheels, Edwards's metaphor of, 116–17
Whiston, William, 18n6, 32, 33, 53–54
Williams, Rowan, 4, 15
Wilson, Andrew, 77–79, 81
Wilson, John F., 89, 90, 92, 93–94
Winslow, Ola, 3
Withrow, Brandon, 2
Wollebius, Johannes, 62, 119, 135
Work of Redemption. See *History of the Work of Redemption*
works, covenant of, 90–91, 123, 127, 136, 170
Works of Jonathan Edwards, The (Edwards), 2

www.ingramcontent.com/pod-product-compliance
Lightning Source LLC
Chambersburg PA
CBHW051636230426
43669CB00013B/2331